CW01506925

THE AFGHANISTAN FILE

By Prince Turki AlFaisal Al Saud

THE AFGHANISTAN FILE

By Prince Turki AlFaisal Al Saud

Former Director of the General Intelligence Directorate
(1977–2001) Saudi Arabia

Arabian Publishing

The Afghanistan File

First published in 2021 in Great Britain by

Arabian Publishing
50 High Street
Cowes
Isle of Wight
PO31 7RR

www.arabian-publishing.com

Reprinted in 2021

Written by Prince Turki AlFaisal Al Saud and Michael Field
Edited by Eleo Carson and Arthur Clark
Cover designed by Albino Tavares

Printed and bound in Great Britain by Clays Ltd., Elcograf S.p.A.

ISBN UK (hardback) 978-0-992980-88-7
ISBN KSA (hardback) 978-603-03-8293-4
ISBN (eBook) 978-1-911487-57-9

King Fahd National Library Cataloging-in-Publication Data
958.103 dc 1442/11070
L.D. no. 1442/11070

In association with

KFCRIS
KING FAISAL CENTER FOR
RESEARCH AND ISLAMIC STUDIES

Contents

List of Illustrations & Maps   vi

Maps   x

Note on spelling and place names   xii

Main people mentioned in the book   xiii

Foreword   An Extraordinary Train of Events   xvii

Chapter 1   Invasion – and Response   1

Chapter 2   A Troubled Independence   18

Chapter 3   The Birth of the Mujahideen   27

Chapter 4   The Arms Pipeline   39

Chapter 5   The War – The Early Years   49

Chapter 6   Charities and Volunteers   60

Chapter 7   The Office of Services and the House of the Supporters   75

Chapter 8   The War – Turning Point and Withdrawal   81

Chapter 9   The Loya Jirga at Rawalpindi   99

Chapter 10   Interlude – The Kuwait Crisis   107

Chapter 11   The Fall of Dr Najibullah   122

Chapter 12   Bringing Home the Volunteers   130

Chapter 13   The Rise of the Taliban   143

Chapter 14   The Taliban and Bin Laden   159

Chapter 15   Aftermath   184

Endnotes   196

Acknowledgements   199

Index   201

List of Illustrations & Maps

1. 28 April 1979. Supporters of the Afghan communist regime march in the capital Kabul to mark the first anniversary of the communist April Revolution. (Getty Images)

2. 30 December 1979. Muslim fighters pose with an assortment of weapons during a break in weapons training in Barikot in the Pakistani province of Khyber Pakhtunkhwa. (Associated Press/Steve McCurry)

3. 1 February 1980. Mohammad Zia ul-Haq, President of Pakistan, at a rally of tribal chiefs in Peshawar. (Getty Images)

4. 14 February 1980. Members of an Afghan Mujahideen patrol move through a rocky mountainous area in Kunar province of Afghanistan, 50 kilometres from the Pakistan border. (Associated Press)

5. 2 February 1983. US President Ronald Reagan meets with leaders of the Afghan Mujahideen in the Oval Office. (Alamy)

6. 1983. Ahmad Shah Massoud, military commander of the Mujahideen group Jamiat-i-Islami. (Shutterstock)

7. 1986. President Mohammad Najibullah. (Alamy)

8. 17 January 1987, Peshawar. Gulbuddin Hekmatyar, right, leader of Hizb-i-Islami, confers with Professor Abd Rabb Al-Rasul Sayyaf, Imam of Ittihad-i-Islami, during a meeting of Mujahideen listening to their leaders announcing the rejection of Kabul's offers of ceasefire and coalition government. (Getty Images)

9. 11 September 1988. Burhanuddin Rabbani, left, leader of Jamiat-i-Islami, sitting with Abdullah Izzam, an Arab Mujahid. (AMRC)

10. 1989. Osama Bin Laden, left, with anti-Soviet fighters in Afghanistan.

11. 12 December 1989. Multan Battalion Commander, Lieutenant General Hamid Gul, during Zarb-e-Momin exercise-manoeuvres simulating an India–Pakistan battle. (Getty Images)

12. 15 February 1989. A convoy of Soviet vehicles leaving Afghanistan via the Friendship Bridge over the Amu Darya river on the border between Afghanistan and Uzbekistan. (AKG Images)

13. 12 February 1989. Soviet soldiers parading at the withdrawal of troops from Afghanistan. (AKG Images)

14. 15–16 October 1990. Benazir Bhutto, former Prime Minister of Pakistan, campaigning for the Pakistan People's Party in the week before the Pakistani general election. (Getty Images)

15. 4 May 1992. The evening sky is lit with tracer bullets and flares above Kabul during the nightly display by rival Mujahideen guerrilla groups continuing to battle for control of the city. (Getty Images)

16. April 1992, Peshawar. The author with Pakistani Prime Minister Nawaz Sharif organising a conference call between Ahmad Shah Massoud and Gulbuddin Hekmatyar to try to persuade them not to fight in Kabul. (Abdullah Mastour Al-Zahrani)

17. 1992. Mujahideen rebels take Kabul. (Shutterstock)

18. 1992. Abdul Rashid Dostum controlled the private buffer state on the southern borders of Turkmenistan and Uzbekistan. (Shutterstock)

19. 1 May 1992. Hazrat Sibghatullah Mojaddedi acknowledging a crowd of supporters. (Getty Images)

20. 29 May 1992. The author and Pakistani Prime Minister Nawaz Sharif arrive in Kabul and walk with Interim President Sibghatullah Mojaddedi. (Getty Images)

21. 29 May 1992, Kabul. After the fall of Kabul, Sibghatullah Mojaddedi arrives at the airport with, on his right, Sharif Nawaz, Pakistani Prime Minister, and, to his left, the author. (Reuters)

22. 7 March 1993, Islamabad, Pakistan. The author with General Muhammad Eid Al-Otaibi and his secretary, Ahmad Badeeb, Saudi Ambassador to Pakistan Yosuf Mutabaqqani, and Abdullah Mastour, the author's personal assistant, talking with Afghan leaders. (Abdullah Mastour Al-Zahrani)

23. 7 March 1993, Islamabad, Pakistan: Afghan leaders (sitting), along with representatives of several Islamic countries, pray after the signing ceremony for an Afghan peace agreement. (Getty Images)

24. 11 March 1993, Islamabad, Pakistan. Left to right: the author, Afghan President Burhanuddin Rabbani, Pakistani Prime Minister Nawaz Sharif and Gulbuddin Hekmatyar at a news conference. (Reuters)

25. 1993. King Fahd of Saudi Arabia and Sheikh Abdulaziz bin Baz, Grand Mufti of Saudi Arabia, in Makkah, meeting Pakistani Prime Minister Nawaz Sharif and the Mujahideen leaders after the signing ceremony for an Afghan peace agreement. (Saudi Press Agency)

26. 19 February 1994, Kabul. Two Shiite teenagers of the minority Hizb-i-Wahdat faction armed with Kalashnikovs peer around their bunker during an exchange of small-arms fire with troops belonging to the Afghan President. (Getty Images)

27. 15 March 1994, Kabul. A man is captured by members of an enemy faction. (Getty Images)

28. 20 October 1996. Ahmad Shah Massoud's Mujahideen capture Bagram from the Taliban. (Getty Images)

29. 1998, Khost, Afghanistan. Ayman El-Zawahri poses for a photograph with Osama Bin Laden. (Shutterstock)

30. 16 December 2001. Anti-Taliban Afghan fighters watch explosions from US bombings in the Tora Bora mountains in Afghanistan. (Reuters)

31. Plaque given to the author by CIA head William Casey. The words in Arabic state 'Never Trust the Russians', a maxim of one of the Afghan kings. (Abdullah Mastour Al-Zahrani)

32. 7 October 2019, Riyadh. The author receiving the decoration for the Afghan award of 'Ghazi Mirbajah Khan'. (Abdullah Mastour Al-Zahrani)

Maps

Map One - Modern-day regional map   x

Map Two - Afghanistan (1980s provincial borders)   x

Map Three - Afghanistan/Pakistan (modern-day provincial borders)   xi

Modern-day regional map

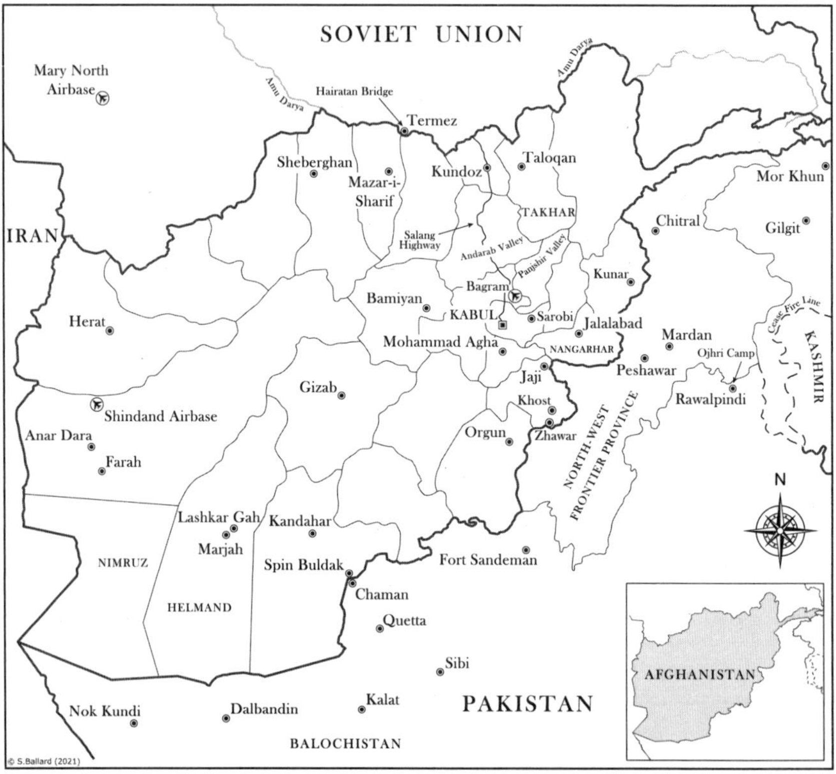

Afghanistan (1980s provincial borders)

Afghanistan/Pakistan (modern-day provincial borders)

Note on spelling and place names

The names of people, places and organisations mentioned in this book are rendered in commonly used anglicised spellings whenever available. Technical transliteration has been avoided for the sake of readability.

Main people mentioned in the book

Saudi Arabia

Khalid bin Abdulaziz, King of Saudi Arabia, 1975–82.

Fahd bin Abdulaziz, Crown Prince, 1975-82, King of Saudi Arabia, 1982–2005 and uncle of the author.

Salman bin Abdulaziz (Prince), Governor of Riyadh, 1963–2011, King of Saudi Arabia from 2015 and uncle of the author.

Sultan bin Abdulaziz (Prince), Minister of Defence and Aviation, 1962–2011, Crown Prince, 2005–11, and uncle of the author.

Saud AlFaisal (Prince), Foreign Minister, 1975–2015, and brother of the author.

Turki AlFaisal Al Saud (Prince), Director of the General Intelligence Department (GID), 1977–2001, son of King Faisal (1964–75) and author of this book.

Sattam bin Abdulaziz (Prince), Vice-Governor of Riyadh Province, supported Sheikh Saleh Ali Al-Suhaibani's fundraising for Afghan resistance fighters.

Abdulaziz bin Baz (Sheikh), Islamic scholar, Head of Presidency for Religious Research, Ifta, Dawah and Guidance, 1975–93, Grand Mufti of Saudi Arabia, 1993–99, supported Sheikh Saleh's fundraising work.

Saleh Ali Al-Suhaibani (Sheikh), imam in Riyadh, raised funds to assist resistance fighters in Afghanistan, an initiative that later became the basis of the National Public Committee for the Support of the Afghan People.

Mohammad Eid Al-Otaibi (General), army officer, GID and later Saudi Ministry of Foreign Affairs member, based in Kabul for four years.

Pakistan

Zulfikar Ali Bhutto, Prime Minister of Pakistan, 1973–77, executed 1979.

Mohammad Zia ul-Haq, President of Pakistan, 1978–88.

Benazir Bhutto, daughter of Zulfikar Ali Bhutto, Prime Minister of Pakistan, 1988–90 and 1993–96, assassinated 2007.

Nawaz Sharif, Prime Minister of Pakistan, 1990–93, 1997–99 and 2013–17.

General Akhtar Abdul Rahman Khan, Director-General of Inter-Services

Intelligence (ISI), 1977–87, then Chairman of the Joint Chiefs of Staff of the Pakistani Armed Forces, 1987–88.

Lieutenant General Hamid Gul, replaced Akhtar Abdul Rahman as Director-General of the ISI, 1987–89.

Brigadier Mohammad Yousaf, head of the Afghan Bureau of the ISI, 1983–87, and author of *Afghanistan the Bear Trap: The Defeat of a Superpower* and other books.

Brigadier Naseerullah Babar, Minister of the Interior under Benazir Bhutto, 1993–96.

United States

Dr Zbigniew Brzezinski, President Jimmy Carter's National Security Adviser, 1977–81.

William Casey, Director of the CIA, 1981–87.

Robert Gates, Acting Director of the CIA, 1986-87, Director, 1991–93.

Afghanistan

Mohammad Zahir Shah, King of Afghanistan from 1933 to 1973, when he was deposed.

Sardar Mohammad Daoud, seized power in 1973, pro-Soviet, remained President of Afghanistan until 1978 when he was overthrown and murdered.

Nur Mohammad Taraki, President of Afghanistan, 1978–79, leader of the communist Khalq (Masses) movement, murdered 1979.

Mohammad Najibullah, Pathan politician, chief of Khadamat-e Aetla'at-e Dawlati (KHAD) State Intelligence Agency, President of Afghanistan, 1986–92. Murdered by the Taliban 1996.

Burhanuddin Rabbani, Tajik party leader, head of the Jamiat-i-Islami (Islamic Group), President of Afghanistan, 1992–2001.

Ahmad Shah Massoud, Tajik, military commander of the Jamiat-i-Islami, 1975 to assassination in 2001.

Gulbuddin Hekmatyar, Prime Minister of Afghanistan 1993–94 and 1996–97, Pathan party leader of Hizb-i-Islami (Islamic Party), 1975–2006, renowned guerrilla fighter, powerful but unreliable leader.

Maulvi Yunus Khalis, Pathan leader of the Hizb-i-Islami, kept the same name after breaking away from Hekmatyar's party.

Maulvi Mohammad Nabi Mohammadi, Vice President of Afghanistan under the Mujahideen, 1993–96, Pathan leader of the moderate Harakat-i Inqilab-i-Islami (Islamic Revolutionary Movement) party, 1965–2002.

Pir Ahmad Gailani, leader of the Qadiriyyah Sufi order and founder of the moderate National Islamic Front, 1979.

Hazrat Sibghatullah Mojaddedi, President of Afghanistan, April–June 1992, founder of the Afghan National Liberation Front.

Abd Rabb Al-Rasul Sayyaf, Professor of Religion, Pathan leader of Ittihad-i-Islami (Islamic Unity) party, chosen as spokesman of the Mujahideen, 1980–81.

Jalaluddin Haqqani, Pathan, very effective commander with Maulvi Yunus Khalis's forces, later with the Taliban, 1980s–2018.

Abdul Rashid Dostum, Vice President of Afghanistan, 2014–20, Uzbek leader, established a KHAD militia loyal to himself, regional commander in north Afghanistan. Loyal to Najibullah's government, later changed sides.

Mullah Mohammad Omar, Pathan, Supreme Leader of the Taliban government, 1994–2013.

Mohammad Rabbani, second-in-command to Mullah Omar, the Taliban's spokesman for foreign affairs, 1996–2001.

Abdullah Azzam, Palestinian university professor, later involved with relief work in Peshawar. Established the Maktab al-Khadamat (Office of Services) guesthouse to support new volunteers, 1984–88.

Osama Bin Laden, born in Saudi Arabia, travelled to Pakistan, where he met Abdullah Azzam (q.v.). Became fundraiser for the Maktab al-Khadamat, subsequently opened his own guesthouse, the Dar al-Ansar. Founded Al-Qaeda, 1988, killed in 2011.

Ayman El-Zawahiri, Egyptian doctor, volunteered for work in Peshawar, became mentor to Osama Bin Laden. His views became the hallmark of Al-Qaeda and then the Islamic State of Iraq and Syria (ISIS).

Foreword
An Extraordinary Train of Events

I served my country as head of the General Intelligence Department (GID) – Saudi Arabia's foreign intelligence service – for twenty-four years, from the end of 1977 to August 2001. This department had responsibility for our dealings with Afghanistan and it happened, quite unexpectedly, that during almost my whole time in the post I was concerned above all with that unhappy country. My work fell into three phases. First, there was our support for the Mujahideen resistance to the Soviet occupation of Afghanistan, which began late in 1979 – an operation on which we worked with Pakistan, the United States and, on a smaller scale, Britain, France and Egypt. Then, after the Soviet withdrawal in 1989, when sadly the Western powers seemed to lose interest in the country, we launched a series of initiatives to try to stop the Mujahideen factions from fighting each other and tried to help them form a stable government. In this, we were working with Pakistan. Lastly, after the Taliban came to power in 1996, we spent several fruitless years trying to persuade that regime to surrender Osama Bin Laden.

Each phase of the story was in itself extraordinary, as readers of the following pages will see. But the events which stemmed from the war in Afghanistan were in many ways even more remarkable and, as far as one can see, mainly bad. I will summarise these events in briefest outline. The Russians' failure in Afghanistan contributed to an internal social demoralisation which was a major cause of the collapse of the Soviet Union at the end of 1991, less than three years after its military withdrawal. The war against the Soviets and the instability in Afghanistan that followed produced and nurtured Al-Qaeda, and it was Al-Qaeda that carried out attacks on Saudi Arabia starting in 1995, followed by the assault on the United States on 9/11, which led to the 'War on Terror'. Almost immediately this produced the US-led invasion of Afghanistan – a military commitment from which America had still not completely extricated itself nearly twenty years later. And as of early 2021 Afghanistan still has no government that can be described as stable.

The Afghanistan operation was followed in early 2003 by the US-led invasion of Iraq, seen by the American government as related to the war on terrorism and intended to remove a further source of instability in the Middle East. The Iraqi regime of Saddam Hussein was thoroughly dangerous; it had invaded Iran in 1980 and Kuwait in 1990. In fact, the occupation of Iraq produced chaos and bloodshed which continues today. It produced ISIS, the Islamic State of Iraq and Syria – a delusional attempt to recreate the Islamic Caliphate by a group of people who had no regard for human life or any of the norms of civilised behaviour. The war against ISIS became an extension of the civil war in Syria, which began in 2011.

The story, though, is not only of one disaster leading to another. There is an appalling theme which runs through all these events, and which has become a curse of the modern world. It is the emergence and empowerment of mainly young people of little intelligence, minimal education and absolutely no understanding of the complexities of the world who have come to believe they have a mission to change the world through violence. They are the types of characters who will believe in conspiracy theories rather than make any attempt to learn and understand the workings of economics, international politics and modern societies. They see themselves as outcasts and they hate the complicated world they see around them. They do not seem able to define the purpose of their mission – they cannot say just how their violence is going to change the world or what the end result should be. They are the people who make up what remains of Al-Qaeda and its many offshoots in different countries, the remnants of ISIS and its spin-offs, the northern Nigerian group Boko Haram (meaning roughly 'Western Education is Forbidden') and what seems to be a large number of little groups of terrorists operating all over the world.

The origin of this way of thinking in recent times lies with the emergence of Al-Qaeda, meaning 'the Base', established by Bin Laden in Afghanistan in 1988. Bin Laden and his followers persuaded themselves that they had played a major role in winning the war against the Soviet occupiers, though as far as I have been able to discover, they played no role at all. The battle that Bin Laden claimed to have fought in Afghanistan appears to have taken place only in his imagination.

It seems that in a muddled way Al-Qaeda's followers mixed together their feelings of separateness and rejection, a simplistic understanding of Islam and a sense of inspiration and excitement which came from being on the fringes of a war to persuade themselves that they were powerful and important. As I describe in Chapter 10 on the Kuwait crisis, after he left Afghanistan in 1990 Bin Laden came first to me to suggest that his people might single-handedly overthrow the Communist government of South Yemen, and a little later approached the Ministry of Defence to suggest that there was no need for an international military coalition and that the same band could evict the Iraqi invaders from Kuwait. What chain of thinking led him to this conclusion I cannot imagine. In his later pronouncements he called on his sympathisers everywhere to wage jihad against an extraordinary combination of Zionists, the United States – which he falsely claimed was occupying the Holy Places in Saudi Arabia – the Saudi government, and its Arab and Western allies. He made no distinction between Muslims and non-Muslims.

The same type of deluded thinking apparently inspired ISIS. Admittedly this body defeated an ill-trained and demoralised Iraqi army in 2014, helped by the alienation of the Sunni Muslim population of northern Iraq from the Shia-dominated government in Baghdad. But then ISIS went on to declare the creation of its own state on Syrian and Iraqi territory and commit a series of atrocities which were bound to turn the whole world against it. Yet it continued to attract large numbers of young followers from the Middle East, North Africa, Europe and elsewhere. In due course it found itself fighting Saudis, Americans, Russians, Syrians, Kurds and Iranians – a remarkable combination, but one which would inevitably defeat it. Its state was destroyed and its leaders and many of its followers were killed, but some of those who survived have scattered to join terrorist splinter groups elsewhere.

The sort of nihilistic thinking – not linked to any national cause – that guides these characters has appeared before in terrorists; one saw it in Europe and Japan in the 1970s. But in the Middle East it has arisen only since the end of the war against the Soviet Union in Afghanistan in 1989. And I have to say that it seems to have its origin with the Muslim Brotherhood ideology, which had a deep impact on Bin Laden and the group of followers he gathered around himself on the Pakistani-Afghan frontier in the mid-1980s. In every way Bin Laden was ill-informed, naïve and a believer in the most simplistic solutions, yet I am sorry to say he has been very influential. His ability to broadcast his vitriol through the Al Jazeera television network gave him a growing audience of adherents and acolytes. The story of the damage he and his movement have caused goes back through my attempts to extract him from Afghanistan in the late 1990s, through a series of initiatives undertaken by Saudi Arabia and Pakistan in the mid-1990s to create a stable government in Afghanistan, and through a ten-year military campaign against the Soviet occupation of Afghanistan in the 1980s.

Alongside Bin Laden and his terrorists and coinciding with the Soviet invasion of Afghanistan came the Iranian Revolution, which inspired a revolutionary ideology that is still wreaking havoc in Lebanon, Syria, Iraq and Yemen. Through the effort to export its resolution to the rest of the Islamic world, Ayatollah Khomeini's Iran recruited youth from Shia communities around the world to do its bidding. But that is another story which will have to be told by others. As far as I was concerned the Afghanistan story began one evening in late December 1979 when I turned on the radio at home in Riyadh ...

Chapter 1
Invasion – and Response

I have always followed the habit of my father, the late King Faisal, in listening to the BBC news at 7 p.m. My father listened on a battery-powered Zenith radio, hearing the BBC news in Arabic and then turning the dial to get the Voice of America headlines. Then he would switch between the two stations to get what he hoped would be the best of both. Half an hour later a secretary would bring him the full texts typed out on paper.

So it was on the BBC World Service at 7 p.m. Riyadh time on 24 December 1979 that I heard the news that the Soviet Union had invaded Afghanistan. The operation had begun about three hours earlier as darkness fell in Kabul. From the Soviet point of view, with an eye on the Western reaction, Christmas Eve no doubt seemed like a good moment to 'bury bad news'. If this was Moscow's thinking, it failed.

The news was grim, but not altogether unexpected. For months we had sensed that the Russians were moving towards direct military intervention in Afghanistan. Early the next day – 25 December – I went to see my father's successor, King Khalid, and Crown Prince Fahd. They were concerned about how far the Soviets might go in Afghanistan. For a hundred and fifty years it had been Russia's ambition to acquire a warm-water port and a door onto the Indian Ocean, through the Gulf, the Arabian Sea or indirectly through the Mediterranean. Much of the thrust of the 'Great Game' – the competition between Britain and Russia in Afghanistan and Central Asia in the nineteenth century – had been Russia's desire to break through to the Indian Ocean and Britain's desire to stop it. Now it looked to us as if the Russians were going back to their old strategy.

We wondered whether they would push on through Afghanistan to Pakistan, perhaps fomenting trouble in the provinces of Sind or Balochistan and moving on to occupy them. This was of immediate and vital concern to us. Karachi, the capital of Sind, is less than a three-hour flight from Riyadh. Pakistan is very nearly our neighbour and it is a close friend. A great number of Pakistanis work in Saudi Arabia. Our Kingdom does not have a port on the Arabian Sea, but the Arabian Peninsula as a whole has a long Arabian Sea coastline. Which countries are active in a military sense in that sea and in the Indian Ocean is important to us.

'What do our friends have on this?' asked Prince Fahd, referring to the intelligence services of America, Britain and France. I remember I told him that we had not yet heard anything, but two hours later when I was back in my office at the GID reports from these three allies began to come in, along with cables from our own embassy in Kabul. Later the same day General Zia ul-Haq, the President of Pakistan, telephoned and spoke to both King Khalid and Prince Fahd. The Soviets had launched a full-scale invasion.

Looking back, it is significant that in those first twenty-four hours we were already in contact with the countries that were going to play the biggest role with us in fighting the Soviet occupation during the next nine years.

* * *

The first substantial reaction to the invasion occurred in Pakistan, which was natural enough given that Pakistan was the neighbour of Afghanistan and the country that was going to be most affected by events. It was on the day after the invasion that President Zia sent for his Director of Inter-Services Intelligence (ISI), General Akhtar Abdul Rahman Khan, and asked him to prepare an 'Appreciation' of the situation, with recommendations for action. General Akhtar produced his report within days.

He was immediately concerned that the Soviet Union, an atheist power, had invaded a Muslim country to back socialist leaders whose declared purpose was to establish a secular, indeed Communist, state. Neither he nor General Zia feared that this would undermine the religious nature of Afghan society, but it seemed to Akhtar that Pakistan was morally obliged to defend Islam in its neighbour. No reader of this book should underestimate the moral and emotional commitment of Muslims to help other Muslims; this is a very powerful element in modern politics.

Akhtar also had military concerns. Like us he was very much aware that once the Soviets gained control of Afghanistan, which they seemed bound to do, their forces would be in the southern provinces of Kandahar and Helmand, bordering Balochistan – and Balochistan was the province they would need to subvert or invade to reach the sea.

Another fear concerned how Pakistan might be affected if a Communist government in Kabul were to establish close relations with the government of India, which at that time had excellent relations with the Soviet Union. Akhtar could see that in the event of another war with India – there had already been three between the two powers – Pakistan could find itself threatened from two sides. Even in less extreme circumstances an Indian-Afghan alliance could put pressure on Pakistan by increasing the armament of the Pakistani tribes on the North-West Frontier, which would increase their already strongly independent instincts and defiance of central authority. Given that Afghanistan had never accepted the border between itself and Pakistan in that area, the subversion of the frontier tribes could easily be followed by a claim to a slice of the North-West Frontier Province.

Akhtar saw Afghanistan as Pakistan's forward line of defence against the Soviet Union and to some extent against India. He recommended forcefully to his President that Pakistan should back the Afghan resistance, which had already been operating for some years against the socialist regime. His thinking struck a chord with his boss, not only because General Zia shared his military concerns, but also because earlier in the year he had ordered the execution of the former Pakistani Prime Minister, Zulfiqar Ali Bhutto, who had been convicted on charges of corruption. The hanging had provoked worldwide (and national) condemnation, and Zia could immediately see that by supporting the Afghans' resistance to the Communist superpower he would divert attention from his deed and win himself sympathy both in the West and in the Muslim world. In effect there was a neat coincidence of moral, strategic and political considerations, all pointing towards Pakistan committing itself to the Afghan fighters – the Mujahideen.

Akhtar argued for a large-scale guerrilla war, aimed ultimately at defeating the Soviets. His plan involved Pakistan supporting the guerrillas with arms, money, intelligence, training, operational advice and – above all – the offer of the border areas of the North-West Frontier Province and Balochistan as a sanctuary. For any guerrilla movement a safe haven is enormously important. In this case Akhtar was turning to the advantage of Pakistan and the resistance the wild nature of the border, which might be exploited by the country's enemies if Afghanistan were to come under hostile control.

This border had been drawn in 1893 by a senior official of the Indian Civil Service, Sir Mortimer Durand, and ever since it had been known as the Durand Line. He had been concerned to give India (then including the territory that became Pakistan in 1947) every tactical advantage in controlling the important borderland heights, but in doing this he inevitably ignored tribal and ethnic politics. His line went right through the homelands of the Pathans, putting bits of most of the major tribes on both sides of the frontier. The British were not particularly concerned about this because they never seriously thought of subduing those of the tribes on their side of the border. If the tribes here became too rebellious, the British would mount expeditions, which provided excellent training for their forces – and once they had achieved some limited objective they would retire. When Pakistan took over the territory at the time of Partition (1947) it adopted exactly the same policy. It allowed the Pathans to move to and fro across the border as they pleased, and within the North-

West Frontier Province it designated 'tribal areas' in which the tribes were allowed to exercise their own government. These areas naturally became the sanctuary for the Pathan elements of the Afghan Mujahideen.

Very soon after he read the 'Appreciation', President Zia telephoned King Khalid to say he wanted to send General Akhtar to Riyadh. He arrived in the first few days of January 1980. I remember we went straight away to pay calls on the King and Crown Prince Fahd. We met in what had been my father's private office, next to the entrance of his palace. King Khalid preferred to use this rather than his official office in the Royal Diwan, in downtown Riyadh. I think this was because it was in the Diwan office that my father had been assassinated some four and a half years earlier, and it still held bad memories for us.

Both the King and Prince Fahd had met Sardar Mohammad Daoud, the Afghan leader who seized power in 1973, when he had made an official visit to Saudi Arabia in 1976. Both had warned him of the dangers of including Communists in his government. They remembered their meeting well.

They now told General Akhtar they had advised Daoud, in effect, to 'have the Communists for breakfast before they have you for lunch' – which is exactly what happened in April 1978 when Daoud was overthrown and killed, along with his family and bodyguard. Later in the day Akhtar and I had a long discussion in my office and then, on what I remember was a very cold evening, we had dinner with my secretary, Ahmad Badeeb, at the Al Khozama Hotel. I know that in Pakistan Akhtar came in due course to have a rather sinister reputation – partly because he was so powerful – but I must say I liked him. He was a big Pathan, fair in complexion, pleasant and cheerful – and he struck me as a very straightforward and loyal colleague of his boss. His message from General Zia was that Pakistan was already playing host to several Afghan political parties and embryonic guerrilla organisations – some of them established in the time of Mohammad Daoud. It was intending to back these guerrilla groups in a war against the Russians – and it needed help, financial and material.

General Akhtar spent only two days in Riyadh, and we decided to help straight away. It was only a few days after he left that we sent Ahmad Badeeb to Islamabad with $2 million in cash in suitcases. The money was in $100 bills – 20,000 of them – and walking across the tarmac with his precious load, which he did not want to let out of his sight for an instant, Ahmad found they weighed a lot more than he had expected. The reason the money had to be in cash was that right from the beginning we and the Pakistanis (and later the Americans) did not want our help for the Afghans to be traceable. Had we transferred the money through the banking network and government departments it might have been noticed by Soviet intelligence, possibly at the point where it arrived in Pakistan. We were also all aware that $100 bills would have a certain appeal to the Mujahideen factions.

Ahmad went straight to the President's residence, where he met General Zia and General Akhtar again, and Zia told them both to go to Akhtar's house and count the money. Ahmad was not to leave until this had been done. Once again Ahmad discovered that counting 20,000 bank notes – or having two of Akhtar's assistants count them – took a long time. He was planning to leave on the return flight of the aircraft on which he had arrived, but clearly the counting was going to continue well beyond the departure time. At this point he discovered that General Akhtar was delaying the flight for him. He felt a bit sorry for the passengers waiting at the airport – at least he says he felt sorry – and out of good manners he mentioned this to Akhtar. 'Don't worry,' said the general, 'Pakistanis are all supporters of the Afghan jihad, and if they knew their flight was being delayed because of you and your support, they would be happy.' So, Ahmad got back to Riyadh late that night, and the Pakistani government was left with $2 million to spend as it wished. Part of the money, I know, paid for a batch of hand-held rockets which was taken from Pakistani army stocks.

A fortnight later I went to Pakistan myself, with my brother Saud AlFaisal, our Foreign Minister – God rest his soul. The occasion was the meeting of the Foreign Ministers of the Organisation of the Islamic Conference in Islamabad on 27–29 January, but we went a day or two earlier for a private meeting with Zia and Akhtar. This was my first meeting with

Zia – the first of many as it turned out. I was immediately impressed by his looks, particularly his piercing dark eyes. He struck me as a man who believed passionately in whatever he was saying. I also noticed the very modest army quarters in which he lived in Rawalpindi, which still had the character of a British Indian garrison town: nondescript red-brick houses, each with its number, small, pretty flower gardens, entered through a gate, and creepers growing up the walls. The four of us meeting in Zia's house agreed that it seemed to be the Soviets' intention to reach the Indian Ocean, and we promised each other that we would do our best, as we put it, 'not to allow Pakistan to become the next Afghanistan'.

Our resolution was reinforced by the Islamic foreign ministers in the next two days. It was an unusually large meeting of forty-one delegations, including the Palestine Liberation Organisation. It began with a powerful speech by Zia calling on the Soviet Union to terminate its 'military intervention' in Afghanistan, and later Professor Burhanuddin Rabbani, who will play a big part in this story, spoke to the Political Committee of the Conference on behalf of six Afghan resistance groups. The Conference passed resolutions that underpinned and legitimised the actions we were to take with Pakistan and America during the next nine years. It urged members to support the Afghan people – particularly the refugees; it declared its solidarity with the countries neighbouring Afghanistan against any threat to their security or well-being; and it authorised the Secretary General of the Organisation of the Islamic Conference to receive contributions from Muslim states, organisations and individuals and disburse them to the authorities that needed them. Lastly it called on members to consider withdrawing participation in the Moscow Olympic Games, which were scheduled for July.

The Foreign Ministers' Conference was one element of a broad international movement against the Soviet invasion. There was widespread international concern about what seemed to be the USSR's expanding ambitions in the Indian Ocean basin. The Russians were already well established in Ethiopia, Somalia and South Yemen, and there were still some flickerings of Communist insurgency, backed by South Yemen, in the southern Omani province of Dhofar. The Russians were friendly with our socialist northern neighbours, Iraq and Syria. Now their intervention in Afghanistan seriously worried not only Pakistan and our own government, but also the Gulf countries, Egypt and the Western alliance as a whole.

The Americans were particularly concerned because, less than a year before, their major military ally in the region, the Shah's government in Iran, had collapsed and been replaced by an Islamic republic which was admittedly strongly anti-Communist – but much more passionately anti-American. Inside the Western governments' foreign ministries and intelligence services memoranda circulated discussing previous Russian/ Soviet drives towards the Indian Ocean, initially in the context of the nineteenth-century Great Game. The outcome of the Game had been that the Russians annexed the Central Asian khanates – now Uzbekistan, Turkmenistan, Tajikistan and Kyrgyzstan – and the British established a government in Afghanistan which was independent but broadly friendly.

Afghanistan became in effect a buffer state, a position it held for a hundred years. Then on several occasions in the early twentieth century Imperial Russia occupied parts of northern Iran. And fifty years after the end of the Game, the Soviet Union had made another push southwards. In 1940 its Foreign Minister, Vyacheslav Molotov, suggested to Hitler that Germany should recognise the Soviet claim to pre-eminence in the region south of the Caucasus. A year later, after it had been attacked by Germany, the Soviet Union invaded northern Iran – mainly to secure its routes for military supplies from Britain and America. Eighteen months after the end of the Second World War it withdrew from Iranian Azerbaijan, but only under great international pressure.

Worried by their analyses of Soviet strategy, and by the increasing Soviet military involvement with the Afghan government in the year before the invasion, the Americans had already begun sending help to the Mujahideen. On 3 July 1979 President Jimmy Carter had signed a Presidential 'Finding' which authorised the CIA to begin covert activities in Afghanistan – spending $500,000 on radio equipment, medical supplies and cash grants for the Mujahideen. In line with what was to become normal practice the physical supplies were shipped via a third state, in this case West Germany, and given to the ISI to distribute. Dr Zbigniew Brzezinski, Carter's National Security Adviser, wrote a note to the President that day saying that this aid would encourage further Soviet military involvement and possibly even direct military intervention. However, the overall view of the Administration was that the Soviets could not simply be allowed to establish Afghanistan as a client state. An attempt had to be made to stop the process. Two months later it was beginning to look as if Brzezinski was going to be right in his prediction, and President Carter asked him to prepare a list of options for US action in the event of a full-scale invasion.

So, in spite of the outrage and indignation we all expressed, none of the allies who came to support the Mujahideen was particularly surprised by the Soviet invasion – which is why we all reacted rather quickly. On 24 December 1979, the day of the invasion, Brzezinski wrote a memorandum to President Carter in which he made the famous remark that the United States now had 'the historic chance to give the Soviet Union its Vietnam' – though he was not too sure that this would be an easy task.

'The guerrillas are badly organised and poorly led,' he wrote in another memorandum, 'Reflections on Soviet Intervention in Afghanistan', on 26 December. 'They have no sanctuary, no organized army, and no central government – all of which North Vietnam had. They have limited foreign support, in contrast to the enormous amounts of arms that flowed to the Vietnamese from both the Soviet Union and China. The Soviets are likely to act decisively ...'. (He later said he was surprised by how ineffective the Russians turned out to be and by their reluctance to commit a really large number of troops, which is what one would have expected, given their vast army.) In spite of his reservations Brzezinski recommended 'more money as well as arms shipments to the rebels, and some technical advice'. 'It is essential that Afghanistani resistance continues,' he wrote. 'To make [this] possible we must both reassure Pakistan and encourage it to help the rebels ... We should concert with Islamic countries both in a propaganda campaign and in a covert action campaign ...'

This memorandum led to another Presidential 'Finding' at the end of December, which permitted the CIA to send weapons secretly to the Mujahideen. The purpose was to make the Soviet intervention as costly as possible to get the USSR 'bogged down', as Brzezinski put it later, and to discourage other military interventions, though the CIA and the Mujahideen were not expected to win outright on the battlefield. One of the specific instructions in the 'Finding' was that the CIA was to work through Pakistan and defer to Pakistani priorities.

Within a week of the 'Finding' there was a meeting of the United Nations Security Council, under French chairmanship, convened at the request of fifty-two governments. The resolution put forward was vetoed by the Soviets, but on 10 January 1980 the General Assembly adopted by a huge majority a resolution which called for the 'immediate, unconditional and total withdrawal of Soviet troops' from Afghanistan.

Then on 23 January came President Carter's last State of the Union address and what soon became known as the Carter Doctrine. This laid down the principle that the security of the United States was interdependent not just with the security of Western Europe and the Far East – as had been accepted since 1945 – but with the security of the Middle East as well. The key words were: 'An attempt by any outside force to gain control of the Persian Gulf region will be regarded as an assault on the vital interests of the United States of America, and such an assault will be repelled by any means necessary, including military force'.

The President further said, '… we are prepared to work with other countries in the region to share a cooperative security framework that respects differing values and political beliefs, yet which enhances the independence, security, and prosperity of all'. The doctrine was modelled very much on the Truman Doctrine laid down after the Second World War in response to the Soviet threat to Greece and Turkey. It was not intended to imply that Afghanistan was an area of vital interest to the United States or to threaten any direct American response to the invasion – but it made plain that the Indian Ocean basin beyond Afghanistan and particularly the Arabian Gulf states were areas of vital interest. Here, it was now clear, Soviet intervention would precipitate an engagement with the United States.

The United States gave immediate practical expression to its anger over the invasion. A meeting of the National Security Council at the White House on 28 December made it clear to the Soviets that their action had buried any hopes they still had – at the end of a poor period generally for US-Soviet relations – of a wide-ranging accommodation between the two powers with a Strategic Arms Limitation Treaty as its centrepiece. Bit by bit in the following weeks sanctions were imposed. A big cut was announced in US grain sales. Soviet fishing privileges in US waters were curtailed. All exchanges and co-operation projects were stopped. The United States ambassador was recalled from Moscow. Later in January the US announced that it would withdraw from the Moscow Olympics – and Japan, China and other countries followed suit.

On 2 and 3 February 1980 Brzezinski and the Deputy Secretary of State, Warren Christopher, went to Islamabad to meet General Zia. They discussed how to give concrete form to their desire to help the Mujahideen and embarrass the Soviets. Zia stressed to his guests the importance he attached to Pakistan working with Saudi Arabia and he asked them to pass on this point to the Saudis. On their way back to the United States, Brzezinski and Christopher came through Riyadh – and it was at this point, in meetings with me, my brother Saud and Crown Prince Fahd, that our two governments put together the outline of our co-operation on Afghanistan.

King Khalid had already given instructions in principle to the Crown Prince to do what was necessary to help our Pakistani friends and the Afghan Mujahideen. We now worked on some details of this assistance and our co-operation in related areas. We undertook to help with some Pakistani arms purchases. We asked for more intelligence on the Soviet and East German presence in South Yemen – to which the Americans agreed. It was also agreed in principle that America would look more favourably on our own arms-purchase proposals. Most important of all, it was at this meeting that the principle emerged of Saudi Arabia and the United States matching each other's funds in helping the Mujahideen.

Brzezinski said at one point that the United States was initially going to send $75,000 in further help to the Mujahideen, and Crown Prince Fahd said, 'We'll match this – and whatever else you send in future'. The sum was tiny, almost symbolic, but money goes a very long way in Afghanistan and at the time the Mujahideen were too few to be able to use large amounts of equipment.

At this meeting we also discussed the idea of channelling the money through bank accounts jointly established by ourselves and the Americans in third countries, and we agreed on the principle of letting the ISI, which knew the guerrilla groups best, decide how the money should be allocated. This was the beginning of what became known as the CIA/ GID/ISI arms pipeline. We and the Americans paid, the Americans and to a smaller degree the Pakistanis acquired the arms, and the Pakistanis handed them out among the Mujahideen parties. We and the Americans were periodically to review the arms-purchasing policy – and spending – and the performance of the Mujahideen in action.

In Saudi Arabia the payment of the money and liaison with America and Pakistan – in fact, virtually all aspects of our policy in Afghanistan – were assigned to the GID. It tends to be the Kingdom's policy to have just one department and one small team of people around the head of that department handling any particular issue. The benefit is that we do not suffer from the departmental turf wars, rivalries, switches in policy and manoeuvrings for the ear of the head of state that afflict the governments of some of our allies – though, on the other hand, our practice means that there is not a great deal of internal politics to be described when we talk about any aspect of our policy. Afghanistan was very definitely GID territory; the Foreign Ministry and the Ministry of Defence and Aviation provided diplomatic and military support, when needed.

Over the next twenty years I became the Saudi government official who had the greatest contact with the Afghans, the Pakistanis and the Americans on this issue – at least it was I who represented Saudi Arabia in official dealings on this matter. And our policy during the period until the Soviet withdrawal in February 1989 underwent very little change. The amounts of money we handled increased enormously, but we stuck to the principles of matching US funding and letting the Pakistanis decide on arms distribution and giving practical help to Mujahideen operations. In our own interests we kept a close eye on these activities. We reviewed Pakistan's disbursement of arms and funds and, when possible, our agents interviewed Mujahideen commanders in Peshawar and in the field.

* * *

At this point I must introduce myself and explain how I came to be Director of the GID at the time of the events we are discussing.

I was born in 1945. My father was Prince Faisal bin Abdulaziz (who later became King, and was then governing the Hijaz, the western region of Saudi Arabia, for his father) and my mother was Iffat bint Mohammad bin Saud Al-Thunayyan. The Thunayyans were a branch of the Saud family descended from Thunnayan bin Saud, who was a brother of the founder of the first Saudi state in the eighteenth century. When I was five I was sent to the Taif Model School for Boys and Girls for eight years, and then I was sent to a private school in the United States – what the Americans call a 'prep' school and the English a 'public' school. At the age of eighteen, in 1963, I went to Princeton to study engineering, and I am sorry to say that from an academic point of view it was a disaster. I failed all my engineering courses and was politely asked to leave. From there I went to Georgetown, where I ended up studying business administration.

Finally, in 1973, I returned to Saudi Arabia. I went to see my father, who was now King, with the intention of saying something along the lines of, 'I am available to do any work which the government would like me to do, and how would you advise me to go about this?' But unfortunately, my speech came out, in effect, as, 'I would like you to give me a job'. My father, who was an austere, frugal and incorruptible figure, was not at all impressed. He turned to me heatedly and said, 'I did not give jobs to your brothers, so why should I give one to you?', and he used a phrase which still rings in my mind: 'He who seeks a position shall not be given it'. The expression is an old Arabic one, which expresses very well how things ought to be, though not how things always work out in reality in the Arab world.

My father dismissed me by telling me to go and find a job for myself as my brothers had done before me. I was lucky in that others had noticed my return to the Kingdom and were thinking of how I might be trained in government. The person who helped me was Kamal Adham, an uncle through my mother who, from 1962 to 1977, served as head of the Foreign Liaison Bureau, in charge of contacts with foreign intelligence agencies of friendly countries. Kamal found me a job as a 'counsellor' – more or less an intern in the early stages – in the Royal Court, a position which involved secondment to the Bureau. Here it happened that my work related to the Yemen, whose file had always been regarded as the professional province of my uncle, Prince Sultan bin Abdulaziz, the Minister of Defence and Aviation. Therefore, in my first job, my boss for practical purposes was Prince Sultan.

After a time I was made a deputy director of the Liaison Bureau and then, at the end of 1977, I was suddenly promoted to be the head of the whole Saudi intelligence service. The occasion was a major reorganisation of our operations. In previous years – from the 1960s – we had two intelligence units. One was the Foreign Liaison Bureau, headed by Kamal Adham, which had been established to work with the intelligence services of our allies. During my father's rule, which effectively ran from 1962 to 1975, this unit worked very closely with him. Adham was a close confidant of my father. The other unit was the GID, which engaged in normal intelligence-gathering activities and was headed by the late Omar Shams. At the end of 1977 there was a crisis affecting both units when they utterly failed to predict or prevent the sudden visit of the Egyptian President, Anwar Sadat, to Israel – an event which we and the other Arab countries felt totally undermined the Arab negotiating position vis-à-vis Israel and the United States. Adham and Shams both retired. The Bureau was merged into the GID and I was appointed to head the expanded unit, with the title of Director.

I was to run the GID for the next twenty-four years and this book will tell the story of what was by far my biggest concern while I was in this job. The idea for the book came originally from the late King Abdullah, Crown Prince at the time, who had noticed that 'everybody else' – the Pakistanis, Americans, Russians and Europeans – had told the story of Afghanistan from their points of view and had blamed Saudi Arabia for much of what went wrong. Now, the Crown Prince felt, Saudi Arabia should give its own version of events, and he told me, in effect, to write my Afghan memoirs.

Looking at what others have written I find it extraordinary how much is attributed to Saudi Arabia without any evidence at all, except, perhaps, hearsay or the prejudices of others who have spoken to the writers. I have read, for example, that my department financed guerrilla groups in Afghanistan outside the context of the CIA/GID/ISI pipeline and that later we financed the Taliban – particularly in its campaigns against the major Afghan cities. I have been told we gave the ISI money for cash bonuses to be paid to particular officers and expanded its budget by providing it with cheap oil to sell. All of this is completely untrue. It seems that, because Saudi Arabia does not continually publicise all that it does, whenever a journalist or 'analyst' or politician has wanted to explain some Afghan payment that was not announced as being from a specific source, he has been able to claim it came from Saudi Arabia – and in particular from the GID. In effect Saudi intelligence has been a source of last resort for anyone seeking an explanation for any flow of funds not easily attributable to another source.

As I authorised, in person, every payment my department made to any party involved in Afghanistan from 1980 until 2001, I can say that during the period of the Soviet occupation all the money we distributed to the Mujahideen was in the context of the CIA/GID/ISI pipeline. Payments outside this went to the Afghan refugees in camps around Peshawar and Quetta in Pakistan. The same went for other Saudi government departments. In 1990, one year after the Soviet withdrawal from Afghanistan and by which time the Mujahideen were already fighting among themselves, King Fahd ordered that all official Saudi monies to Afghanistan were to be stopped. Later, from 1992 when the Communist government in Kabul collapsed, we tried to help create a new, stable Afghan government. We sponsored a series of peace initiatives, intended to prevent the Afghan factions fighting each other – all to no avail. As a matter of principle, we would never provide funds for one Afghan party to fight another and we never provided money for the Taliban.

Of course, during the period I am discussing there were large private Saudi donations to many Afghan causes. Most of the money went to help the three million refugees on the Afghanistan-Pakistan border, but some must have gone to political parties and been used for military purposes. In a financial and economic sense Saudi Arabia is and was then a very free society. There was (and is) virtually no direct personal tax – the only exception being the religious tax, *zakat*, which is levied at a rate of 2.5 per cent on a person's liquid assets. There were no exchange controls whatsoever.

People were free to do exactly what they liked with their money – much freer than people were, or are, in the West. If a person wanted to take a million dollars out of the country in a plastic carrier bag (or in several carrier bags) nobody would ask any questions. In the 1980s the government very much encouraged the private sector to make donations to charities sending money to Afghanistan, and it was only at the beginning of the 1990s that we became aware of how some of this money was financing extremism in Afghanistan and opposition at home and in other Arab countries. This is when the United States and our other Western allies also became aware of the problem. Since the events of 9/11 we have – for good or ill – restricted our citizens' freedom to do as they like with their money, particularly when it comes to giving it to charities or transferring it abroad. This has not been easy for a society which is not used to curbs on its financial freedom.

It is the story behind the few ideas I have mentioned here that I am setting out to tell. This book tells the story of Afghanistan in three broad phases: the war against the Soviet occupation and the Communist Afghan government from 1979 to 1992; the failed attempts to create a broadly based, stable Afghan government between 1992 and 1996; and, lastly, our dealings with the Taliban and our attempts to get Bin Laden out of Afghanistan from the mid-1990s onwards. It includes the stories of the Saudi charities, and those of the volunteers who went to Afghanistan, their radicalisation and our attempts to get them, too, out of the country once their services were no longer needed after the fall of the Communist regime.

Chapter 2
A Troubled Independence

I dare not claim to be an expert on Afghanistan. There is always more to learn and less to take for granted about that country. But before describing the events from the time of the Soviet invasion, I ought to say something about Afghan society and Afghanistan's history during the last century.

The Afghans are not a single people. Their country is made up of a collection of different races and linguistic groups. This dominates their history, hugely complicates their politics today and is one of the problems which immediately concerns any foreigner who becomes involved in the country.

In the south and east are the Pathans (or Pashtuns), who speak their own tongue, Pashto, which is a mixture of Indo-Persian languages. They are a fierce, independent, warlike people, divided into several different 'nations' and many tribes, much concerned with family honour – which normally revolves around the behaviour of their women and others' behaviour towards them – and very prone to blood feuds which can run on for generations. The Pathans are by far the most numerous of the Afghan peoples. They make up some forty per cent of the population. They are also among the bravest people I have dealt with.

The second group, the Tajiks, live in the north and east of the country and in the neighbouring republic of Tajikistan. The heart of their territory in Afghanistan is the famous and beautiful Panjshir (Five Lions) Valley, which was the scene of several Soviet campaigns in the early 1980s. The Tajiks are an Iranian people; they speak Persian. Persian, and its local variant, known as Dari, are the languages of government, the Kabul professional classes and much of the press. Their courage is equal to that of the Pathans.

Other Afghan peoples are the Uzbeks and Turkomans in the north – both Turkic peoples from Central Asia – the Nuristanis south of the Panjshir Valley, the Baloch in the south-west and the Hazaras of the centre. The Hazaras were originally from Mongolia, but they speak Dari and centuries ago were converted by the Persians to the Shia Islamic sect. The other peoples of Afghanistan are Sunnis, followers of the legal teaching of the Hanafi school.

For the purposes of the present story the modern history of this complex land goes back to the last two decades of the nineteenth century, to the time of the Amir Abdel-Rahman Khan, the 'Iron Amir'. He was a Pathan, like all the Afghan monarchs and almost all the presidents since the end of the monarchy in 1973. He emerged as ruler in 1880 at the end of the Second Afghan War, which was Britain's second unhappy attempt to control the government of the country. He was not in any sense Britain's client, but his freedom of action was somewhat constrained by treaties with Britain.

Generally, Abdel-Rahman worked well with the British. He was a tough, independent man, one of the most effective monarchs of his age, and from the British point of view he was just what an Afghan ruler was supposed to be – the right man to have between themselves in India and the Russians in the north. The British gave him arms and subsidies. On his country he imposed stern law and order; he was especially hard on non-Pathans and rebellious mullahs. He used to tell visitors that 'more wars and murders have been committed in this world by ignorant priests than by any other class of people'. When he crushed a rebellion of the Hazaras he made a minaret of their skulls. He had a rapist put in a hole in the ground in winter, and then had water poured over him until he was encased in a block of ice – to cool his ardour. Petitioners went pale with fear in his presence.[1]

He also wanted to modernise his country. He created a standing army and a reasonably modern administration. An English tailor designed Western uniforms for his officials and the royal family and its entourage, male and female, adopted European dress. The workshops established by his predecessor were expanded to make civilian goods as well as munitions.

After Abdel-Rahman died in 1901, possibly poisoned by his son, his policies were continued by his successors, Amir Habibullah (1901–19) and King Amanullah (1919–28). Amanullah was a tireless worker. He founded many schools, usually named after himself or his wife, and sent the first Afghan students to university in Europe. He brought in doctors and architects from Turkey, France and Germany – but not from Britain or India. Turkish educational and military missions arrived and a large number of former Ottoman officers were installed in the Afghan army, earning much resentment. He redoubled his predecessors' efforts to introduce European dress, which was made compulsory in the districts of Kabul located around the court. In 1928, on his return from a visit to Europe, he ordered that the wives of all senior officials should remove their veils. In September that year, when an assembly of tribal representatives, a Loya Jirga, was summoned, the members were ordered to appear in suits and ties, which none of them had ever worn before. Assembled for a photographer, they made a remarkable picture.

In any conservative, traditional society, such as Afghanistan was in the first half of the twentieth century (and in many respects still is), it is very important that a ruler does not run too far ahead of the rest of society in his attempts to modernise – especially in such sensitive or visible areas as the role of women, modes of dress and the adoption of foreign practices. If he ignores this principle he will be seen as arrogant, out of touch with his people and not caring about their sensibilities. This is a mistake that Mohammad Reza Shah made in Iran in the 1960s and 1970s, and which my family has always been extremely careful not to make in Saudi Arabia.

King Amanullah totally disregarded these rules with the result that in

December 1928 a Tajik highwayman, Habibullah Ghazi Bacha-i-Saqao, rose in revolt. The army failed to support the King, the rebels took Kabul and Amanullah went into exile in Italy. There followed ten months of chaos before Habibullah Ghazi was captured and shot in the moat outside the palace in Kabul. His body was exposed to the public gaze.

The monarchy returned. From 1929 to 1973 first Mohammad Nadir Shah and then Mohammad Zahir Shah continued policies of modernisation and reform – though more cautiously than their predecessors. Both monarchs kept their country at arm's length from Britain. Under a treaty that had been signed with the British at the end of the First World War, Afghanistan had been allowed to conduct its own foreign policy, which in the days of Amir Abdel-Rahman had been subject to supervision from Calcutta. The rulers remained very conscious, though, of the British imperial presence over their southern border.

When Britain withdrew from India in 1947 this informal constraint on their freedom of action was removed and bit by bit Afghanistan came under the influence of its northern neighbour, the Soviet Union. The Russians developed the relationship very cleverly and with great patience – never pushing the pace, inviting students (particularly officer cadets) to Moscow and periodically giving aid projects. No power to the south worked to counter this. Pakistan had little influence, and India was actively pro-Soviet. Indeed, India was rather happy to see the Russians involved in Afghanistan because it saw that the effect might be to isolate Pakistan. My father was concerned by how strong the Russian connection was becoming in Afghanistan when he visited the country in 1970. Saudi Arabia and Afghanistan had already had considerable diplomatic contact by this time. Afghanistan had been the first Muslim country to recognise my grandfather, King Abdulaziz (Ibn Saud), as King of the Hijaz and Najd (later Saudi Arabia) in the 1920s. My father visited the country a few years later, in 1932, and Zahir Shah came to Saudi Arabia in 1951.

My father was quite right to have been concerned. In 1973 the process of 'modernisation' and the Soviet connection took a big step forward when Zahir Shah was deposed by his cousin and brother-in-law, Sardar

Mohammad Daoud. The new regime had the backing of some leftist officers in the army, and a small urban-based Communist party, *Parcham* (Flag), led by the staunchly pro-Soviet Babrak Karmal. An Islamic opposition movement was crushed and its leaders – Gulbuddin Hekmatyar, a Pashtun, and Burhanuddin Rabbani and Ahmad Shah Massoud, both Tajiks, all of whom will play a major part in this story – sought refuge in Pakistan.

Mohammad Daoud turned to the Soviet Union for help with a programme of socialist modernisation and infrastructure construction, and the Soviets responded generously. Foreign aid, mostly from Moscow but from other sources as well, came to account for forty per cent of the government's budget. The ruler, though, was not entirely a Russian puppet. On a visit to Moscow in 1977 he lost his temper with President Leonid Brezhnev, banging his fists on the table and shouting that Afghans made the decisions in Kabul. He paid dearly for his outburst. In April 1978 the Russians sponsored a coup in Kabul by a group of Soviet-trained army officers. Mohammad Daoud was killed.

The people who replaced him were openly Communist, but they were split into two factions, Babrak Karmal's *Parcham* and the *Khalq* movement of Nur Mohammad Taraki. Moscow decided to back Taraki, mainly because Brezhnev – by then an old man of much reduced mental and physical capacities – had met him and believed he would 'do a good job'. Karmal was packed off to Prague as Afghanistan's ambassador to Czechoslovakia, and then the *Khalq* faction set about killing the *Parcham* supporters, many of whom had been recruited as agents of Soviet intelligence, the KGB.

The Communist regime had no understanding whatsoever of Afghan society – indeed it had no desire for understanding. It treated the people with contempt. It only wanted to impose change upon them. It launched a compulsory literacy campaign for women – admirable as an idea, but unwise in the way it was executed. The campaign showed a lack of respect for the people, their traditions and the society of the small towns and villages. The government was overtly opposed to religion and to the traditional ruling class of the countryside. Land was confiscated and given to party supporters. Anyone who objected was murdered. There were mass executions of 'reactionary elements' in the Pul-i-Charkhi jail in Kabul.

Red replaced green as the national colour. Public buildings were painted red and, out of fear, shopkeepers competed with each other to display the biggest portrait of Taraki. They painted their doors and windows red. By the spring of 1979 stocks of red paint in the bazaar were exhausted.

Almost immediately the religious leaders, the mullahs, and the rural chiefs, the khans, declared jihad against Taraki's Communist regime. Much more seriously, there were mutinies in the army. In March 1979, after the government announced its female literacy campaign, an uprising began in the western city of Herat. It started with a demonstration which led to an attack on the jail to release political prisoners. Two days later the troops in the garrison joined the movement, shooting some of their officers – and then the entire Afghan army division in the city mutinied, led by Captain Ismail Khan, who was to become the most famous Mujahideen commander in the west.

In the chaos that followed the people showed their hatred of the Soviet military advisers and their families. More than fifty Communists were rounded up, tortured and cut to pieces. Their heads were stuck on poles and paraded through the city. The government sent its most loyal armoured forces from Kabul – a fast-diminishing band – and eventually retook the city at a cost of some 5,000 mostly civilian lives. It was not a very decisive victory. In the following months almost every Afghan garrison mutinied. Taraki and his regime called on Moscow to send its own troops.[2]

The Kremlin by this time was having second thoughts about the wisdom of choosing Taraki. It sent a mission of seven generals to Kabul to assess the situation and they were severely shaken by what they saw. They reported that indiscriminate killing was pushing people to join the growing resistance and that the Afghan army was on the point of collapse.

The Russians have since released records of Politburo meetings held at the time – publication was part of the glasnost policies of President Boris Yeltsin in the 1990s – and they make interesting reading. In one of their meetings on 17 March 1979 at the time of the Herat uprising the Defence Minister, Dimitri Ustinov, declared, 'the problem is that the leadership of Afghanistan does not sufficiently appreciate the role of Islamic fundamentalists'. The head of the KGB, Yuri Andropov, who later became President, agreed: 'It is completely clear to us that Afghanistan is not ready at this time to resolve all the issues it faces through socialism. The economy is backward, the Islamic religion predominates, and nearly all of the rural population is illiterate. We know Lenin's teaching about a revolutionary situation. Whatever situation we are talking about in Afghanistan, it is not that type of situation.'

It was agreed at this meeting that the Prime Minister, Alexei Kosygin, should telephone Taraki to persuade him to change his policies. He did this the next day and the conversation was not a success. When Kosygin asked what had happened to the hundreds of Afghan officers who had been trained in the Soviet Union, Taraki said they were mostly with the 'reactionaries'. Taraki appealed for military help, particularly for regiments made up of Soviet citizens from the Central Asian republics who would look like Afghans. 'You are of course oversimplifying the situation,' replied Kosygin.[3]

Taraki remained difficult and obtuse during the summer. Yuri Andropov wrote to him urging him to stop quarrelling with his rivals and soften his stance towards Islam. He advised him to recruit mullahs onto the Communist payroll and to work at 'convincing the broad mass of Muslims that socioeconomic reforms will not affect their religious beliefs'. Taraki kept demanding troops. So, in September the Kremlin organised an official visit for him to Cuba and when he returned to Kabul all had been arranged for his removal. He was arrested, and then tied to a bed and suffocated with a pillow.

His successor, Hafizullah Amin, had worked under Taraki as Prime Minister. Amin, like Taraki, was apparently Brezhnev's choice. The KGB was suspicious of the man because he had once been a student at Columbia University in New York and it was thought he might have links with the CIA. There were fears that the Americans, having just 'lost' Iran, might see if they could cultivate Afghanistan under Amin as a replacement.

There were thoughts that the Americans might want to base Pershing missiles in Afghanistan or even use the country as the first building block in the creation of a new Islamic community or empire in Central Asia, incorporating some of the Soviet republics. In fact, the CIA did try to establish contact with Amin – but it failed.

Both Moscow's fears and the CIA's more tentative hopes turned out to be baseless, because Amin proved himself to be as bloody and incompetent a tyrant as Taraki. The Islamic opposition grew in strength and the Russians began to worry that the Communist regime might be overthrown and replaced by a government similar to the new revolutionary government of Ayatollah Khomeini in Iran. This would have given them two militant Islamic regimes on the borders of their own nominally Islamic republics. There came a time in December when they decided they had to act decisively or risk 'losing' Afghanistan. The records of the Politburo meetings show that those present were well aware that they would be labelled as aggressors and condemned internationally. Eventually a decision was taken to mount an invasion. The people involved were just a few generals and members of the Politburo; the full Politburo and the Foreign Ministry were not informed.

Amin at this time appealed once again for help. His appeals were heard, but they did not have the consequences he intended. The Kremlin acted first, so it seemed, to ensure his personal safety. His Soviet advisers asked him to move from his office in central Kabul to the old Darul Aman Palace on the city's outskirts, which was said to be easier to defend. New palace guards and cooks were introduced – Soviet Uzbeks and Tajiks. The palace was renovated at Soviet expense. Amin was suspicious. He kept switching his food and drink, and sometimes – but not always – he used his own chefs.

On 24 December 1979 Amin invited his inner circle and their wives to lunch to welcome a colleague who had just returned from Moscow. When the soup was served only this man, Dastagir Panjshiri, refused it, saying his doctor had forbidden him fats. The soup, of course, was poisoned. Sometime later, when a doctor from the Soviet Embassy was summoned, he found the guests strewn around the dining room, dead or dying, some still in their chairs, some on the floor. Amin was still just alive. He was taken to his private apartments and doctors tried to revive him, but by this time the invasion had begun. Amin's wife, in another room, heard the shooting start and rushed to his bedside. According to her testimony, Amin sat up and asked what was happening. He reached for a telephone, but the line had been cut. Then units of the Russian Special Forces burst in, saw Amin and shot him dead.[4]

During the attack on Darul Aman Palace the Special Forces also killed by mistake some of their own presidential guardsmen, the Tajiks and Uzbeks the Russians had imposed on the Afghan president. Other units at the same time were taking control of all points of strategic importance in Kabul – the radio and television buildings, the Ministry of Internal Affairs, the secret police headquarters, the Pul-i-Charkhi prison and the airport. Then a stream of Soviet troop transports began arriving at the airport, one every two or three minutes. One of these, flying directly from Moscow, brought in the new President, Babrak Karmal, the leader of the Parcham faction of the Afghan Communist Party, the recent ambassador to Prague and the man whose supporters had been murdered a year before by the Taraki regime.

Chapter 3
The Emergence of the Mujahideen

The Afghans' resistance to the Communists began soon after the party came into government in the wake of Mohammad Daoud's coup in 1973. Many politically minded Afghans were immediately worried by Daoud. They saw him as laying a road towards Communism, and they noticed that almost immediately anyone who might be considered a threat by the regime came under pressure. People lost their jobs. There were arrests. Conservative and religious political figures, and those who wanted simply to enjoy their traditional freedoms, began to think of leaving the country – or going to the tribal border regions of Afghanistan and Pakistan, which were beyond the reach of either central government.

Professor Burhanuddin Rabbani left Kabul in 1974 and went to live with the eastern Mohmand border tribe. I got to know him well in later years and he told me his story. Soon after he had settled into his new 'home' he was contacted by Brigadier Naseerullah Babar, who at the time was Governor of the North-West Frontier Province of Pakistan and adviser on Afghan affairs to the Prime Minister, Zulfiqar Ali Bhutto. (Later, under Bhutto's daughter, Benazir, he became Minister of the Interior.) The Pakistani government had been worried about Afghanistan from the time of Daoud's coup and it had decided to welcome Afghan exiles. Initially Babar wanted a meeting with Rabbani, which took place, but in due course he suggested that Rabbani should move to Peshawar, the principal town on the Pakistani side of the border. Rabbani agreed.

Once installed in Peshawar Rabbani established contact with the Saudi Arabian ambassador in Islamabad – he had previously known our ambassador in Kabul – and a message was sent to my father, who promptly invited him to come to Saudi Arabia on pilgrimage. He told my father when they met that, though Daoud might appear to be a man of the people, he was in reality a bridge for the Communists. It was a message my father was very willing to accept so he invited Rabbani to stay in Saudi Arabia if he wished, but he felt he had a more important mission in Afghanistan and he returned to Peshawar.

Other exiles joined Rabbani in Peshawar. They included Ahmad Shah Massoud and the redoubtable Gulbuddin Hekmatyar. Their resources at first were nothing. Rabbani told me that in 1974 his only piece of equipment was a typewriter, which was of little use because none of his group knew how to type. The Pakistanis, however, began a basic military training course for some 5,000 young exiles, and in 1975 Massoud led some of these back into Afghanistan and raised the standard of revolt in the Panjshir Valley. His uprising got nowhere and he rapidly retreated to Peshawar.

At this point the opposition split. So far it had been rather loosely tied together in a body known as the Jamiat-i-Islami (Islamic Group) headed by Rabbani. Now Massoud stuck with Rabbani, but Hekmatyar formed Hizb-i-Islami (the Islamic Party). They made little progress during the next two years, until Taraki's coup in April 1978 led the Pakistani government to quietly increase its support and encourage the opposition to resume action inside Afghanistan. Massoud began operations in Kunar province, which is on the Pakistan border in the Nuristan Mountains, south of the Panjshir Valley, and after a short time his campaign forced the Communist *wali* (governor) in Panjshir to retreat to Kabul. At this point Massoud established his dominance of the valley, which he maintained for the next twenty-two years. Hekmatyar, who remained based in Peshawar, also operated in Kunar.

They had very few arms. One very basic source was the village of Darra Adam Khel, which was a centre for 'informal' weapons manufacture. Much better than this was a NATO weapon they obtained in small quantities from Pakistan. This was always known in Afghanistan as the 'Twenty Rounds', but in NATO it was called the SLR, the Self-Loading Rifle, which was the standard infantry weapon until the late 1980s. The biggest and best source for the opposition was the Afghan army itself. Out of fear, greed or sympathy – mainly the second two – the Afghan soldiers parted readily with their weapons. In this way the Mujahideen groups acquired rifles, mortars, rocket launchers, machine guns and all sorts of other small arms.

By the time of the Soviet invasion, or soon afterwards, six distinct opposition parties had appeared.

The one that was to be perhaps the best known and most important during the next fifteen years was Gulbuddin Hekmatyar's Hizb-i-Islami. Hekmatyar, a Pathan from Kunduz in the north, was among the youngest of the leaders: he was born in 1946. He had received a good education – he had a degree in engineering from Kabul University – and while at university he had become involved in politics. In 1972, quite soon after he left university, he was imprisoned for two years for anti-government activities, and when he was released, under the Mohammad Daoud regime, he promptly joined the opposition in exile.

As a character Hekmatyar was the most difficult of all the Mujahideen leaders. He was arrogant, incapable of seeing another person's point of view, unable to compromise, suspicious – a man who needed to control everything around him – and jealous even of his own junior commanders. He was also ruthless and a stern disciplinarian – but well organised, an excellent administrator and scrupulously honest in his financial dealings. In the war against the Soviets he was one of the toughest, most vigorous and effective of all the guerrilla leaders, but he was impossible to deal with politically.

There was a good example of this when he visited the United Nations in New York in 1985. He publicly refused to meet President Ronald Reagan. He came under great pressure to change his mind, but he was unmoved. He maintained that for him to be seen talking to Reagan would play into the hands of the KGB and the Afghan secret police, the KHAD, both of which always claimed that the war in Afghanistan had nothing to do with a fight for independence but was part of American foreign policy. His view was quite logical, and correct, but at the same time he could not see that in the US domestic political context it was important that anyone receiving American aid was shown – ideally on television – to be grateful for that aid. Nor could he see that his refusal would give the Americans the impression that he was a dangerous fundamentalist, no friend of the West and not the sort of man they would want to see installed one day in government in Kabul.

On this occasion there were faults on the American side as well. Nobody in the Administration seemed to understand that for Hekmatyar, and the other Afghan leaders, to publicly acknowledge gratitude for American help would be humiliating. Brigadier Mohammad Yousaf remarks in his book *Afghanistan the Bear Trap: The Defeat of a Superpower* that in the US 'aid donations are publicised so much that the receiver loses face and becomes resentful rather than grateful'. Hekmatyar's party, Hizb-i-Islami, was mainly Pathan but had members from most of the other Afghan peoples. Many of his fighters came from the Pavan area north of Kabul, a region of mixed Pathan and Tajik population. He also had an important Ferghanachi element. These were young men from émigré families who had fled the Ferghana valley in Uzbekistan in the 1920s – during the brutal period in which the Soviet system was imposed – and had settled in Hekmatyar's home region of Kunduz.

The binding force in Hekmatyar's party was ideological. His was one of what became known as the 'fundamentalist' groups, inspired very much by the Jamaat-i-Islami party of Pakistan, founded by Abul-Ala Maududi in 1941. This party, which was a strong force during Zia's presidency, rejected nationalism, tribal divisions and traditional class structures based on landholding. It wanted instead to create a truly Islamic society. This would have no divisions among believers and would be led by strong, just men guided by the Quran and consulting with their people. This, in the view of Maududi, Hekmatyar and the other fundamentalist leaders, was the right formula for a Muslim society facing the challenges of the modern world.

The other important Afghan party, on a par with Hekmatyar's, was the Jamiat-i-Islami, which had Burhanuddin Rabbani as its political leader and Ahmad Shah Massoud as its military commander. The group had much the same Islamist ideology as Hekmatyar's party and its forces came largely from the Panjshir Valley and the Pavan province north of Kabul, an area in which Hekmatyar was also strong. This contributed to the rivalry of the two groups.

In the main Massoud's forces were Tajik rather than Pathan, but what really distinguished his party from Hekmatyar's was the utterly different personalities of the leaders. Rabbani was a university professor, a scholar and a linguist – he spoke six languages. He understood politics and was the ideal representative of the Afghan opposition at conferences such as the Islamic foreign ministers' meeting in Islamabad in January 1980. Massoud had been educated at the Lycée Istiqlal in Kabul. He had become involved in politics when he was at the university, and when Mohammad Daoud came to power in 1973 – when Massoud was twenty – he immediately found himself in opposition. From the late 1970s he showed himself a superb military commander, not just in guerrilla raids but also in broader engagements such as his defence of the Panjshir Valley and his capture of Kabul in 1992. He was a charismatic figure, adored by his troops and impressive to all who met him. He was as much a politician as a party leader. He and Rabbani often tried to get the different groups to work together, but they never succeeded.

The third Islamist party, closely connected to Hekmatyar's, was the Hizb-i-Islami of Maulvi Yunus Khalis – Maulvi, meaning 'scholar', is a traditional title given to clergy in Afghanistan. The party had the same name as Hekmatyar's because it had the same origin. Khalis was originally part of Hekmatyar's organisation, but he broke away a short while before the Soviet invasion and, because he considered that he was as good a representative of the original party as Hekmatyar, he kept the name. His party mainly consisted of Pathans. Its base was Jalalabad in the south, south of Kunar, but it was quite active in carrying out operations far into the interior of the country.

At the time of the invasion Maulvi Khalis was nearly sixty, a relatively old man who had an established reputation as a religious leader. Before the war he ran his own madrasa, a religious school. Nominally his party subscribed to the same Islamist ideas as Hekmatyar and Rabbani. But it was different in that it was more conservative and more tribally based, and whereas the two big parties supported the idea of elections as a means of choosing a future Afghan government, Khalis supported the traditional Loya Jirga, a gathering of tribal representatives, to select the leadership. The tribal link was the strength of Khalis's party. Several people who later became important in the Taliban, including that movement's leader, Mullah Omar, at first joined Khalis, partly on the basis that he was from their own home province. They also noticed that he had good access to money and supplies.

The three other opposition parties were normally referred to as 'moderate' or 'traditionalist'. Broadly speaking they favoured the restoration of the monarchy of Zahir Shah. The moderates had much more contact with the Americans than did the Islamists. Their leaders travelled frequently to the United States during the war (at American expense) and they were certainly the people the Americans would have liked to become the leaders of the Mujahideen movement as a whole. But they were less effective on the battlefield. They followed the Sufi tradition of Islam.

The most prominent of the moderate parties was the Harakat-i Inqilab-i-Islami (Islamic Revolutionary Movement – a misnomer designed to disguise its true character) of Maulvi Mohammad Nabi Mohammadi. Like Khalis, Mohammadi had been a well-known scholar, teaching in his own madrasa. His strength lay in his Pathan tribal links in the south; one of his early recruits from Kandahar was Mullah Hassan, later another important personality in the Taliban. Yet what Mohammadi led was hardly a party in the sense of the Hizb-i-Islami of Hekmatyar. It was more a loose alliance of tribal chiefs and independent guerrilla commanders, with no formal structure. Furthermore, Mohammadi was not a strong or effective leader. He left the running of his movement's affairs to his two sons, both of whom were later accused of retaining for their own use funds that they were supposed to hand over to their military commanders. This very much discredited their operation.

A rather similar loosely knit body was the National Islamic Front (another carefully chosen misnomer) of Pir Ahmad Gailani. The movement was strongly tribal, drawing much support from the Durrani Pathan tribes around Kandahar, and its leader was a strong advocate of the return of the monarch Zahir Shah, which was a popular idea among the Durrani tribes. (The monarchy had been Durrani Pathan since 1747 and Kandahar was its original home.) Gailani, however, was not a forceful character. He was a soft-spoken, liberal democrat, fond of the easy life and happy to spend much of his time abroad. He had little control over his party.

Lastly there was the Afghan National Liberation Front headed by Hazrat Sibghatullah Mojaddedi. Mojaddedi was a linguist and philosopher of repute. His main claim to fame was that he had tried to assassinate the Soviet President, Nikita Khrushchev, when he visited Kabul in the early 1960s, and for this he had spent four years in prison. He was not a forceful leader. He was let down by the people around him; their dubious financial activities brought his party into disrepute. The Afghan National Liberation Front and the other two moderate parties enjoyed popular support abroad as well as inside Afghanistan.

From the very beginning of the fight against the Soviets and the Babrak Kamal regime it seemed logical to the Saudi government, and to the Pakistanis and Americans, that the Mujahideen parties should be united in a single organisation. If they could be made to work together there would be obvious benefits in coordinating military strategy, organising the distribution of arms and money, and presenting the movement to Afghans and the rest of the world as a plausible future government of Afghanistan. It would also, we all hoped, prevent them from fighting each other. We made no progress on this, partly because the man who was best qualified to be leader, Professor Rabbani, would not be accepted by Hekmatyar.

Then, in the latter part of 1980, a man appeared in Peshawar who seemed to be the answer to our prayers. He was Professor Abd Rabb Al-Rasul Sayyaf. (His rather unusual first name means literally slave – *Abd* –

of the Lord – *Rabb*, which in this context refers to God, of the Messenger/ Prophet – *Al-Rasul*.) Sayyaf, a Pathan, was a professor of religion from Kunar in the east of Afghanistan. He had studied in Egypt and was a graduate of the Islamic university of Al-Azhar, and he spoke excellent Arabic. In 1978 he had been thrown into prison by the Communists, but he was released in the chaotic period that followed the Soviet invasion. He slipped out of Kabul and soon afterwards arrived in Peshawar.

At this point the Saudi government was organising a summit meeting of Muslim leaders to be held under the auspices of the Organisation of the Islamic Conference in Makkah and Taif at the end of January 1981. Pakistan and Saudi Arabia both invited the Mujahideen to attend, but it was obviously necessary that at the meeting they should speak with a single voice. The delegation that arrived in Taif, in the mountains above Makkah, a few days before the summit opened included Abd Rabb Al-Rasul Sayyaf.

Its members came to see me in a group in my office in Taif and I asked which of them was going to speak on behalf of the Mujahideen. 'You cannot all speak,' I said. 'If you cannot choose a single spokesman, you cannot go to the conference.' There was an immediate undignified argument. I told them that they should go to a separate room to make up their minds. I said I had no intention of breaking up their meeting until they had come to a decision. It seemed a straightforward statement which left the choice up to them, though the leaders knew that I favoured Sayyaf and that it was the Saudi government which had invited him to Taif. My secretary, Ahmad Badeeb, conducted them to the meeting room and closed the door. I have no idea what happened inside, but after a while they all chose Sayyaf – I believe on the grounds that he spoke the best Arabic.

At the Islamic summit on 25–28 January Sayyaf performed very well. He was an imposing figure. He made an eloquent speech asking for the support of the delegates. Three of the leaders – Saddam Hussein of Iraq, Hafez Assad of Syria and Yasser Arafat of the Palestine Liberation Organisation – opposed a motion condemning the Soviet invasion, but Sayyaf very ably countered by saying to Arafat, 'God willing, after we have liberated our country, we shall liberate yours'.

During the meeting the Mujahideen leaders agreed to establish the Islamic Union for the Liberation of Afghanistan, generally known as the Ittihad-i-Islami, with Sayyaf as its *Imam*, leader. They gave him *bayah*, the oath of allegiance. After the conference was finished we took the group to Makkah and they swore in front of the Kaaba to work together. But as soon as the leaders went back to Afghanistan, they totally forgot their oath, ignored Sayyaf and periodically fought each other. Sayyaf kept the money that he had been given for the Ittihad-i-Islami and established his own party with the same name. The Ittihad became a seventh Mujahideen party and the smallest of the four Islamist groups.

Sayyaf received much support from the Saudi public – he was popular in the Kingdom, mainly because he spoke Arabic. He was the man who introduced the Afghan cause to the Saudi public. Yet in Afghanistan he was quite a small force, probably because his was the last of the groups to be established. His commanders operated mainly in the Paghman mountain range immediately to the west of Kabul and also in the region south of the capital and around Jalalabad.

The disunity of the Mujahideen was to be the story of the next twenty years. It not only weakened the campaign against the Soviets, it also cost thousands of lives and much human misery in the decade after the Soviets left. During this period I must have gone to Pakistan a dozen or fifteen times, and on every occasion before I went King Fahd, God rest his soul, would tell me to make a point of urging the leaders to be united. We did everything we could to this end. On one occasion, in May 1982, we invited the Mujahideen leaders to Makkah and opened the Kaaba. This was a most unusual event. Normally the Kaaba is opened just once a year after the Hajj (Pilgrimage) when it is washed in the presence of either the King or his representative and invited dignitaries – mostly heads of state – from the Muslim world. The interior walls are of marble, hung with tapestries on which are embroidered inscriptions of verses from the Holy Quran.

The Mujahideen leaders were much impressed by our gesture. They went inside and, overcome by the emotion of the occasion, cried on each other's shoulders and swore that they would never fight each other again.

Then we arranged transport for them to go to Madinah, which is the second city of the Muslim world after Makkah – and to our exasperation and despair they started arguing again and nearly came to blows in the bus.

My own view of the Afghans is that they share bad and good qualities. They are cruel, fractious and unreliable – but they are also generous, open, very patient and willing to suffer incredible pain and adversity and yet remain steadfast. They are also immensely brave. On the Salang highway, where it winds up into the mountains eighty kilometres north of Kabul, there is a little monument on a hairpin bend above a precipice. It commemorates a young man who saw a minibus coming down the road out of control. He threw himself onto the front wheels of the bus so that his body would act as a brake. There is unbelievable courage and self-sacrifice in that deed.

I respect the Afghans for their strength and bravery, but the qualities I find endearing are their directness and ability to laugh at themselves. There was an occasion in Pakistan in February 1989, at the time of the end of the Soviet occupation, when we were working painfully towards putting together some sort of provisional government, and the Pakistani President was canvassing the views of the leaders. He asked each one for his views on who should be in the government, how it should work and what Pakistan could do to help. The last man to speak was a member of Sayyaf's party, a person called Ahmad Shah Ahmadzai, who had been appointed provisional prime minister. 'Well,' said Ahmad, 'if you want the Afghans to achieve their just and honourable objective, you ought to take all the seven leaders here, keep them in Pakistan and put them in prison.'

* * *

If we found the Afghans difficult, the Russians in the period after the invasion misunderstood them totally. The Kremlin in the summer of 1979 might have made a shrewd assessment of the shortcomings of the leaders it had put in power, but Russian policy in Afghanistan was generally inept and insensitive. The people who ran operations seemed to have an utter lack of sympathy for the Afghans, no feel for the conservative and religious character of society, and no understanding that in a country such as Afghanistan the need for independence, honour and self-respect is more important than the achievement of material prosperity. In the last of these ways, they were not unlike the Americans in similar circumstances.

The average Russian soldier and official viewed Afghanistan as backward, chaotic and totally unenlightened. His feelings were a mixture of contempt and a belief that material aid and education could improve what he saw as these wretched people. And he thought if he provided these things he would not only be helping Afghanistan modernise itself but would also win his country friends. These at least were the common attitudes immediately after the invasion; in time, as Russians learnt about the brutality of the war they were fighting and began to understand the Afghans' lack of appreciation, their feelings changed.

In the early 1980s they poured in material goods – intended partly to show their own country, quite untruthfully, as a successful, productive land of plenty. A young man from Termez, the town across the border on the main crossing of the river Amu Darya (formerly the Oxus) between Uzbekistan and Afghanistan, told the author Monica Whitlock, 'We saw loads of cooking oil and flour and medicine crossing the Amu every day and we were very proud to see that we were helping the poor Afghans'.[1] Cheap loans were given for the purchase of Russian equipment for factories. There were cultural exchanges, conferences and exhibitions. Sports teams went to and fro.

Rather more sinister was the movement of thousands of Afghan children to schools and children's homes in the Soviet Union. The wife of the new Afghan President became the chairwoman of an institution called the Household Nursery, which sent boys and girls aged between seven and nine to special Soviet institutions, mainly in the Central Asian republics, to be brought up as the first Afghan cradle Communists, the hoped-for nucleus of future party cadres. The Nursery was intended to look after the orphaned children of 'martyrs of the revolution', but many poor families said later that soldiers seized children from bombed villages without checking whether their parents were alive or dead.

The new system was backed up by the KHAD, which was given advisers seconded from the KGB. The KHAD began to conduct surveillance of people in the same way that the KGB did in the Soviet Union and the Stasi did in East Germany. It set up networks of informers, compiled loyalty dossiers and very quickly destroyed the old fabric of society in the cities by creating an atmosphere in which nobody felt able to trust anyone else, even within families.

The Afghan response, inevitably, was hostile from the moment of the invasion. Within a week or so leaflets began to circulate in the bazaars. 'Sons of Lenin, what are you doing here?' asked one that spread through the bazaar in Kandahar in January 1980. As dusk fell one misty evening, hundreds of people in Kandahar climbed onto their roofs and shouted for hour after hour, '*Allah-u Akbar*' (God is Great).[2] The same thing happened in Kabul on the night of 21 February. Quiet killings of Russians and Afghan Communist Party members began. The Afghan army, which was supposed to be strengthened by the Soviet presence, fell apart. There were mass desertions.

Quite quickly we, the Americans and the Pakistanis came to realise that the Afghan resistance had more potential than we had originally thought. More and more Afghans, including middle-class people from the towns, went over to the Mujahideen. By the end of 1981 the guerrillas were operating in most parts of the country. There were regular attacks on Russian convoys. Ahmad Shah Massoud, Gulbuddin Hekmatyar and Yunus Khalis were already active, as was Jalaluddin Haqqani, one of Khalis's more independent commanders, who operated in the area around Khost, south of Kabul near the Pakistani frontier. There was a very active commander, known as Zabihullah, a high school teacher associated with Burhanuddin Rabbani's party, who radioed reports every day of Russian losses inflicted in the area around Mazar-i-Sharif, capital of Balkh province in the north. At this stage there was much action around Kandahar. We also saw the emergence of some commanders, linked to all the parties, who for reasons of prestige and money were mostly concerned with talking to journalists in Peshawar and projecting themselves and their fairly minor exploits to the outside world.

Chapter 4
The Arms Pipeline

From the beginning of the war against the Soviet invasion force the task of managing the Mujahideen groups, in so far as this was possible, was left to the Pakistanis. And the people who had most influence on the overall strategy of the war – on the theatres of action, the intensity of operations and the allocation of supplies – were President Zia and the chief of the ISI, General Akhtar Abdul Rahman Khan. The two were masters of the game. They showed great attention to detail, perfect judgement, diplomatic finesse and caution.

The game was not an easy one. If they overplayed their hand and provoked the Soviet Union too much – or alternatively if the Soviets found themselves quite easily able to control Afghanistan – there was the ultimate danger of a Soviet attack on Pakistan itself. More likely would have been a determined Soviet effort to subvert and promote the independence of the southern Pakistani provinces of Sind, the home of the family of the executed Prime Minister Bhutto, and Balochistan. As it was, Pakistan soon came under pressure.

Within a year of the invasion there were more than a million refugees in the border areas of Pakistan, living in a string of camps running from Chitral in the north to the region south of Quetta. Most of them were Pathans, and the population of the border areas was Pathan; in fact there were, and are, more Pathans in Pakistan than in Afghanistan.

These people presented the Soviets and the Communist government in Afghanistan with a perfect opportunity for subversion, working through the agents of the KHAD. The Pathans of the frontier had never liked the central government in Islamabad and the tribes might be only too happy to be given the means to increase the already substantial degree of de facto independence they enjoyed. The refugees might be persuaded that they were not being helped sufficiently by the Pakistani government or that their plight was all the fault of the Pakistanis, who could be presented as prolonging an unnecessary war by backing the Mujahideen.

So, KHAD agents began giving arms to some elements in the border tribes. Propaganda was distributed. Teachers were recruited to the Communist cause in the refugee camps. Bombs were placed in bazaars in the North-West Frontier Province and in Sind. To reinforce their message to the Pakistani government the Soviets periodically fired shells across the border. There were hundreds of infringements of Pakistani airspace by Soviet aircraft. All this showed General Zia that he had to be extremely careful in the amount of support he gave to the Mujahideen. As he said to General Akhtar immediately after the invasion, 'The water in Afghanistan must boil at the right temperature'.

Even so, the two saw at an early stage that the Mujahideen had more advantages than Zbigniew Brzezinski thought in 1979 when he wrote his memorandum warning President Carter not to be 'too sanguine' about their prospects. Admittedly, they were disunited, which was a major problem, but it soon emerged that they were backed by practically the whole population. They believed absolutely in their cause, they were willing to sacrifice themselves and they were fighting on very favourable mountain terrain in which it was easy for them to hide and move undetected. The guerrillas also benefited from a safe haven – once Zia had decided to back them – in the border areas of Pakistan, and there were many routes across the border. Most conveniently a piece of Pakistan jutted into Afghanistan in a mountain area south of Jalalabad, bringing the frontier to about 100 kilometres from Kabul.

The challenge for the allies of the Mujahideen was to make our help as effective as possible. In the early years our system of distributing aid and weapons was made less effective than it should have been by the fragmentation of their forces. The ISI began by giving arms to individual commanders, most associated with one or other of the seven parties, but many operating completely independently. There were some hundreds of these individuals, all clamouring for recognition, exaggerating their exploits and demanding bigger allocations. The system was confused and open to corruption, and in the summer of 1983 it led to what became known as the 'Quetta incident' in which three officers of the ISI accepted bribes from commanders in exchange for issuing them with weapons well above their proper allocations.

The extra weapons were sold in the frontier areas, where they fetched good prices and might help the Soviets in their attempts to undermine central government authority. In due course the officers were detected, arrested and court-martialled. In the aftermath of the incident, in September 1983 General Akhtar appointed Brigadier Mohammad Yousaf to head the Afghan Bureau of the ISI. He also decided to stop issuing supplies to individual commanders and to have everything in future channelled through the parties. This was easier said than done. Akhtar found it impossible to get any form of agreement among the parties on what quantities of aid and munitions each deserved, which areas should be their spheres of operations and how they might co-operate in a military sense. Some of the leaders would not even sit in the same room with each other.

Akhtar persevered. By early 1984 he had decided that there had to be some sort of alliance between the parties to create a recognised high-level body that could act at least nominally to allocate arms and money, and through which the Afghan Bureau could attempt to coordinate some of the action inside Afghanistan. For weeks Akhtar argued with the leaders in vain. He asked me to come to Pakistan to address them, which I did willingly – to no avail. President Zia lent himself to the task, but still found the leaders recalcitrant – and then his patience snapped. At 2.00 a.m. one day he issued a directive that there was to be an alliance of the seven parties and that they were to issue an announcement to this effect within seventy-two hours. The leaders knew that without Zia's backing they were finished – so they formed an alliance, though even now Hekmatyar insisted that all important decisions be made unanimously, not by majority vote.

From now on it became a firm principle that every Mujahideen commander had to belong to one of the seven parties; otherwise, he would get no support. The parties formed a Military Committee, with one representative from each, which worked with Mohammad Yousaf's Afghan Bureau on supplies, financial help, training and some operations planning. Yousaf met the representatives in Peshawar at least monthly. The alliance did not by any means solve all the problems among the groups, but at least it made possible some coordination of military operations, and it imposed some order on the competition for arms and money. From now the Arms Pipeline, as it was known, operated on a stable and effective basis until close to the end of the Soviet occupation in 1989.[1]

The purchasing of weapons and ammunition was managed mainly by the CIA, and at the start it was agreed among us, the Pakistanis and the Americans that supplies should be of Warsaw Pact origin so that it would appear to the Russians that the Mujahideen had captured them or bought them from the Afghan army. Alternatively they could be of old Western manufacture, the sort of material that the Mujahideen might have bought on the international arms market or in the frontier region. At all costs we wanted to avoid showing that our three countries were involved as suppliers. This policy continued until 1985, by which time our involvement had become obvious.

The CIA found it was able to buy some of its supplies directly from Poland and Czechoslovakia, where officials could quite easily be bribed and in any case showed themselves none too loyal to the Communist regimes for which they were supposed to be working. Other sources were Egypt, Turkey and, for some of the older types of weapons, Pakistan itself. Lastly there was China, which proved an extremely helpful and efficient supplier. The quality of its materiel was excellent; it was delivered promptly and in exactly the quantities promised. The Chinese were very formal in their dealings. They signed an arms protocol with the ISI every year, invited General Akhtar and Brigadier Yousaf to an official dinner at their embassy in Islamabad to seal the event and insisted on absolutely accurate accounting.

Most of the materiel from Communist sources was good. The problems came with old Western equipment, or where politics obliged the CIA or the Pakistani government to buy arms that the Afghan Bureau's officers working with the Mujahideen knew would not be effective. There were various scandals. A shipment of arms and ammunition was found to be totally unserviceable, with rifles rusted together and covered in dirt and 30,000 mortar bombs with cartridges so swollen by damp that they could not be fitted to the bombs before firing. On another infamous occasion in 1984 a Pakistani dealer bought a vast quantity of old .303-calibre ammunition from Pakistani army stocks, sold it to the CIA as being from some other source, secretly shipped it out of Karachi, and had the ship turn round and sail back to Karachi again. Then the ammunition was trucked up to Rawalpindi, where every round was found to be stamped with the initials POF, standing for Pakistan Ordnance Factory. It all had to go back to the POF so that the letters could be taken off.

A year later, by which time we were less concerned about weapons being seen to be of recent Western origin, the British persuaded the Pakistani government to buy their Blowpipe anti-aircraft missile. This was an optically guided system which worked properly only against aircraft that were directly approaching or going away from the user. It was heavy and its operators needed long training. It had been a disappointment in the Falklands and as far as I know it did not destroy a single aircraft in Afghanistan. It was bought mainly because General Zia wanted to lock the British firmly into supporting the anti-Soviet war effort. A much better weapon, used from the early stages, was the L-42 sniper rifle, which was produced by the British for their Special Forces.

I regularly met my colleagues in the CIA and the ISI to review the supply operation. I went to Pakistan almost every month for briefings at the ISI headquarters and I often flew to America. Likewise, Pakistani and American officials often came to Riyadh. I remember one meeting at the end of 1981 with William Casey, the head of the CIA. Casey came to Pakistan and Saudi Arabia once a year and on this occasion I went to Riyadh airport to meet him. He arrived, as he always did, in a huge Starlifter aircraft which had been specially designed for him. The plane was totally dark – no lights, no windows – and I asked him about this. The point, obviously, was that he wanted his flights to be as invisible as they could possibly be – and to expand on this he invited me on board. Inside the aircraft he had a totally enclosed apartment, which was taken out of the plane when it was back at its base, kept in the most secure conceivable conditions so that it could not be bugged or tampered with, and loaded on again when he wanted to fly. My private thought about this level of security, which was truly obsessive, was, 'Thank God, I don't have to use this'. Personally, when I fly I like to be able to look out of the window.

On this occasion and in other similar meetings we discussed the progress of operations. In Islamabad I would be briefed by the Pakistani officers who were in contact with the different Mujahideen groups. Likewise, we reviewed relations with our arms suppliers and how we could help with new sources of supply. The GID's role in the arms pipeline was sometimes to approach well-disposed Arab countries which we knew had stocks of Warsaw Pact weapons. More often we helped with end-user certificates, or EUCs. Any country which sells arms will want to know where those arms are going – or in this case it would want for its records some documentation which indicated that the arms were going to an acceptable user, even if its officials knew that they were destined for the Mujahideen. Our role was to provide our own EUCs, or more usually EUCs from friendly Arab governments. Egypt was very helpful in this respect.

At the next stage we helped with transport. A large proportion of the weapons acquired by the CIA were sent by air or by sea to Dhahran in Saudi Arabia's Eastern Province. Here they were transferred to rented non-government aircraft or to sea vessels and sent to Pakistan, normally to Karachi. The attraction of this route was that, because there was so much regular traffic between Saudi Arabia and Pakistan, a few extra flights and sailings were inconspicuous.

28 April 1979. Supporters of the Afghan communist regime march in the capital Kabul to mark the first anniversary of the communist April Revolution. In 1978, the Afghan *Khalq* (masses or peoples party removed and killed Sardar Mohammad Daoud, the republican President, in a military coup to rule the country until 1992 and to allow the Soviet 1979-89 invasion.

30 December 1979. Muslim fighters pose with an assortment of weapons during a break in weapons' training in Barikot in the Pakistani province of Khyber Pakhtunkhwa. The rebels had been fighting Marxist Afghan government troops and now faced the pro-Soviet government of Babrak Karmal, who took power in a bloody coup.

1 February 1980.
Mohammad Zia
ul-Haq, President of
Pakistan, at a rally
of tribal chiefs in
Peshawar.

14 February 1980. Members of an Afghan Mujahideen patrol move through rocky mountainous area in Kunar Province of Afghanistan, 50km from the Pakistan border, as they continue to resist the Soviet military intervention in their country.

2 February 1983. U.S. President Ronald Reagan meets with leaders of the Afghan Mujahideen in the Oval Office.

1983. Ahmad Shah Massoud, military commander of the Mujahideen group Jamiat-i-Islami.

1986. Mohammad Najibullah. From 1980-85, he was the secretary of the Central Committee and Director-General for the state information service, KHAD. In 1985 he became the general secretary of the People's Democratic Party, and in 1986 the Soviet Union selected him to replace Babrak Karmal as the President of Afghanistan.

17 January 1987, Peshawar. Gulbuddin Hekmatyar (R) leader of Hizb-i-Islami confers with Professor Abd Rabb Al-Rasul Sayyaf, Imam of Ittihad-i-Islami, during a meeting of Mujahideen listening to their leaders announcing the rejection of Kabul's offers of ceasefire and coalition government.

11 September 1988. Burhanuddin Rabbani, left, leader of Jamiat-i-Islami, sitting with Abdullah Izzam, an Arab Mujahid.

1989. Osama bin Laden, left, with anti-Soviet fighters in Afghanistan.

12 December 1989. Multan Battalion Commander, Lieutenant General Hamid Gul during Zarb-e-Momin exercise-manoeuvres simulating an India versus Pakistan battle. Between 29 March 1987 – 27 May 1989 he served as Director-General of ISI, Pakistan's military intelligence department.

15 February 1989. A convoy of Soviet vehicles leaving Afghanistan via the Friendship Bridge over the Amu-Darya border river between Afghanistan and Uzbekistan.

12 February 1989. Soviet soldiers parading at the withdrawal of troops from Afghanistan.

15-16 October 1990. Benazir Bhutto (1953-2007), former Prime Minister of Pakistan, campaigning for the Pakistan People's Party (PPP) in the week before the Pakistani General Election.

4 May 1992. The evening sky is lit with tracer bullets and flares above Kabul during the nightly display by rival Mujahideen guerrilla groups continuing battle for control of the city.

April 1992, Peshawar. The author with Pakistani Prime Minister Nawaz Sharif organising a conference call between Massoud and Hekmatyar to try to persuade them not to fight in Kabul.

From Karachi some thirty per cent of munitions were trucked to Quetta, a supply base opposite the Afghan province of Kandahar. The rest went up to the headquarters of the Afghan Bureau at Ojhri Camp on the northern outskirts of Rawalpindi. This was an impressive establishment, but utterly inconspicuous, being an anonymous, vaguely military compound in a city made up entirely of other military buildings. It covered some thirty hectares and contained a huge transit warehouse and garage facilities for 300 vehicles – civilian, of course. All of its staff, 450 officers, NCOs and enlisted men – mainly Pathans – wore civilian clothes. Their most basic task was to break down the shipments of munitions and send them to the forward base at Peshawar, opposite the Khyber Pass, where they were handed to the representatives of the seven parties and moved into their own warehouses.

Ojhri Camp also housed units that dealt with psychological warfare – radio broadcasts, the distribution of leaflets, press interviews – and, most important, with operations and training. Operations meant collecting intelligence, selecting targets and, as much as possible, allocating tasks to the Mujahideen. Training, in Rawalpindi, partly meant Americans training Pakistani instructors. The ISI was very concerned to keep the CIA at arm's length from the Mujahideen. It always resisted the periodic American attempts to influence the way it distributed weapons, which normally meant resisting suggestions that more be given to the 'moderate' parties. It never let Americans train Mujahideen; it did this itself at various locations, mostly near Peshawar. And, with one exception, it never took any American into Afghanistan.

The exception was Congressman Charles Wilson, from Texas, who was the Mujahideen's most committed ally in Washington – and even he was only taken a short way across the border so that he could be photographed wearing Afghan dress, surrounded by fighters, against genuine Afghan mountains. The reason for the extreme caution was not just that the Pakistanis wanted to be left to run operations in their own way, as we had all agreed at the beginning, but that the border areas, and Rawalpindi and Islamabad, were well infiltrated by KGB and KHAD informers and they did not want to give the enemy solid evidence of American involvement. The Pakistani authorities and the Mujahideen were very sensitive to Soviet and Afghan government propaganda which claimed that they were just pawns in America's rivalry with the Soviet Union.

The ISI's Afghan Bureau allocated arms on the strict basis of the parties' combat effectiveness, which did not coincide at all with the size of the parties or their own claims of achievements. The system had the advantage of giving the Bureau some influence over military operations. Although it could not issue orders, it did find that the Mujahideen responded to the allocation or withholding of supplies or training, and to the promise that if they undertook a particular operation they would receive additional supplies. They were also incentivised by being told that success in that operation would gain them yet more supplies. They were particularly keen to obtain heavy and modern weapons – and for this they would sometimes show surprising willingness to listen and follow instructions.

One criterion used in assessing battlefield competence was the location of a party's military commanders and the willingness of the commanders to fight outside their own areas, which might sometimes mean outside their own valleys. There was an obvious bias in favour of supplying parties whose commanders operated around Kabul, the Bagram air base, the Salang highway and the northern provinces near the Soviet border. More important was the frequency of successful attacks by commanders. Here the Bureau relied very little on the Mujahideen parties' own reports, though Hekmatyar's party, in particular, was good at reporting frequently and quite accurately on its operations. The Bureau's sources of intelligence were careful debriefings of commanders, reports of CIA and British intelligence (MI6) agents, CIA satellite photos and the ISI's interception of Afghan government and Soviet radio communications. It also found that it was useful to visit the parties' warehouses in Peshawar and Quetta.

If a party's warehouse were full for months on end, this would suggest either that it was not managing to transport the arms to its commanders or that it was not so enthusiastic about prosecuting the war. Maulvi Nabi's party was a prime culprit, in spite of having good commanders and a large following. On the other hand Abd Rabb Al-Rasul Sayyaf's warehouses always had minimal stocks – because he had the great advantage of receiving large-scale financial support from private Arab sources, which enabled him to transport his supplies to his areas of operations.

Transport was a big problem and a huge cost for the parties. By the mid-1980s the cost of moving munitions from the Pakistan border to the northern provinces was running at $15–$20 per kilo. Moving a mortar to the Mazar-i-Sharif area cost about $1,100; moving one bomb cost $65. The parties' total transport spending was running at about $1.5 million a month. This covered all forms of transport – men, mules and vehicles, including vehicles which Mujahideen commanders borrowed, for a fee, from Afghan army personnel. There is no question that the cash allocation for transport from the official pipeline was always inadequate. In *Afghanistan the Bear Trap: The Defeat of a Superpower*, Mohammad Yousaf remarks, 'It was largely Arab money that saved the system. By this I mean cash from rich individuals or private organisations in the Arab world, not Saudi government funds. Without these extra millions the flow of arms actually getting to the Mujahideen would have been cut to a trickle.'[2]

The same point was made to me by Burhanuddin Rabbani. 'We got cash from many places – even a donation from Poland – without this private sector money we would never have been able to win,' he said. A characteristic of this private money was that it went mostly to the party leaders whose representatives were most active in fundraising in Saudi Arabia and the Gulf, particularly Sayyaf and Hekmatyar.

As far as the pipeline funds were concerned, the percentages were never fixed, but in the mid-1980s allocations of arms and cash by the Afghan Bureau worked out roughly as follows: Gulbuddin Hekmatyar 18–20 per cent; Burhanuddin Rabbani and Ahmad Shah Massoud 18–19 per cent; Abd Rabb Al-Rasul Sayyaf 17–18 per cent; Maulvi Yunus Khalis (whose party was quite small but vigorous) 13–15 per cent; Maulvi Mohammad Nabi Mohammadi 13–15 per cent; Pir Ahmad Gailani 10–11 per cent; and Hazrat Sibghatullah Mojaddedi 3–5 per cent. The first four of these, the leaders of the 'fundamentalist' parties, were the ones who received by far the biggest amounts of additional private funding.

During the war the amounts of money going into the pipeline increased enormously. In 1980 Saudi Arabia and America together put in $300,000, though at this stage there were various other direct payments made, including the $2 million we sent in cash with Ahmad Badeeb in January that year. In 1981 the two countries put in $60 million, by 1984 the figure had reached $400 million and by the end of the Soviet occupation it was running at around $1 billion. The actual movement of the Saudi contribution was into a Swiss account of the CIA.

Of course, individual Afghan party leaders, Sayyaf in particular, frequently came to me to ask for some additional direct funding, or they would approach other members of my family and ask them to persuade me, or put pressure on me, to give their parties more. In every case I refused. But I stress that the money I controlled and that went into the CIA/GID/ISI arms-and-cash pipeline was only part of the funding that flowed from Saudi Arabia to the Mujahideen and to Pakistan. The Mujahideen received funds from many Saudi individuals, including of course members of the royal family. The Saudi government had various aid agreements with Pakistan, and several Saudi charities and a great many individuals channelled a huge amount of money to help Afghan refugees.

Chapter 5
The War – the Early Years

The Soviet forces' strategy in the early stages in Afghanistan was defensive. It was impossible for them to hope to dominate the whole country and we soon saw that they were concentrating on controlling the major towns and air bases, notably Bagram on the plain north of Kabul, and the Salang highway, which went from Termez, the frontier town just inside Soviet Uzbekistan, to Kabul. This road, running over the Hindu Kush mountains and through an eight-kilometre tunnel below the Salang Pass, was their only line of communication with the capital. It was enormously important to the Russians for all their heavy supplies, equipment and munitions – and for fuel which was carried by a pipeline that ran parallel to the road. They also attached importance to the northern provinces, the relatively flat country north of the Hindu Kush around Mazar-i-Sharif. This was a sensitive area not only because it produced some oil, gas and minerals, but because the Uzbeks and Tajiks lived on both sides of the border and the Soviets did not want their own elements of these peoples infected by anti-Communist ideas.

The eastern areas of Afghanistan were significant mainly as theatres of operations against the Mujahideen; but the west and south were not important, except as a buffer zone between Communist Afghanistan and Iran, and for Shindand, which was Afghanistan's second air base, south of Herat. In all the regions of Afghanistan the mountains, the villages and the tiny settlements in the valleys were left to the Mujahideen.

The number of troops the Soviets committed to Afghanistan was quite small – they maintained their forces at about 85,000 throughout the occupation. To put this figure into perspective, in 1968 they deployed 250,000 troops to crush the 'Prague Spring' in Czechoslovakia. And in Vietnam the Americans increased their forces from 16,000 in 1964 to half a million in 1969. Most of the Soviet forces in Afghanistan, nine out of ten soldiers in the estimation of the ISI, were committed to static defensive duties, escorting convoys or doing administrative work.

It was interesting that the Soviets never expanded their occupying force, though they had a huge army to draw on. It seems the reasons were a mixture of political, economic and military considerations. The invasion had greatly damaged their relations with the West. It had no doubt helped Ronald Reagan win the American presidential election in November 1980, and it seemed likely that a big expansion of the Soviet effort would make relations even more difficult. At the same time the war had a high economic cost. The Afghan economy was ruined, the cities (as well as Pakistan's side of the frontier) were full of refugees, and Moscow was spending some $12 million a day on military costs and assistance to Afghanistan. And from a military point of view the Russians were very casualty conscious and they obviously wanted to control the level of fighting. In addition, a big increase in the size of the army would have necessitated much-improved supply lines to the north; the Salang highway was just not adequate for this. In the Afghan Bureau in Rawalpindi, Mohammad Yousaf decided in 1983 that if the Soviets had not already reinforced their army they would probably not do so in future. 'Possibly,' he said to himself, 'they have no trumps in their hand.'[1]

The Soviets suffered further from the poor quality of their troops. Almost all their soldiers were conscripts, enlisted for two years at the age of eighteen. They hated the army. They had received little training, they had bad food and bad accommodation and their only ambition was to survive Afghanistan and go home. Many were only too happy to sell their weapons and ammunition or exchange them for food or hashish. They were reluctant to leave their bases, and in battle they preferred to stay in their armoured vehicles. Recognising the incompetence of most of their forces, the Soviet commanders came to rely increasingly on air power – particularly on the MI-24 Hind helicopter – and on their Special Forces, the Spetznaz, and on air assault and paratroop units. These men were also conscripts, but they were the best of the intake, well trained, better equipped and led, and, above all, highly motivated. The gradual increase in the intensity of fighting in the first half of the 1980s came from the use of greater numbers of these forces, combined with heavier bombing and attacks by helicopter gunships – not from any increase in the overall number of troops.

At the beginning of the occupation the Russians clearly believed they could achieve their aim of stabilising the Communist regime by providing a garrison which would support Babrak Kamal's government and give the Afghan army sufficient confidence to go out into the mountains and valleys and flush out the guerrillas. This plan was an immediate and total failure. In fact the invasion had the opposite effect from that intended. In the first two years – later known as the 'Revolving Door' period of the Afghan army – the Afghan authorities found that, however hard they tried to round up conscripts, even greater numbers deserted to the Mujahideen. Sometimes whole units disappeared, with their weapons. Commanders took to confining their men to base – which is not at all what the Soviets originally had in mind. From 100,000 men shortly before the invasion, the Afghan army shrank in the early 1980s to 25,000. Even in the mid-1980s, when its situation stabilised, the ISI calculated that the army suffered an annual loss of 20,000 men from desertion, demobilisation and death.

Given the ineffectiveness of the Afghan army the Russians found themselves obliged to play a more active role than they originally envisaged. They turned their attention first to the Panjshir Valley, which was the base of Ahmad Shah Massoud. The valley ran for 160 kilometres into the Hindu Kush in the north-east of the country, and its entrance was close to the Salang highway and Bagram air base. Any forces based in the valley were therefore a threat to Soviet communications and in the first few years of the war Massoud did very well in keeping his forces clothed, fed and armed by attacking convoys on the Salang highway.

But the Soviets had another reason for making Massoud their target, which was explained to me after the war by an officer from Russian military intelligence. It had to do with the internal ethnic politics of the Afghan regime and the fact that Soviet operations were always launched in consultation with the Afghan government. The Soviet advisers in Kabul generally found that the different ethnic elements in the government, Pathans and Tajiks, would feed them information which would encourage them to launch attacks against the other group and, in this case, they came under some pressure from the Pathans to attack the Tajiks. It was natural for them to respond to this, because they were very much aware that the Pathans were the most numerous of the Afghan peoples and made up the biggest group within the Afghan forces. As an unpopular occupying power, they wanted to gain from the Pathans what extra support they could.

The first Soviet attack on Panjshir came in the spring of 1980, and in the next two and a half years five further assaults were launched, each bigger than the one before. The last of the series, Panjshir 6 in the autumn of 1982, involved 10,000 Soviet troops and 4,000 Afghans. The attacks followed what came to be a fairly predictable pattern. Massoud would always find out from his agents in the Afghan army that an attack was being prepared weeks before it actually happened. This would give him time to move his forces and much of the non-combatant population of Panjshir into the small side valleys. Then, the day before the attack began, the Russians would bomb the valley. Their bombing was notoriously inaccurate. They could hit villages, but specific military targets they often missed by half a kilometre. It became a joke among the Mujahideen and foreign journalists who went into Afghanistan that the safest place to be during an air raid was on the target.

No attempt would be made to block the side valleys to prevent the escape of the Mujahideen (or their counterattacks), or to coordinate air strikes with a swift approach by ground forces. There would be a slow, methodical advance up the valley in daylight by tanks and armoured infantry vehicles. On arrival at a village the Afghan officers with them would call on anyone who was still alive or had not fled to come out, then the troops would open fire with machine guns and mortars and finally they would enter to search and destroy, with the emphasis much more on destruction than on searching. When they had the opportunity the Mujahideen would come out of the side valleys and attack the columns from behind.

The Russians' assaults were intended partly to 'teach the villagers a lesson', to stop them supporting the Mujahideen, and partly to drive the people into exile, with the purpose of depriving the Mujahideen of its pool of manpower and increasing the burden on Pakistan. In reality the campaigns only increased the numbers of young men, further embittered by the killing of their families and the destruction of their villages, who went to join the resistance.

It would be wrong, though, to suggest that these early campaigns were totally ineffective. Their persistence and the sheer volume of ordnance deployed wore down the defenders in the Panjshir. In the spring of 1983 Massoud felt forced to agree a truce with the Soviets. This came as a shock to the other Afghan resistance groups and to their backers, though in a sense it also raised his prestige among the Mujahideen in that it showed that he had become sufficiently powerful and important to be able to deal with the occupier in his own right. He used the ceasefire to let his people rebuild their homes and harvest their crops and to give his forces a chance to replenish their stocks of food and weapons. He also used it to attack a group allied to Gulbuddin Hekmatyar, which had been operating in the Andarab Valley close to Panjshir and had cut his supply lines. His action was the beginning of a small, intermittent civil war between his troops and Hekmatyar's.

Not surprisingly the truce with the Soviets did not last very long. In the winter of 1983–84 little incidents began to undermine it, and in March Massoud received intelligence of preparations for a major Soviet attack. He evacuated the people of many villages into the side valleys, mined the road that led up the valley and made a very successful ambush on the Salang highway in which he destroyed some seventy vehicles. He also blew up two bridges on the highway.

Nevertheless, the Russians launched Panjshir 7 in April 1984 on a much bigger scale than anything they had unleashed before. They began with high-altitude bombing, flying sorties from the big bases in the Soviet Union at Termez in Uzbekistan and Mary North in Turkmenistan. As usual the bombing was not very effective. Then they advanced up the Panjshir Valley – this time with large numbers of airborne Spetznaz troops and MI-24 Hind helicopters with armoured undersides which withstood the Mujahideen's small-arms fire. The helicopters were armed with rockets, heavy machine guns, bombs, mine pods and chemical canisters. Generally they worked in pairs, with one protecting the other. They caused serious casualties among the Mujahideen. The attack, which lasted well into May, was much more successful than its predecessors. It seemed to shift the advantage in the war slightly in favour of the Soviet Union. It was after this attack that the ISI, on behalf of the Afghan parties, made its first formal request to the Americans for Stinger anti-aircraft missiles.

The Panjshir Valley was not the only scene of action in the early years of the war. It became well known just because it was the scene of the biggest Soviet offensives. Elsewhere the war was fought on a smaller scale and it was mainly the Mujahideen who took the initiative. Mostly they attacked vehicles on the roads and small Afghan army posts, but some of their attacks were on bigger targets. In 1983 there was a series of attacks on the small garrison towns of Orgun and Khost near the Pakistan border. Eventually the Mujahideen surrounded Khost, but as winter approached the Afghan government forces counterattacked and easily reopened the road that linked Khost to Kabul. The Mujahideen never liked fighting during the winter and on this occasion the forces around Khost also wanted to join their colleagues around Orgun, because they felt they had a better chance of capturing that town and did not want to miss out on their share of the loot, mainly arms, clothing and food.

There were several successful attacks on Bagram air base, particularly in 1984. Some twenty aircraft were destroyed on the ground that year, and in one particularly successful attack a commander attached to Hekmatyar's party hit the main ammunition dump, which produced a gigantic explosion. Another attack, carried out by one of Maulvi Nabi's commanders, gave a good indication of the financial and logistical difficulties the Mujahideen faced. It involved the transport of multi-barrel rocket launchers, rockets and other munitions from the Pakistan border to Bagram. This required seventy-five pack animals and their drivers. The contractors charged over $30,000 and it took Maulvi Nabi two weeks to organise the funds. In the end his commander destroyed four aircraft.

Throughout the war the Mujahideen attacked Kabul. This was clearly a very important target. Attacks here had the potential to undermine the Communist regime in its home, reminding the population all the time that a war was being fought, showing that the guerrillas were not being defeated, and humiliating the government and undermining its propaganda. The attacks took three forms. One type was to cut the power lines and water pipes that ran from the dams in the mountains near the city. They also carried out assassinations, bombings and sabotage inside Kabul. The targets were mainly Soviet citizens, KHAD agents and government officials, and the buildings they used. Educational institutions were considered fair game because the staff members were all Communist and they were indoctrinating Afghan children with Communist ideology. The attacks on Russians were so successful that in due course all bazaars were declared "off limits" to Soviet personnel and their families.

The third type of attack was the firing of long-range rockets, which became almost a daily event. The Afghan Bureau of the ISI produced a list of more than seventy suitable targets in the city – mostly military installations or government offices. Top of the list was the Soviet Embassy. A big event in the bombardment campaign was the arrival in the Mujahideen arsenal in 1984 of the Chinese multi-barrel rocket launcher (MBRL). It was heavy and difficult to transport, but it had range, firepower (twelve barrels) and accuracy. The Mujahideen eventually received 500 of these weapons, and three-quarters of them were deployed against Kabul.

Some of the more sophisticated sabotage operations were carried out with the help of American and British Special Forces, who also worked in training the Mujahideen inside Afghanistan. The personnel were all retired, so that if they were killed or captured they would be 'deniable' by their governments. There were Americans with Gulbuddin Hekmatyar's commanders, and the British from 1983 were involved mainly with Ahmad Shah Massoud. A few ex-military Arabs joined these and other Mujahideen groups.

Some of the work the Special Forces did was important but quite basic and unspectacular. They taught commanders how to do a proper reconnaissance, how to site anti-aircraft guns and how to issue proper orders for an operation, with a model of the target. They also supplied various types of communications equipment. One ingenious idea involved tapes to carry messages. In those days, everybody's proud possession in the developing world was a cassette tape recorder. On the tapes there was a very thin strip down the middle between the A side and the B side, and it was possible, with the right equipment, to record on this strip. Messengers would carry the tapes between party headquarters, commanders and small Mujahideen units, and if they were stopped and interrogated all the KHAD agents or the Russians would hear would be popular Afghan songs. A different type of technology, which was a big success, was jamming devices. These could be put in the ground in a place where an attack was expected and activated just before the attack was launched. They would jam quite a wide bandwidth, say 100–200 megahertz.

Much of the Special Forces' work inside Afghanistan was sabotage and demolition. A very effective material used by the British and Massoud's guerrillas was boron carbide, which was put into the enemy's fuel supplies. The classic method was to inject it into the pipeline which ran beside the Salang highway. The pipeline was heavily guarded, with guard posts or armoured vehicles every 200 or 300 metres, but the ground in between was very uneven, providing plenty of cover, and at night the Russians never patrolled between posts. So it was less difficult than one would think for two men to crawl up to the pipe, put a clamp on it, drill a hole and inject the powder. Alternatively, the boron carbide could be formed into lumps and made to look like charcoal or goat dung, both used as fuel in Afghanistan. These could be given to Afghans who worked in the Soviet bases, to put into jerrycans or vehicle fuel tanks. Once the boron carbide got into the engine of a tank or helicopter the results were spectacular. The engines would overheat and seize up within minutes. The effect on a helicopter was as good as hitting it with a missile. It simply dropped out of the sky.

The Special Forces were given the commanders' elite troops to train and they found them excellent pupils – superb at sniping and sabotage. On missions there was much camaraderie and humour but, according to one of the British advisers, 'in the early days it was terribly difficult to get the boys to keep quiet, even near the Russian posts'.

In response to the increasing intensity of operations the funds going into the arms pipeline grew every year, and from 1983–84 there was a big expansion of Saudi involvement. The biggest jump in US and Saudi government funding came in the fiscal year running from October 1984. In the early autumn of every year the Mujahideen's sympathisers in Congress, led by Charlie Wilson, would comb through the US defence budget in search of unspent funds, and then Congress would order some of these funds to be used for Afghanistan. In October 1984 the Afghan supporters managed to appropriate enough extra cash to bring the programme budget up to $250 million, which the Saudi government matched. The $500 million we spent together in 1985 was nearly as much as we had spent in all the previous years put together.

The increase in funding suited William Casey, the director of the CIA. His goal was much more ambitious than the one President Carter had endorsed in 1979–80.

Carter's aim was to embarrass the Soviet Union and make the cost of occupying Afghanistan as high as possible. Casey wanted to restore independence to the country, and he was in part responsible for the directive which President Reagan signed in March 1985. The existence of this document could not legally be revealed, but its purpose was to encourage the Mujahideen and the ISI to ask for more sophisticated equipment. Under the American system there had to be a formal request for supplies – they could not be despatched to Pakistan just on the initiative of the CIA. The new equipment included various weapons of American manufacture and 'burst communications' sets, which could compress a long message into a short transmission to prevent Soviet interception of Mujahideen radio traffic. In the same directive the CIA was authorised to use satellite photos to help the Mujahideen plan attacks. By this stage it was obvious to the Soviet Union that America, Pakistan, Saudi Arabia, Britain and other Western countries were heavily involved in backing the Mujahideen. The question that worried the allies was whether issuing more effective weapons would provoke the Soviets to retaliate heavily against Pakistan.

In 1985 and early 1986 the fighting in Afghanistan grew fiercer still. The Russians deployed Spetznaz and intelligence teams to try to seal the border with Pakistan. When their watchers saw a convoy of pack animals they would radio the news, and helicopters would be sent to destroy it. The tactic was to fly ten to fifteen kilometres into Pakistan and then swing round and attack the convoy from behind. The Spetznaz also began to operate in disguise as Mujahideen.[2] In August and September the Soviets launched a major operation against Mujahideen bases in Paktia, south-west of the 'parrot's beak' of Pakistani territory that juts into Afghanistan.

In the winter, as always, the Mujahideen went home to their villages, and the Soviet forces took the opportunity to extend the secure defensive perimeters around Kabul and important military bases. This meant that to attack these targets in the following year the Mujahideen needed longer-range weapons, which were heavier and more difficult to transport. For the Mujahideen one of the highlights of 1985 was Ahmad Shah Massoud's seizure of a heavily defended post at Peshgar in the Panjshir Valley. He killed the Afghan Central Corps chief of staff and took 450 prisoners, including five colonels who were on a visit from Kabul.

The spring of 1986 saw another big Communist attack in the Paktia area, which was notable for showing a remarkable improvement in the capabilities of the Afghan army. The focus of the attack was the village of Zhawar, near the border, which the Mujahideen had made into an important base. It was used particularly by Commander Jalaluddin Haqqani, an important tribal personality attached to Maulvi Yunus Khalis's party. Haqqani had quite impressive facilities at his base – and he had captured a number of tanks – and he found it useful to show what he had to important foreign visitors, notably rich private-sector donors from

Saudi Arabia and the Gulf states. He was a man who believed in taking and holding positions. On this occasion his strategy cost him dearly. The fighting caused heavy casualties on both sides and the Zhawar base was lost for forty-eight hours.

In the aftermath of the battle the Afghan Bureau of the ISI concluded that the Mujahideen would have done better if they had built proper defences in the way they had been advised to do months before. It also decided, not for the first time, that the fighters needed a good surface-to-air missile – something better than the Blowpipe, which had proved useless in this battle.

The general feeling at this time was that the war was getting bigger and more professional. There was some Western press talk of the Mujahideen 'losing', but the more accurate picture was one of escalation, in which the advantage seemed to be shifting a bit in favour of the Soviets and the Afghan government.

Chapter 6
Charities and Volunteers

The flow of refugees from Afghanistan began well before the invasion. Under the regimes of Mohammad Taraki and Hafizullah Amin tens of thousands of Afghans were imprisoned or murdered, or simply disappeared, and this led to many thousands more crossing the border. In late 1980, a year after the invasion, there were a million refugees in the border areas of Pakistan. In 1990, after a decade of war and the Russian withdrawal, but with the Communist regime still in power in Kabul, the total number of refugees was five million – three million in Pakistan and two million in Iran. In Pakistan there were some 350 camps of different sizes, the biggest with 125,000 inhabitants. The camps were administered by Pakistani officials, with assistance from the United Nations High Commission for Refugees.

One talks of 'camps', but it should not be imagined that these places were completely shut off from the Pakistani economy and society. The people who lived in them did not spend all their days in tents merely surviving while they waited for handouts of food and clothing. Refugee camps quickly came to resemble small townships, and the big camps around Peshawar were virtually indistinguishable from the town's suburbs.

From the beginning the government of General Zia treated the refugees almost as Pakistani citizens, or one could say more accurately as additions to the tribal population of the North-West Frontier Province.

This was logical, given that the people were the same on both sides of the border, but it was also generous. The refugees were allowed to keep their arms – it is not easy to disarm the Pathans – seek employment and start their own businesses. They worked as truck drivers, traders and dealers in all sorts of goods, including drugs and weapons. Pakistan received political credit for this in the Muslim world, but it paid an economic price.

The refugees pushed down wages, and prices, in some sectors, they helped the growth of mafia-like practices in businesses such as trucking, and they introduced great quantities of drugs and weapons. The actual financial cost of the camps and the aid given to the refugees was borne by United Nations bodies and the international community in general – notably by international charities and by governments, charities and private donors in the Gulf states and Saudi Arabia.

From the beginning Saudis were shocked by the numbers of refugees who came out of Afghanistan. They read about them in the newspapers and saw them on television and, feeling themselves relatively rich, they wanted to help fellow Muslims in their distress. I reacted in the same way as every other Saudi, and I felt even more strongly about the situation after I first visited a refugee camp in Peshawar in 1981. Seeing the suffering of these strong, dignified people, driven out of their homes and living in these (then) squalid camps, would have made an impression on anyone. From then on, I felt a sense of pride as I continued to visit the camps around Peshawar and Quetta in later years and could see all the good being done by Saudi charities and individual donors.

Bit by bit we saw better housing, schools, hospitals and rehabilitation centres. The last were for people who had lost a leg, a foot or an arm by mines or bombing, or by the really appalling tricks the Soviets played – throwing from the air toy-like objects which were actually bombs, and which exploded when children picked them up. I know several Saudi ladies who funded rehabilitation centres and orphanages entirely with their own money. Throughout the war Saudis would often come to me and ask how they could help the refugees. Usually I referred them to aid agencies, but sometimes they preferred to work on their own.

A few people got involved with helping the Afghans from the beginning. One of these was Sheikh Saleh Ali Al-Suhaibani, whose story serves as a good example of how charitable operations worked in the early days – and how Saudi government and society interact. At the time of the invasion in December 1979 Sheikh Saleh was the young imam – a leader for prayers – of a mosque in Riyadh. He was much concerned by what had happened. He saw Communism as atheistic and evil, and he started immediately to think how he might help in the fight against it.

He followed events every day during January and February 1980 in newspapers and magazines and at the end of each week he made a summary which he put in the sermons he gave to his congregation on Friday. At the same time he encouraged the people to make charitable donations to the Afghans – for the Mujahideen parties and the refugees. He felt a bit nervous about raising money in this way because, two months before, a band of religious fanatics, believing they were the harbingers of a new order for mankind, had seized the Grand Mosque in Makkah. They had managed to organise a significant force and raise money and buy vehicles, arms and supplies without the authorities noticing – so naturally enough in early 1980 private fundraising initiatives were a sensitive matter in the Kingdom.

Saleh decided he would be wise to go to Prince Sattam bin Abdulaziz, then the Vice Governor of the province of Riyadh, to explain what he was doing. Prince Sattam very much appreciated Saleh's initiative. He said the Soviets represented a threat to Saudi Arabia and that Saudis should 'reach out' to help the Afghans – and he added that Saleh should keep him informed about what he was doing. Then, to receive further endorsement and strengthen his hand as a fundraiser, Saleh went to the man who at the time was Saudi Arabia's senior religious scholar – the blind, highly principled and widely respected Sheikh Abdulaziz bin Baz, the head of the Presidency for Religious Research, Ifta, Dawa and Guidance.[1]

Bin Baz gave him a letter of support, but, mindful of the Makkah incident, urged him always to tell the government about his work. Saleh said later that his basic view of government had always been one of suspicion; he thought government agencies were corrupt and that they would embezzle his funds. But he came to discover that having the government's endorsement made people trust him. He also found in due course that government agencies could provide him with material help.

Armed with bin Baz's letter Saleh went to see some rich potential donors, and then went back to Prince Sattam. Sattam ran his eye down the list of donors and was struck by one particularly rich businessman who had given only 100,000 riyals, about $30,000. It seemed to him that this was a rather modest sum, so he telephoned the man and told him simply that Saleh would be calling on him. 'But I've already seen him,' said the man. 'I still think he'll be coming back,' replied Prince Sattam – nothing more. When Sheikh Saleh called again the businessman added another 400,000 riyals. He said he had been worried about giving too much because of the Makkah incident.

Soon after this, in February 1980, Saleh made his first visit to Pakistan. He had been contacted by some Afghan students at Saudi universities who had heard about his good works, and it was through them that he was put in touch with the Pakistani religious party, Jamaat-i-Islami – not to be confused with Burhanuddin Rabbani's Afghan party of a similar name. The Jamaat arranged for him to visit the camps around Peshawar and introduced him to the three fundamentalist Afghan parties. He met Rabbani, Gulbuddin Hekmatyar and Maulvi Yunus Khalis. He did not fail to notice that the Jamaat was giving its very strong support to Hekmatyar. He was also very struck by a conversation he had with Khalis. The Maulvi shook hands with Saleh and said to him more or less straight away, 'Brother, I have a message for you to give to bin Baz – tell him to tell Hekmatyar to stop his bad works – he has killed two hundred of our Mujahideen'. (The figure was no doubt an exaggeration.) 'I was shocked,' Saleh said afterwards. 'Up to that moment I had seen the Mujahideen as angels.'

A more thoughtful and worldly Sheikh Saleh reported back to Prince Sattam and bin Baz in Riyadh, and with bin Baz he began discussing how he should distribute the money he had raised. In almost two months he had collected 24 million riyals (around $7.1 million) and bin Baz said he had himself received donations of some 18 million riyals. Both men already knew the six original Afghan parties, and both were a bit unsure about giving to the three less religious 'moderate' parties, partly on the grounds that they seemed to be less active inside Afghanistan and partly because Maulvi Nabi Mohammadi and Pir Ahmad Gailani were Sufis.[2]

Bin Baz came to the conclusion, however, that they should help all the groups, 'those who are not active, as well,' he said, 'so that they will be able to become active'. To advance the matter the two men decided to form a committee to include representatives of the Pakistani Jamaat and the Muslim World League, as well as Saudi, Qatari and Kuwaiti scholars. In March Sheikh Saleh travelled back to Pakistan to discuss the allocation of the 42 million riyals so far collected. The committee met in Islamabad, and there was a heated discussion in which the Jamaat representatives insisted that most of the money should go to Hekmatyar. Eventually they were forced to back away from this position and it was agreed that seventy per cent of the funds should be divided equally among the three 'fundamentalist' parties while the three 'moderate' parties would get ten per cent each.

Returning once more to Saudi Arabia, Sheikh Saleh took a plot of land in the Riyadh industrial zone to act as a reception area for gifts people were bringing in kind. Donations were coming in from all classes and often they were quite small in value – clothes, bottles of cooking oil, cooking utensils – but together they made up a considerable volume. Initially Saleh appealed to the Minister of Defence and Aviation, Prince Sultan bin Abdulaziz, and got him to make available a C-130 Hercules aircraft to transport the material to Peshawar. Then, as the volumes increased further in the summer, Saleh, with the help of Prince Sattam, organised shipments from Dammam port to Karachi.

Meanwhile, Saleh went again to Pakistan with the intention of making his own assessment of which parties were really the most effective in the military sense and most worth helping. In Saudi Arabia he was coming under pressure from people lobbying on behalf of Rabbani and Hekmatyar, and he wanted to be able to argue with them on the basis of experience. Once again, he found his visit very informative.

When he met the party leaders he decided, quite rightly, that all were exaggerating the numbers of their members and their military effectiveness. He also realised very soon that the Mujahideen were prepared to switch their loyalties from one party to another according to which was seen to be getting the most weapons. He asked to visit the parties' training centres. Hekmatyar and Rabbani immediately agreed and on the basis of what he saw he decided that these two must have the biggest forces.

The other parties were more diffident. One leader said that Saleh could not visit his training camp because it was 'secret'. Saleh explained that he had to report back to bin Baz and it would not look good if he were forced to say that one camp had been closed to him. So the leader of this party agreed and three days later Saleh went to his camp. He found a queue of Afghans who did not look much like Mujahideen, or even recruits. They were just standing in a line in front of some weapons. 'How long have you been here?' he asked them. 'Just today,' they replied. 'You mean you're not training here?' he asked. 'Oh no,' replied the Afghans, 'we're from the refugee camps. We've been paid to come here.' Saleh had roughly similar conversations with implausible recruits in all the minor parties' camps.

During the rest of 1980 Saleh's fundraising – in both cash and kind – grew steadily and he and bin Baz expanded their management committee to include representatives of all the major government departments. The committee played a major role in the establishment of two hospitals, one in Quetta sponsored by the Ministry of Defence and Aviation, and the other in Peshawar sponsored by the Saudi Red Crescent. In later years the management committee became the basis of the National Public Committee for the Support of the Afghan People, which was headed by the then-Governor of Riyadh, Prince Salman bin Abdulaziz, who became King in 2015. This body had the role of national fundraiser and coordinator of the aid efforts of private-sector charities.

Sheikh Saleh Ali Al-Suhaibani was maybe the most enterprising and energetic of the early volunteers, but there were dozens of others. The very first had gone to Pakistan to help in the camps when the flow of refugees began after Mohammad Daoud was overthrown in April 1978. Once in

Pakistan almost all the volunteers at this stage worked for the Saudi Red Crescent, which was the only Saudi body established on the ground. They distributed relief goods – tents, blankets, foodstuffs, medicines and materials so that the refugees could make their own quilts or clothes. Some of the braver volunteers took supplies into Afghanistan. With the Pakistanis the Saudi volunteers spoke English; with the educated Afghans they spoke Arabic, which is the language of the Quran and therefore the language which any Muslim who has studied his religion and law will know at least in outline.

In the mid-1980s there was a big expansion of Saudi involvement. By this stage the Saudi Red Crescent was running two small hospitals and ten clinics. It was joined by the Islamic International Relief Organisation, which is part of the World Muslim League, and by the World Assembly of Muslim Youth (WAMY), which operated through its Benevolence Committee. These two bodies established offices in Peshawar and they were concerned mainly with medical and educational services. The latter, inevitably, included a certain amount of religious education – *dawa* – not least because most of the children being taught had received a partly or wholly religious-based education in Afghanistan. A charitable body which was more active in *dawa* was the Haramain Foundation, then not yet tainted by its later connection with Al-Qaeda. Both the Islamic International Relief Organisation and WAMY kept their aid for refugee purposes; they were very careful to see that their money did not go to any of the seven parties for military use.

Many young Saudis went to work for international bodies, principally the United Nations High Commission for Refugees, and for the Afghan parties. Those who were trained helped in schools and clinics. To encourage the volunteers, on the recommendation of Sheikh Abdulaziz bin Baz, from 1987 the Saudi government gave a seventy per cent discount on Saudia tickets to anyone flying for relief work. There is no record of the total number of Saudis who went to Pakistan to help in the aid and military effort between 1980 and 1989, but my own guess is that the figure would be around 15,000. As for the total amount of funds given by the Saudi private sector between 1980 and the fall of the Communist regime in Afghanistan in 1992, the estimate of Prince Salman's office was 17 billion Saudi riyals (about $4.5 billion).

Included in both the numbers who travelled and the aid figure is a certain amount of activity by people who operated entirely separately from the charities. Some said to themselves, 'Why go through organisations, with their bureaucracy and administrative costs? I want my money to go directly to end-users.' Many people all over the world feel this way about charitable giving, and in Saudi Arabia a large number of people are sufficiently rich to put the idea into practice. Also, perhaps, Saudis are less institutionally minded than people in the Western world; they like to get involved in business, investment, charities and in all sorts of other areas of life on a direct person-to-person basis.

Such people generally made contact with the Afghan parties and then went to Islamabad and Peshawar. They would be taken to the refugee camps, shown something of the parties' training facilities perhaps, and maybe even taken a short way across the border. Then they would make a donation. A big donation might be one million Saudi riyals, nearly $300,000. My former press adviser, the late Jamal Khashoggi, who worked as a journalist in the region, remembered seeing a Saudi religious teacher arriving in Peshawar in the mid-1980s with almost this sum in cash in a bag – though it is quite possible that he was carrying the money on behalf of more than one person. Perhaps private donations of this sort were equal to about ten per cent of the money that went through the agencies, but it is impossible to make an accurate assessment.

Something which appealed greatly to these people, and to Saudis of all types who went to the Pakistan-Afghanistan border – and later into Afghanistan – was how the country resembled what they imagined was once the world of the Prophet Mohammad. They often commented on this when they returned to Saudi Arabia. They were struck by the simplicity of the Afghans' style of life, by the way people worked, by the tools they used in their fields. Their fathers and grandfathers would have known something like this life in Arabia in the 1920s and 1930s, but they themselves had never seen anything like it.

The same rich people and others less wealthy also made contributions to the Afghan parties' representatives in Saudi Arabia. The representatives often came to the Kingdom, normally with the ostensible purpose of performing Umra, a pilgrimage to Makkah and Madinah made outside the month of the Hajj. They did not say they were on fundraising missions, and they certainly did not advertise for funds, but money was the main purpose of their visits. They quickly developed networks of contacts through the mosques. Religious scholars interested in the Afghan cause would introduce them to potential donors, and then donors would pass them on to their friends or organise meetings of small groups at which the parties' representatives would give a short talk. The system was not unlike the way in which funds for good causes are raised in Europe and America.

The most successful fundraisers were the parties of Abd Rabb Al-Rasul Sayyaf and Gulbuddin Hekmatyar. Sayyaf was the more popular. He often came to Saudi Arabia and because he spoke excellent Arabic he was interviewed on television and was able to present his cause directly to the Saudi public. He was also able to speak directly to potential donors. Hekmatyar was popular because he had charisma. He was seen through press and television reports as being effective, tough and independent-minded.

At the same time as the financial flows increased from the mid-1980s, Saudis started to become more involved in Afghanistan in a direct military sense. I have heard it said that this was in response to the suggestion of William Casey, the Director of the CIA, in 1986, but this is a misunderstanding. Certainly, Casey and I talked about the Saudis who went to Afghanistan to fight – and by this time neither of us was concerned about concealing the Saudi involvement – but what we were discussing was a process that was already under way. Saudis would not have been in the least impressed if they had thought the CIA was asking the Saudi government to authorise or encourage them to go to fight. Any suspicion of this would probably have caused most of them to stay at home.

The Saudis, and the other Arabs, who went to Afghanistan did not contribute much to the Mujahideen campaign. Apart from the few who had been in the Saudi armed forces, they had no military training. As a government we did not think it desirable to give them training, or for that matter military experience, because we did not want to make Saudi society military in any way. We simply tolerated people going to fight if they wished. And we were not surprised that they proved ineffective. They did not speak Pashto, the language of the groups they joined, and, unlike the Pathans, they had not been brought up from childhood with a gun in their hands. The Mujahideen had to teach them the most basic military skills, and organise their feeding, clothing and accommodation. They were not accustomed to the harsh life of the Afghan mountains. Most of them, the Mujahideen commanders confessed, were more of a hindrance than a help in the fighting. Their general view was, 'Don't send us fighters – we have enough men – what we want is volunteers who will help with the refugees'.

During the whole period of the war against the Soviets there were probably only a few scores of Saudis who participated in the fighting, and most of these were involved at the end of the war in 1987 and 1988 when the Soviets were launching attacks near the Pakistan border. This was a period when the war was receiving a great deal of publicity in Saudi Arabia.

Typically the volunteers were young men with mixtures of motives. They were partly inspired by the romance of going to Afghanistan to fight for freedom and justice, and partly they wanted to devote themselves to God's service. Most of them felt that if they were killed, they would become a *shahid* – a martyr – which is the best way for a man to leave this life. They would arrive on the frontier, make contact with a party, cross the border and maybe spend only a week or so inside Afghanistan. They would be lucky if they saw any fighting. The comment of Saudis, and Afghans, working in the camps was that most of these people wanted simply to get inside Afghanistan, 'get their feet dusty' and return home saying that they had 'fought the Communists'. For the Afghan parties the advantage of the volunteers' presence was that it increased the publicity they got in Saudi Arabia and helped their fundraising.

* * *

From time to time there was friction between Saudis and Afghans in the border areas, caused by the different ways in which the two peoples saw their religion. I should explain that Saudi Arabia stands for a very pure form of Islam based entirely on the Quran, which is the actual word of God revealed to the Prophet Mohammad, and the Sharia, which is Islamic law based on the Quran and the Hadith – the sayings of the Prophet. It is Islam stripped of the various accretions – certain doubtful sayings and traditions of the Prophet, various mystical beliefs and ideas from other religions – which in some societies have become attached to it during the last 1,400 years.

The people of central Arabia adopted this pure form of Islam in the eighteenth century, led by the teachings of Sheikh Mohammad bin Abdul-Wahhab. The sheikh began his career as a student. He travelled to Basra and Madinah and it was here that he talked to scholars who were concerned to improve the quality of religious life in the Islamic world. In central Arabia at the time, people were following a very corrupted form of Islam in which they had come to believe in the holy properties of particular trees and wells. They prayed at tombs, believed in saints, djinns, faith healers, the evil eye and magicians, and had all sorts of other superstitious ideas. Mohammad bin Abdul-Wahhab decided to devote his life to introducing proper Islamic learning and he found an ally in my ancestor, Mohammad bin Saud, who in the early eighteenth century was the amir of the settlement of Diriyah, next to modern Riyadh.

Mohammad bin Abdul-Wahhab's preaching was simple. It was that men should believe in God alone and that their lives should be guided by the law – the Quran and the Hadith – and nothing else. He condemned belief in saints, prayers to anyone except God, worship at tombs – or the construction of tombs, which he argued was likely to lead to undue reverence for the structure rather than for God – and all superstitions. He and his followers, in other words, were strict Unitarians – in Arabic *muwahhideen*, from the word *wahid*, meaning 'one'. Ironically, in later years his followers became known in Europe after his own name, as Wahhabis. However, this is not a term that is ever used in Saudi Arabia.

The alliance between Mohammad bin Abdul-Wahhab and Mohammad bin Saud led to a campaign of conquest and conversion which won over most of the Arabian Peninsula to the Unitarian cause and created what became known as the First Saudi State. This was destroyed in the early nineteenth century by Ibrahim Pasha, son of the Ottoman Governor of Egypt. It was succeeded by a second and then a third Saudi State – the last created between 1902 and 1932 by my grandfather, King Abdulaziz. Throughout this whole period the links between my family and the family of Mohammad bin Abdul-Wahhab, the Al-ash Sheikh, the 'Family of the Teacher', have remained strong.

The Sauds have provided political leadership and the Al-ash Sheikh much of the religious leadership of the Kingdom, as well as members of the Council of Ministers. The two families are intermarried – my paternal grandmother was from the Al-ash Sheikh. But, more important, the original commitment to strict Unitarian Islam has remained. It is this commitment that is the raison d'être of the Saudi State. It is reinforced by the fact that the State serves and protects the two holiest places in the Muslim world, Makkah and Madinah.

The Saudi State in the last hundred years has not tried as a matter of formal policy to spread Unitarian beliefs to other Muslim countries. Its attitude is not the same as that of the old Soviet Union with regard to Communism or the present United States with regard to democracy. It does not put any sort of pressure on other Muslim governments to change their people's beliefs. But it does encourage better levels of Islamic learning – an understanding of pure Islam – wherever it can. It is bound to support all sorts of bodies – governmental, semi-governmental and private – that try to spread a proper understanding of Islam abroad. Most Saudi support for building mosques around the world has been in response to requests from Muslim governments or Muslim communities in non-Muslim countries. Inevitably, in our providing this aid Unitarian beliefs are spread in these communities.

In describing the character of Islam in Saudi Arabia, I should also explain something about the different Islamic schools of jurisprudence. In the two hundred years after the death of the Prophet in 633 various scholars, referring to the Quran and the Hadith, codified Islamic law. There were a number of these scholars, and among Sunni Muslims the work of four of them has survived, in schools named after their founders – Hanafi, the first to be developed, Maliki, Shafii and Hanbali. (There is a fifth, Shia, school, known as Jaafari, with its own subdivisions.) Among the Sunni schools there are no differences in religious doctrines. What separates them are a few formal religious rituals and various differences in commercial and family law.

The Hanbali teachings were adopted by Mohammad bin Abdul-Wahhab. They are now applied in Saudi Arabia – and traditionally they were applied in Damascus – and in most senses they are stricter than those of the other schools on issues of worship, though they permit greater freedom in commercial activities. The Saudi Supreme Court, though, also recognises the other Sunni schools. In Afghanistan and most other Sunni Muslim Asian countries – Arab and non-Arab – the populations follow the Hanafi school. All of the Afghan political parties, including the Ittihad-i-Islami of Abd Rabb Al-Rasul Sayyaf, follow Hanafi doctrines.

Likewise, the madrasas which were founded along the Pakistan-Afghanistan border in the 1980s and 1990s were Hanafi. Some of these were sponsored by Pakistani religious parties in the 1980s, often working with the tacit approval of the Pakistani government. Many were backed by the Deobandi movement, which has its roots in a famous madrasa established in the Indian town of Deoband in the nineteenth century. The founders of this madrasa rejected the idea that Islam should adapt itself to a world changing around it. They argued that Muslims should try to live as the earliest followers of the Prophet had lived, eliminating modern intrusions from their lives and avoiding sensuous indulgence in such pleasures as music, fine clothes and decoration in buildings. The Deobandis in the Pakistani madrasas were a profoundly conservative influence.

The Hanbali legal teaching of Saudi Arabia is not in any sense *against* the teachings of the other legal schools. In general the schools exist happily side by side. They are not in themselves political or nationalist, or revivalist/

fundamentalist, or modernist. These types of ideas come from movements quite separate from the legal schools. What Saudi Arabian Unitarian belief opposes is not the legal doctrines of the Maliki, Shafii and Hanafi schools, but any distorting influence, from any sect, movement or party, which introduces into Islam extraneous mystical beliefs, superstitions or political ideas.

Saudi charities and individuals working on the Pakistan-Afghanistan border were not trying to replace Hanafi legal principles with Hanbali ideas, but they were trying to improve the people's understanding of Islam generally. Many of the Afghan refugees, they found, professed Islam in a simple, emotional sense, but knew rather little about its religious and moral principles and laws. The refugees were also living in somewhat chaotic conditions. They had lost their established leaders, who were either dead or fighting with the Mujahideen. Their society was one of women, children and the old. In these conditions the Saudi volunteers, particularly those from the religion-based charities, set themselves to providing leadership and education in order to preserve social values and morals, educate the young, respect the elderly and care for women. As part of their work they distributed Qurans, provided imams, and established schools teaching both secular and religious subjects.

The volunteers were told by the institutions for which they worked that they should respect the schools of law and the customs of the people they were trying to help. The message was, 'Improve their understanding of Islam by education, but do not attack their customs'. Some, however, found themselves shocked by the Afghan religious practices they encountered. A few volunteers disapproved of simple details of the Afghans' religious and social routines. More seriously, a handful were very disturbed by the sight of black-and-green flags and tombstones decorating the graves in the cemeteries. In Saudi Arabia the dead are buried in unmarked graves; there are no headstones – even for kings. As a result, a few years after a funeral nobody can remember where the kings or other important personalities have been buried. In Afghanistan, therefore, it seemed to some of our volunteers that the flags on the graves smacked of idolatry. On a few occasions groups of zealots took it upon themselves to tear down the flags. In most later cases when this happened, the local people found them, gave them a sound beating and chased them out of the province. In isolated cases enraged Afghans killed the young zealots.

Much more common as time went on was a general attitude of hostility on the part of Arabs from several countries – not just Saudi Arabia – to Westerners working in the frontier areas. In some places the attitude of the more nationalistically inclined volunteers was, 'This is a Muslim war against unbelievers, and you have no business being involved here'. There were cases of Westerners being threatened and intimidated.

I must say that from my own point of view, and that of the rest of the Saudi government, the religious zealots were a nuisance. Our purpose in Pakistan and Afghanistan was simply to defeat the Soviet occupiers. Improving religious knowledge, as long as this objective was pursued with respect and sensitivity, was one thing – but zealotry got in the way of the main aim. The message I repeated to the Afghan party leaders and commanders, and to Saudi volunteers, on many occasions was, 'We are all Muslims – we should not be sectarian'.

Chapter 7
The Office of Services and the House of the Supporters

In the early days of the war in Afghanistan many of the Arabs who went to work in the refugee camps were received and helped by the Pakistani party Jamaat-i-Islami, which I mentioned in the last chapter. The Jamaat provided them with an address and, if necessary, put them in touch with the relief agencies. Some of the volunteers had already established contact with one or other of the Afghan parties or with an international agency, in which case it was this agency that looked after them.

As the Arab presence gradually increased it was natural that at some point somebody would set up a reception centre specifically for Arab volunteers – and the person who took this initiative in 1984 was a Palestinian university professor named Abdullah Azzam. Azzam had had a rather troubled career. He was looking for a role in life. He was born near the Palestinian town of Jenin and in the 1970s was educated at Al-Azhar University in Cairo, where he gained a doctorate in Islamic law. Here he had become associated with the well-established nationalist/Islamist political movement known as the Muslim Brotherhood. He created links with dissident Islamist politicians, including the exiled Egyptian, Mohammad Qutb, whose brother, Seyyid, had been executed by the regime of Gamal Abdel Nasser. When he left Egypt, Azzam taught for a time at the university in Amman, Jordan, but the government regarded his views as subversive and he was fired. Then he moved to Jeddah, to work at King Abdulaziz University. He preached at the university mosque and, because he was an eloquent speaker who gave well-argued sermons addressing interesting current topics, he attracted a large regular congregation.

The beginning of the 1980s, when Azzam was in Jeddah, was a time when Islamist activists prospered. There was a widespread feeling that society had become too secular during the period of fast economic growth in the 1970s. Certainly the people – and the government – had been shocked when Juhayman bin Mohammad Al-Otaibi and his followers stormed the Grand Mosque in Makkah in 1979, but it was accepted that religious fanatics appear from time to time in any society.

The official reaction was not so much to tighten security to try to detect other potentially rebellious groups, as to look at the broader social picture to try to allay the causes of religious discontent. This meant looking to our Islamic roots. New mosques were built, more religious programmes appeared on television and the Islamic content of the school curriculum was expanded. These developments led, of course, to a steady increase in the numbers of preachers and religious teachers and, as we later learnt to our cost, to a gradual spread of subversive sentiment. In the early 1980s, however, very few people worried about this. We and the Western world were still much more worried about Communism.

Abdullah Azzam could have done well at King Abdulaziz University in this atmosphere, but he was restless. As a radical and a Palestinian he was attracted to the idea of jihad; for the long term he felt that jihad, the religious commitment to fighting for a just cause – not necessarily in a military capacity – was the only way forward for his own people. But he decided that jihad in Palestine had become tainted by nationalist and Marxist actors. In the early 1980s it seemed to him that the most immediate need for jihad, of a proper Islamic nature, was in Afghanistan, so he left Saudi Arabia and took a job at the Islamic University in Islamabad. He became involved with relief work and helped run a council of Arab and Islamic charities. And it was through this that he saw the need for a body to help organise the Arab volunteers.

In 1984 Azzam established an institution in Peshawar which he called

Maktab al-Khadamat, the Office of Services. In part this operated simply as a guesthouse. It became well known among the Arab community in Pakistan, and Saudis, Yemenis, Egyptians and other Arabs arriving in the country would go there for accommodation. It organised buses to bring people to Peshawar from Islamabad airport, a drive of about two hours. Its small staff would interview the new arrivals, find out what they were able to contribute and then through its web of contacts direct them to clinics, schools or, if they did not have special skills, more ordinary places of work. In so far as it dealt with the Afghan parties, when it received military volunteers it tried to distribute them equally. The office did not encourage the non-military volunteers who passed through it to get involved with any single political party.

To raise money for his operation Azzam travelled to Saudi Arabia and the United States. In 1986 he opened a small office in Tucson, Arizona, where there was a large Arab community. When he needed help with the Pakistani bureaucracy, he looked to the Jamaat-i-Islami. To publicise his operations and promote the cause for which he was struggling he published a magazine in Arabic, which he called *Jihad*.

A short time after the Office of Services had been established a young man by the name of Osama Bin Laden arrived in Peshawar. Bin Laden was born in Riyadh in March 1957. He was one of the younger of the many children of the famous and hugely successful contractor, Mohammad bin Laden, and was the only child of a Syrian mother; he had hardly known his father because Mohammad had been killed in an air crash in 1966. He read engineering at King Abdulaziz University, a few years before Abdullah Azzam taught there, but he dropped out before completing the course.

Bin Laden became interested in Afghanistan in the same way as other young Saudis did in the early 1980s, and travelled there for the first time in 1984 or 1985 and met Azzam. With his connections Bin Laden's main role for the Office of Services, and for other institutions, was as a fundraiser. In the mid- and later 1980s he travelled regularly between Saudi Arabia and Pakistan. In 1986 he brought some Bin Laden company engineers and equipment with him to Pakistan to help build roads and depots, including the Khost tunnel complex, which was a base for arms storage, training and medical care in the Afghan mountains, very close to the Pakistani frontier.

Bin Laden's fundraising work and his relatively high profile, due to his famous name brought him into contact with senior figures in the Saudi government. I met him three or four times at receptions in Pakistan, and I found him a very polite, pleasant young man – enthusiastic but gentle, a person who did not raise his voice when he spoke. Other members of the government who met him formed the same impression. We appreciated what he was doing, and in passing we were interested to hear what he had to say about conditions on the frontier – but he never had any official role for any part of the government. The GID had quite enough links with the Pakistani government, the Afghan parties and their commanders for Bin Laden to be necessary for us in any organised capacity.

In due course Bin Laden founded his own guesthouse and reception centre, the Dar al-Ansar, the House of the Supporters. Historically the Ansar were the people who supported the Prophet Mohammad when he established the first Islamic state in Madinah, after he travelled there from Makkah in 622 – so the name that Bin Laden chose gave his establishment a distinctly religious air. It was opened at a point when Arabs were starting to participate in the fighting on the other side of the border, which meant that it became much more involved than the Office of Services with military volunteers.

Azzam and Bin Laden had different views on how these volunteers should be organised. Azzam believed that the Arabs were too small in number to be effective on their own as a unit, and he also felt that spreading the volunteers among the Afghan parties was a useful way of showing the Mujahideen troops that they were getting international support. He therefore continued with his established practice of sending volunteers to all the seven parties.

Bin Laden wanted an Arab military force and, on a very small scale, this is what he established. He recruited about fifty or a hundred Arab Mujahideen, equipped them with weapons bought in the arms market in

Peshawar and managed to get his force across the frontier into Afghanistan. This was not necessarily an easy task because the Pakistani government remained worried about the potential Soviet reaction to its backing for the war and it feared that too overt a foreign participation might provoke retaliation. Still, it may be that Bin Laden bribed his troops' way across the border, or that he arranged for the Pakistani guards and the ISI to turn a blind eye. Inside Afghanistan Bin Laden built a small, fortified camp based around caves in the mountains by the border village of Jaji, near Khost.

In April 1987 the Soviet forces attacked this compound in one of the offensives they launched in the border area. In a battle lasting several days Bin Laden and his volunteers faced at least twice their number of Russian troops and more than a dozen of the Arabs were killed. As far as I have been able to establish, there were no Saudis among the dead. Bin Laden's own role in the battle is uncertain. Afterwards he gave an account of what happened to a Pakistani magazine. He described how at the beginning of the battle he and his companions were in a trench, facing an overwhelming force of tanks and helicopters. Then at some point, Bin Laden said, he fell asleep for no obvious reason and when he woke up the battle was over. In front of him he saw wreckage. The implication was that there had been divine intervention – that angels rather than men had fought the Soviet troops. Other people's descriptions of the battle, from both sides, had a more secular character.

In one way or another Bin Laden organised much publicity for his heroic stand, in Pakistan and in Saudi Arabia. He gave several interviews and a few public lectures. He emerged as something of a minor celebrity.

It was during the publicity campaign that he met an Egyptian doctor, Ayman El-Zawahiri. Zawahiri was a little older than Bin Laden. He was from a well-to-do Egyptian family and he had become involved in Islamist politics as a member of the Egyptian al-Jihad al-Islami movement, which was an extremist and violent offshoot of the Muslim Brotherhood. He followed the thinking of Seyyid Qutb and Khalid Islambouli. Qutb held that anyone who did not agree with his very literal, fundamentalist interpretation of the Quran could not be considered a Muslim. Islambouli was the man who assassinated President Sadat in 1981. For a short period after the assassination El-Zawahiri was imprisoned for activity on the fringes of the plot. On his release he established contact with the Muslim Brotherhood's Islamic Medical Society, and it was through this body that he travelled to Peshawar and volunteered for work at a hospital funded by a Kuwaiti charity.

The meeting between Zawahiri and Bin Laden was significant because, although the latter was obviously quite a strong and energetic character, he was also impressionable and it seems he liked to have the support of some sort of mentor. Zawahiri, being older and with rather more experience of politics, and of life, than Bin Laden, became that mentor. From now on he was to have an important influence on Bin Laden's career. The intolerant, simplistic ideas that Zawahiri had absorbed from Seyyid Qutb were passed on to the younger man, and in due course became the hallmark of Al-Qaeda – and then ISIS and the various splinter groups and individual Islamist terrorists plaguing the world in the last twenty years.

Chapter 8
The War – Turning Point and Withdrawal

From the Russians' point of view the war in Afghanistan in the mid-1980s did not seem to be going well. They were a lot less happy about the situation than Pakistan, Saudi Arabia and the Western allies supposed they were. Their forces were increasing pressure on the Mujahideen, but they were nowhere near a decisive victory or securing the regime they supported. The war was an embarrassment. It created continuous bad publicity and to some extent isolated the Soviet Union diplomatically. Worst of all, it was undermining morale at home.

The Soviet government's attitude to the war began to change when Mikhail Gorbachev became Secretary General of the Communist Party in January 1985. From that moment on, discussions inside the Politburo became more honest and less doctrinaire. In February the following year Gorbachev told a Communist Party Conference that 'counter-revolution and imperialism have transformed Afghanistan into a bleeding wound'. Nine months later, in November 1986, he told his colleagues in the Politburo that the goal had to be to finish the war in 'one, maximum two' years and withdraw the troops. The alternative was a huge escalation of the war in men, money and equipment – and that was unthinkable.

As a preliminary step the Soviets replaced their client president in Kabul. In November 1985 they arranged for Dr Mohammad Najibullah, the chief of the KHAD, to be promoted to the Afghan Politburo, and at the beginning of May 1986 they had him installed as President. Babrak Karmal, who had just returned from a long visit to Moscow, resigned "for health reasons". Najibullah was a rather better prospect for the Russians than his predecessors. He was a Pathan, whereas Karmal was a Tajik. He was confident, had the appearance of being more independent and was a good speaker. At the beginning of December 1986 he was summoned to Moscow and told of the Soviet government's plans for finishing the war. The idea was that he should start preparing his own government and forces for life with much-reduced Soviet support.

The outside world, including intelligence services, knew very little of Soviet thinking at this time. Obviously, the 'bleeding wound' speech was very significant, but we had no idea in 1986 about just how worried the Russians had become. Together with the ISI and the CIA, we were still mainly concerned with fighting the war and, at that moment, avoiding defeat. We were particularly worried by the losses the Mujahideen were suffering from Soviet aircraft and helicopters.

The Mujahideen were not wholly defenceless against air attack. They periodically destroyed helicopters of all types by firing down on them with rocket-propelled grenades when they were flying close to the ground along the floor of a valley. They had some successes with Soviet-made SAM-7s – shoulder-launched surface-to-air missiles – and on one occasion destroyed a MiG-21 that was being flown from Kandahar to Shindand by a major general.

A British Special Forces adviser achieved a satisfying success when he instructed a Mujahideen unit on the advantages of siting anti-aircraft guns so that they could achieve a crossfire, rather than placing them next to each other. His unit destroyed a MiG the next time it went into action. The problem was that these successes were all too rare, and that the Mujahideen were very vulnerable to attack by helicopters with armour-plated undersides. They needed some really effective anti-aircraft system. The obvious answer was the Stinger missile – a new, highly effective, light-weight weapon which was fired from the shoulder. It had already been mentioned on several occasions in our discussions on arms supplies, and the Pakistanis raised the matter seriously when they reviewed the situation with the Americans at the end of 1985.

The Stinger had been issued to American forces in 1981, but it had never been used in battle and its technology was still secret. The worry was that if it were used in Afghanistan it would sooner or later end up with the Soviets, through being captured or perhaps being sold to a KHAD agent. It might also be acquired by the Iranians or even find its way into the hands of a terrorist group. President Zia himself was nervous about assassination – there had been several attempts on his life – and he was concerned about the missile being used against his own aircraft. In the end what tipped the balance in favour of supplying the missile was the big Soviet offensive near the border in April 1986. President Reagan authorised the supply a few weeks after this and Pakistani instructors flew to the United States for training in June. At the same time a Stinger training school in which the instructors would train the Mujahideen was set up in the Ojhri Camp in Rawalpindi. All training in this facility was carried out in a simulator. The missile was not fired in real life until it was used in Afghanistan.

The Afghan trainees were selected personally by Mohammad Yousaf. They were men who had done well with the SAM-7 missile, half of whom had destroyed at least one aircraft or helicopter. The first training course was for a small group of men from Hekmatyar's party, the second for two from Khalis's. The whole system of issue and use was subject to tight control. The Americans had devised a way of making the missiles inoperable after a certain period, which meant that if a commander had not used a missile within this period he would have to return it to get it replaced. This did happen from time to time. Later, when the war was over, the Americans organised a Stinger 'repurchase' campaign. The purpose of this was not so much to prevent the missiles being used – they should by this stage have become inoperable – as to prevent them falling into the wrong hands and their technology being copied.

In September 1986 the first Mujahideen unit equipped with Stingers went into Afghanistan. It got close to the airfield at Jalalabad, between the

Pakistan border and Kabul. Within a short time it saw a number of helicopter gunships approaching. It fired five missiles and destroyed three helicopters. The action was filmed by a cameraman – a precaution intended to prevent teams making false claims of use, successful or unsuccessful. The man was so excited that he filmed while running around and what he captured, which I watched a little later, consisted mainly of blurred images of sky, bushes and ground. He only steadied himself enough to film smoke pouring from the wrecks at the end. The film was shown to President Reagan, who loved it.[1]

The success gave a big boost to the morale of the Mujahideen and it was a shock to the Soviets. They closed Jalalabad air base for a month. At other airfields aircraft were instructed to make their approaches in tight downward spirals, releasing flares as they went. Transport aircraft approaching or taking off from Kabul had their movements protected by helicopters releasing flares. In action helicopter pilots became reluctant to press home their attacks, or to evacuate wounded soldiers.

In the ten months after it was introduced the Stinger destroyed more than a hundred aircraft and helicopters. This encouraged the Mujahideen to keep operating during the winter of 1986–87, though they were also greatly helped at this time by the issue of proper winter clothing. It may seem strange that they did not have this clothing themselves – but it is the Afghans' habit to stay in their homes during the coldest winter months and hardly venture out beyond their villages. They certainly did not have kit which would have enabled them to survive in the mountains for days at a stretch. The winter of 1986–87 was significant in that it was the first in which the Mujahideen did not lose ground around Kabul.

The Stinger tipped the balance of the fighting in favour of the Mujahideen, and it had a big effect on morale – in opposite ways – among both the Mujahideen and the Soviet forces. It destroyed many aircraft in the last two years of fighting, but over the course of the war probably more aircraft and helicopters were destroyed or put out of action by attacks on air bases, groundfire and boron carbide than by these missiles.

The experience and opinions of Ahmad Hayat, one of Ahmad Shah Massoud's commanders, are not untypical. He was issued with two

Stingers, out of fourteen that Massoud's forces had at the time, and soon afterwards he fired one at a jet flying at 3,000 metres – and missed. The target was too high and Massoud complained that he had wasted a missile. On the other hand, on two occasions, in 1983 and 1986, Hayat successfully injected seven or eight gallons of boron carbide supplied by MI6 into the fuel pipeline running across the Salang Pass to the Bagram airbase. He had no way of knowing *exactly* what effect this had, but, as he said, a small amount of the chemical would ruin a lot of fuel.

His assessment, based on his own experience and what he heard from other commanders, was that the Stinger was very effective against helicopters, but that boron carbide worked well on both helicopters and jets. Hayat was a successful commander – he led many operations and in the later stages of the war was in charge of Massoud's base camp in Panjshir – but, as for many Afghans, the war for him was also a very sad and painful personal experience. It was as much an Afghan civil war between the government and the opposition as a war against an occupying power. Hayat's brother was a pilot in the Afghan air force and during the war he was shot down and killed by another Mujahideen group.

Of course, it was not long before some of the Stingers were lost. In early 1987 a commander equipped with the missiles was ambushed near Kandahar by helicopters carrying Spetznaz forces. Now that the Soviets were known to have the missile the ISI's Afghan Bureau took the risk of introducing the weapon in the area around Herat and Shindand. Almost immediately some Mujahideen from Yunus Khalis's party travelling from Quetta towards Herat strayed into Iranian territory – or maybe they crossed the border intentionally – and were arrested, with four launchers and sixteen missiles, by Iranian border guards. Repeated efforts by Khalis and Burhanuddin Rabbani – who had excellent contacts in Iran – failed to get the missiles back. The Iranians kept delaying their release with a stream of excuses.

The episode marked the last time anyone in Khalis's party was issued with Stingers. Yet, annoying as this was, it did not have serious consequences. The Stinger missile has never been used by the Iranians, or by any terrorist group. Indeed, it has never been used by anyone since the end of the war against the Communists in Afghanistan. In the end all the precautions that surrounded its use were a success.

Another important change at this time was an escalation of operations a little way across the border inside the Soviet Union. The initiative for this came originally from William Casey, the CIA Director, on one of his annual visits to Saudi Arabia and Pakistan. He was very much aware of the potential for destabilising the southern republics of the Soviet Union, which had a mainly Muslim population – the non-Muslim elements were Russians who had been sent there, or had settled there, in Stalin's or Khrushchev's time.

The Muslim population had been treated brutally when the Communist system was imposed on it in the 1920s and 1930s. The Kremlin had always been afraid of a nationalist or Islamic revival in this region. Indeed, one of the reasons it had invaded Afghanistan in 1979 was a fear that the collapse of its puppet regime in Kabul might lead to the emergence of an Islamist state in Afghanistan, which would export its revolution to the southern Soviet republics. Given that Afghanistan was Sunni and had large populations of Uzbeks and Tajiks – including refugees from the northern side of the border – it was potentially much more dangerous to the Soviet Union than to Iran.

Operations began in 1984 in a cautious manner with the distribution of anti-Soviet propaganda and Qurans. About five thousand copies of the Quran were distributed and they were well received. Reports came back of people wanting to help. Some wanted weapons, others to join the Mujahideen and others to participate in operations inside the Soviet Union. The United States at this point became nervous about providing anything which would be traceable back to itself, especially large-scale maps. Likewise, a decision was taken not to try to foment guerrilla activity by citizens of the Soviet republics.

Instead, a campaign of attacks across the border was started in 1985 – but again we were all worried about the consequences of being too successful. There was a plan to blow up the Friendship Bridge (Hairatan Bridge) across the river Amu Darya near Termez, which was the starting point of the Salang highway and a crucial choke point for Soviet supplies. It was called off because President Zia was afraid that the Soviets would retaliate by blowing up similar bridges in Pakistan. It was on the same principle that, in spite of American encouragement, Ahmad Shah Massoud's forces never tried decisively to block the Salang Tunnel. He was afraid that doing this would result in a massive, punitive Soviet invasion of the Panjshir Valley. In limited wars, such as the one in Afghanistan, the sides operate within certain rules. They are always afraid of escalating the war into something much bigger with consequences beyond their control.

The Mujahideen were obliged to limit themselves to quite minor attacks. Mines were laid in the Amu Darya. Limpet mines were attached to the bottoms of barges and boats. Rockets were fired across the river, hitting fuel depots, railway lines and power stations. Most of these operations were carried out by Hekmatyar's forces. On one occasion when the Mujahideen raided the border of the Tajik Soviet Republic to attack hydroelectric power stations, they took two small guard posts – and eighteen Muslim soldiers deserted to them. Clearly these attacks hit a raw Soviet nerve, because every incursion provoked a huge retaliation by aircraft, including helicopters, against whichever village happened to be on the southern side of the border opposite the place attacked.

Then in April 1987 one of the commanders went thirty kilometres inside the Soviet Union and launched some thirty rockets against an industrial plant in the small town of Voroshilovabad in the Tajik Soviet Republic. It is not clear what he hit, but he caused a huge explosion. The Soviets were shocked and furious. Their sensitivity was caused not least by the fact that there had recently been riots in Alma-Ata, the capital of the Kazakh Soviet Republic, not so far to the north. The Soviet ambassador in Islamabad called on the Pakistani Foreign Minister, Sahibzada Yaqub, and made it plain that unless this sort of attack were stopped his country would bomb military installations inside Pakistan. The ISI and the CIA were quite shaken – the attack went well beyond the type of operation the CIA had been authorised to encourage – and President Zia ordered the Afghan

Bureau not to undertake anything similar in the future. As the local CIA chief said to Mohammad Yousaf, 'Please don't start a Third World War'.

Looking back, though, the cross-border operations were a success. They showed the Soviet Union the dangers of its continuing presence in Afghanistan. Also, the attack on Voroshilovabad marked the only occasion during the whole forty years of the Cold War in which a military operation was carried out inside the Soviet Union. For the Mujahideen, it was a major achievement.

* * *

Throughout most of the period of the war – strange as it may seem – the United States and the Soviet Union had been talking to each other about a way in which the Soviet forces might withdraw from Afghanistan and end the fighting. The talks began in 1982 in Geneva and they ran on for six years in parallel with various other US-Soviet negotiations in that city dealing with strategic and intermediate-range nuclear weapons limitation and conflicts involving the presence of Soviet and Cuban troops or advisers in several other countries, including Angola, Ethiopia, Nicaragua and Cambodia.

No progress was made on Afghanistan until after Mikhail Gorbachev came to power in 1985, but in the following year the negotiations became serious. In May 1986 the Soviets offered a four-year withdrawal timetable and, as a token of their serious intent, in July they actually withdrew a small force of 6,000 men. At the same time the number of participants in the talks increased. Originally there were four parties – the USSR, the United States, Britain and the United Nations – and in 1986 this was expanded to what became known as the 'Four Plus Two' – the two being the Communist Afghan government and Pakistan, which represented the Mujahideen. Needless to say, it was not easy for us – the Saudi and Pakistani governments – to get the Mujahideen parties to agree on how they should be represented. We held a meeting in Islamabad at which we tried to get them to establish an interim government which might have enabled them to be represented at the talks directly, but this proved impossible at that stage.

Feeling that it had the upper hand, the United States – with the Mujahideen in the background – was not in the mood to make many compromises. The basic principle of a Soviet withdrawal was an accepted part of the talks from the beginning, and quite soon it was settled that it would happen within a year of an agreement being signed. The difficult issues concerned the composition of the government that would be left behind in Afghanistan and the support that the Soviet Union and the United States would continue giving to their clients, Najibullah and the Mujahideen.

On the first matter the Soviets, naturally, wanted something which would be more or less a continuation of the government they had in place. They were frustrated by the fact that Najibullah had proved quite incapable of creating anything like a government of national reconciliation – and when the idea was floated of Mujahideen participation in a Najibullah government the seven parties rejected it out of hand. On the second issue, in late 1987 it seemed that the Americans might be prepared to end CIA supplies to the Mujahideen, but early in the following year President Reagan said on television that he did not think it would be fair if the Soviets continued helping Najibullah while America stopped supplying the guerrillas. So, by the time the last of the ten rounds of negotiations began in Geneva on 2 March 1988, it had been tacitly accepted that the war was not going to be brought to an end – the Najibullah government would remain in place and the Mujahideen would continue fighting to overthrow it, which they were expected to do rather easily. The actual agreement for the Soviet withdrawal was signed on 14 April, and the first substantial units to be pulled out of Afghanistan – 12,000 men stationed in Jalalabad – left a month later.

Some months after the Geneva agreement, as the final withdrawal of troops was being planned, the Russians became concerned about the movement being carried out in an orderly fashion without too much harassment by the Mujahideen. They wanted to save the lives of their troops and, equally important, save face. They were telling their people at home that they were withdrawing because their forces had finished their job, and it would not look good if troop convoys were destroyed en route and the whole affair made to look like a defeat. Nothing had been said at Geneva about the way in which the withdrawal would take place. Since the agreement, the Russians had made it known to the Mujahideen that if their troops were attacked there would be very heavy retaliation – but they wanted to get some sort of diplomatic agreement on this as well. The Americans were obviously not likely to co-operate, so they decided to approach Saudi Arabia. They came to us via Egypt, which had been very involved on the Saudi-Pakistani-Western side in the war. Egypt had also helped us with arms supplies, and some of the Mujahideen groups had opened offices in Cairo, for diplomatic reasons.

In the early autumn of 1988, I was contacted by my Egyptian opposite number, saying that the Soviet government wanted to send an emissary to talk to me. I made arrangements for this person, a general, to come to see me in Jeddah – keeping the Americans and Pakistanis informed at the same time. When the Soviet delegation – the general and two or three other officers – arrived a few weeks later, we put them up in one of the good Jeddah hotels and I invited them to come to see me in my house. The general explained that his government wanted to talk to representatives of the Mujahideen groups and asked if I could organise this. We agreed that we would try to arrange a meeting in the mountain town of Taif. It would be relatively empty in the winter months, which would help preserve secrecy. Afterwards I gave them dinner. It was all very friendly – there were no recriminations, no blame, no apologies.

The only thing that worried me later was a trivial matter of a bronze plaque which was sitting on top of the television in my living room. We had gone there for coffee after dinner, and out of the corner of my eye I suddenly saw this plaque. I had forgotten all about it. It had been given to me by William Casey on one of his visits, and it had engraved on it in Arabic the words 'Never Trust the Russians', which had apparently been a maxim of one of the Afghan kings. My eye shifted from the plaque to the Russian general, who could read Arabic, and it seemed to me he was looking at it. So I took him by the arm and walked him away from the television, saying something like, 'General, thank you very much, it's been so good to meet you and it's been an excellent evening'. The general did not say anything about the plaque, but I am sure he must have seen it. I only hope he realised it was an American present.

The Russian delegation went back to Egypt the next day, and we got to work on the Mujahideen. It was not an easy task. The different groups had differing views on the desirability of a meeting, and predictably the most difficult was Gulbuddin Hekmatyar. In his view the Russians had lost the war and he saw no reason why he should help them in any way. In negotiating with him I ran through the usual gamut of emotions – admiration, annoyance, exasperation – which were more or less the same feelings the Americans used to experience. I explained that it was necessary for the bloodshed to stop, and that if the Soviet forces could not save face in their withdrawal they would cause as much destruction as possible. I also pointed out that the meeting would mark a significant diplomatic step forward for the Mujahideen because they would be dealing directly with the Russians without the Najibullah government being represented at all. Eventually, with the help of the Pakistanis, who always had the most influence on Hekmatyar, I persuaded him to take part.

The talks were fixed for the weekend of 3-4 December. The Mujahideen delegates arrived first, led by Professor Burhanuddin Rabbani and including Maulvi Yunus Khalis, Hazrat Mojaddedi and Pir Ahmad Gailani, along with representatives of the other three parties. All of them came dressed for Umra, in the seamless white towelling garments Muslims wear for pilgrimage. They promptly set off for Makkah, which is about an hour-and-a-half drive down the escarpment from Taif.

Then the Russians arrived, led by Yuli Vorontsov, who had been Soviet ambassador in Kabul and was later to be the Russian representative at the United Nations. We went into the VIP reception room at Taif airport, sat down, drank coffee and exchanged small talk, and at this point I remarked to Vorontsov that the Afghans had already arrived and had gone to perform Umra. It happened that there was an interpreter with the Russian delegation, Mr. Hakimov, who I think was probably of Tajik descent and was going to translate between the Russians and the Mujahideen. At the mention of Umra, Hakimov promptly sat up and said, 'I want to do Umra'. 'Ah,' I said, 'so you are a Muslim'. 'Of course not,' he replied. 'I am a Communist.' The contradiction was completely lost on him – but I noticed Vorontsov raised his eyebrows.

In the morning, after the Afghans had returned, meetings began in the conference hall where we had first tried to get the Mujahideen to form a united front in January 1981. The talks continued for two days and were conducted directly between the Russians and the Mujahideen. I attended some of the meetings, and in the background, though not in the meetings, was a Pakistani general who had come with the Mujahideen. The Russians and the Mujahideen came to a preliminary understanding – enough progress for them to hold another meeting. This involved a visit by Rabbani and Mojaddedi to the Soviet Union a few weeks later.

After the meeting in Taif I enjoyed showing Vorontsov round the city. He was a distinguished, interesting man who spoke excellent English. I then took him and his delegation to Riyadh, to meet King Fahd. It was the first meeting of a Saudi king or king-to-be since my father had gone to Moscow in 1932 when he was Viceroy of the Hijaz. All went well. The Russians expressed their gratitude for our help and the King and Vorontsov spoke of how they both looked forward to peace in Afghanistan and reminded each other that the Soviet Union had been the first foreign government to recognise the Kingdom of the Hijaz and Najd in the 1920s. It was two years later that we re-established diplomatic relations with the Soviet Union's successor.

I remember a story that Vorontsov told me that was not in itself of any relevance to our negotiations, but which seemed to me very significant as a sign of the way things were changing in the Soviet Union. Up to this time any representative of a non-socialist country dealing with Soviet officials would be used to hearing what was often referred to as 'auto-speak', speeches composed of strings of clichés, normally condemning the reactionary behaviour of imperialist capitalism, etc. But on this occasion Vorontsov's anecdote was of direct criticism of the USSR.

He told me that when Nikita Khrushchev had toured America in the 1950s he had visited a wheat farm in the Midwest and been much impressed by the farmer/owner. He invited him to come to the USSR and give his opinion on what was wrong with Soviet wheat production and how it could be rectified. The farmer went, toured Ukraine and other areas, and at the end came back to Moscow to meet Khrushchev, who expected to be presented with a long report. 'But I don't have to write a report,' said the farmer. 'You've got the wheat, but you don't get it to market. All you have to do is improve your transport system.' This had nothing to do with Afghanistan. I'm sure Vorontsov told me this story simply as a way of showing that the Russians were being open and honest.

From this point on – and indeed as they had for several months previously – our diplomatic efforts and the Russian preparations for withdrawal took place against the background of a perceptible waning of American enthusiasm for the Mujahideen, in spite of what President Reagan had said about continuing to help them while the Soviets continued to help Najibullah. The Americans were turning their thoughts to what sort of government might eventually replace Najibullah in Kabul. They certainly did not want the fundamentalist parties (led by Hekmatyar, Rabbani and Massoud, and Khalis) to come to power and create anything like the government in Iran. They made various proposals aimed at strengthening the position of the moderate parties. At one point they suggested that former King Zahir Shah, in exile since 1973, be brought back – an idea that was anathema to the fundamentalists, given the very secular attitudes of the Afghan royal family. They also pushed for arms to be supplied to individual commanders, bypassing the parties – hoping in this way that more arms would end up with the moderates.

The CIA had never been happy with the fact that the biggest share of weapons went to the fundamentalist parties, but before the war tipped in favour of the Mujahideen they had not been able to argue against it. When the Mujahideen seemed to have the advantage the Americans proposed that all the party leaders should call a *shura* (council) at which they would discuss a future government on the basis of equal representation of each party. The picture was complicated by conflicting views and considerable infighting between departments and personalities within the American government. All the time one could see that, now the Soviets had been defeated and were going to withdraw, the Americans were losing interest in Afghanistan. They had got their revenge for Vietnam.

It may be that the Americans were partly responsible for the removal of Akhtar Abdul Rahman Khan from command of the ISI in March 1987. He was promoted to full general and made Chairman of the Joint Chiefs of Staff Committee – but neither he nor anyone else in Pakistan involved with the campaign in Afghanistan welcomed this promotion. Akhtar had been firmly against American proposals to change the arms-supply system, and he was regarded by the Americans as the champion of the fundamentalists. Also, he had few friends at the top of the Pakistani military establishment. He was regarded by the other generals with envy and suspicion, and he did not get on with the Prime Minister. President Zia could have resisted all these pressures, but now that victory was within sight, possibly he did not want any Pakistani other than himself taking too much credit. So Akhtar went, and was replaced by Lieutenant General Hamid Gul, who had been Director of Military Intelligence at General Headquarters. Mohammad Yousaf stayed on at the head of the Afghan Bureau for five more months but resigned in August 1987.

In April 1988, almost coinciding with the signing of the Geneva Accord, there was an explosion at Ojhri Camp in Rawalpindi which destroyed the entire stock of arms and ammunition held there. It emerged at the subsequent enquiry that a box containing rockets fell from a pile of other boxes and caused a small explosion. It seems that contrary, to all regulations, the rockets had been armed with fuses before being shipped. The explosion injured several people, and during the rush to evacuate them nobody bothered to extinguish the small fire it started. Ten minutes later the entire ammunition dump went up – 10,000 tons of it. A hundred people were killed and more than a thousand injured. Rockets and missiles fell up to 20 kilometres away and secondary explosions continued for another two days. It is still not known if the explosion was the result of incompetent handling by a loading party or was caused by sabotage. It is possible that a small explosive device was put beside the box that fell or was inserted inside it.

The reason such an enormous quantity of munitions was destroyed was that a new distribution system had been introduced. Previously supplies had been shipped to the parties' warehouses in Peshawar as soon as they arrived, but the new procedure was to build up composite packages of munitions for each commander to whom they would ultimately be issued. Because CIA shipments deliberately never contained all the material needed to complete a weapon, different elements had to be held for some time in Rawalpindi. And in April 1988 the stocks were particularly big because bad winter weather on the frontier had prevented packages being despatched in the previous three months. What was very significant for the Mujahideen was that after the explosion there was no rush by the CIA to replace the supplies that had been destroyed.[2]

A final disaster that year happened in August, when an aircraft carrying President Zia, General Akhtar and the US ambassador and military attaché crashed on a flight from a Pakistani military camp back to Islamabad, killing all on board. No definite evidence of the cause ever emerged, but on this occasion it certainly looked like sabotage by the KGB or KHAD.

So, in one way and another the Soviets got the trouble-free withdrawal they wanted. They kept strictly to the timetable agreed in Geneva. Their forces left a battalion at a time, usually at night, overloaded with TV sets and electrical goods the soldiers could not buy at home. There was some Mujahideen harassment, but in most places the guerrillas waited outside the villages or small posts the Soviets had occupied and moved in after they had left. The Soviets were also helped by bad weather. The last forces departed on 15 February 1989 and the very last man to cross the Hairatan Bridge near Termez was Lieutenant General Boris Gromov, the commander of their forces in Afghanistan, who walked over without a backward glance to embrace his teenage son. There were flowers and banners. It all looked very good on Soviet television. And it happened to be my birthday.

On the night of the withdrawal the Soviet Foreign Minister, Eduard Shevardnadze, flew to Kabul and had dinner with Mohammad Najibullah and his wife. He offered them a home in Moscow if they wanted to leave, but they refused. Najibullah's situation did not look good. He had failed to achieve the smallest compromise with any of the Mujahideen parties – let alone include any of them in his government or cause a split in their ranks. At one point he offered the Defence Ministry to Ahmad Shah Massoud, but was refused. Najibullah sent a message back saying that he would leave the post open – but it was ignored.

The only thing that could give him any cause for hope was that the Afghan army was in much better shape than it had been in the early 1980s. It was buttressed by some hundreds of Soviet soldiers left behind in the guise of advisers, some of them with the job of operating the Scud medium-range missiles that had been given to the Afghan army. Since the Geneva agreement the Soviet Union had given huge supplies to the Afghan forces – hundreds of Scuds, more than a thousand armoured vehicles and large supplies of food, fuel and munitions. Their advice to the Afghans was to concentrate their forces in a few important cities, keep well dug in and hold them at all costs, make maximum use of air power and missiles – and keep open the air and land bridges to the Soviet Union. It was not so very different from the strategy of the previous nine years.

* * *

The war in Afghanistan was more a political and military failure than a conventional military defeat for the Soviet Union. Its immediate, obvious failure was in not creating a regime that had sufficient support among the Afghan people to be able to survive. In a military sense it failed to subdue the Mujahideen, but it never suffered a major defeat in battle. The war was never very intense. In most years there were one or two important campaigns; in between, long periods of relative quiet, particularly during the winters, prevailed. In all, the Soviets had 50,000 casualties – 15,000 dead and 35,000 wounded. The worst losses were in the period from 1980 to April 1985, which saw the big campaigns in the Panjshir Valley. On average the number of personnel killed ran at under 1,700 a year, which was fewer than the Red Army used to lose annually through accidents in the Soviet Union.

To put these figures into perspective, American losses during the much shorter war in Vietnam were 58,000 dead. Soviet losses of materiel, according to figures published after the war, included 118 aircraft, 333 helicopters, 147 tanks and 2,683 trucks and armoured infantry vehicles. There were no Saudi military casualties, as far as I know – though some of our people may have died in car accidents or similar mishaps in the frontier area. Our Pakistani allies had a few casualties as a result of the sporadic bombing by Soviet aircraft.

The consensus among the Soviet staff and intelligence officers after the war was that their big mistake had been made early on. They determined that they should have confined their efforts to holding the important cities and highways, supporting the Afghan government and training the Afghan army. This, of course, is what they did in the main – but they also launched attacks on areas from which the Mujahideen were drawing support, particularly the Panjshir Valley. The Russians were very open after the war in admitting that this strategy only increased the numbers of refugees and the numbers of young men joining the Mujahideen, as well as causing increased hatred and bitterness. They felt they did much better from April 1985, when they switched their attention to the areas near the Pakistani border, with the purpose of intercepting the Mujahideen's supplies.

The real disaster for the Soviet Union, though, was the effect the war had on its society at home. The war was a burden on the country's collapsing economy, and it demoralised the Soviet people. By the time of the withdrawal more than half a million soldiers and civilians had served in Afghanistan, for periods of two years for officers and eighteen months for other ranks. They brought home stories of the immense cruelty of the war – and of corruption, incompetence and failure. Seeing what their country was failing to achieve in Afghanistan, hearing tales of the hostility of the Afghan people and contrasting these with the entirely different accounts in the Soviet media only served to make Soviet citizens more aware of the uselessness and hypocrisy of the system under which they lived.

In his book *The Hidden War: A Russian Journalist's Account of the Soviet War in Afghanistan*, published in 1990 during the time of glasnost, Artyom Borovik wrote that the Soviet Union at the beginning was 'obsessed with our own messianic mission and blinded by arrogance. ... [W]e rarely stopped to think how Afghanistan would influence us. ... In Afghanistan we bombed not only the detachments of rebels and their caravans, but our own ideals as well. ... In Afghanistan the policies of the government became utterly incompatible with the inherent morality of our nation. Things could not continue in the same vein.'[3]

The denouement for the Soviet Union as a whole came very soon after the withdrawal from Afghanistan. In the autumn of 1989 all the Communist regimes of Eastern Europe collapsed and in November the Berlin Wall came down. In August 1991 Gorbachev's rivals attempted a putsch in Moscow. For forty-eight hours things hung in the balance, but in the end it failed. On 24 August Gorbachev resigned as leader of the Communist Party and disbanded the party organisation. On the same day Ukraine declared itself independent from the Soviet Union and one by one the other thirteen republics that made up the USSR broke away. On 25 December 1991, twelve years to the day after it invaded Afghanistan, the Soviet Union ceased to exist. Gorbachev resigned as President. The Red Flag was hauled down on the Kremlin, and the white, blue and red flag of Russia was run up in its place. But nobody thought of removing the red stars on top of the towers along the Kremlin walls, and they remain there to this day.

Chapter 9
The Loya Jirga at Rawalpindi

Much changed in 1989, the year of the Soviet withdrawal. Up to this point, the three foreign partners backing the Mujahideen had generally worked rather well together. We had all wanted to push the Russians out of Afghanistan and remove the Communist regime. And the personalities involved had been more or less the same – President Reagan, William Casey and then Robert Gates at the CIA, President Zia and General Akhtar Abdul Rahman Khan, King Fahd and myself. Now our interests diverged – not completely, but it became clear that we had different emphases and in the United States and Pakistan there were new leaders.

The United States had always been most interested in defeating the Soviet Union and weakening it internally – as well as getting its revenge for Vietnam. Once these things happened it saw its mission as being accomplished. Of course, there were differences among various departments. The CIA officials seemed most interested in finishing the war and removing Najibullah; the State Department at this time seemed more worried by the increasing strength of Hekmatyar and the more militant Islamists. At the top of the US administration President George H.W. Bush, who took office in January 1989, was never greatly interested in Afghanistan. For him it was a matter of waning importance – something successfully resolved under his predecessor – and he faced more important and exciting issues, notably the collapse of Communism in Eastern Europe that year and the prospect of a reunited Germany. There was a big cut – more than half – in the money the CIA was allocated for Afghanistan in the fiscal year from October 1989 to October 1990.

Pakistan remained hugely involved with Afghanistan. It still had a hostile neighbour in the Najibullah regime, so it very much wanted the Mujahideen to take Kabul. It also wanted the three million Afghan refugees it had on its soil to go home, and soon. As the Soviet Central Asian republics became independent in the later months of 1991, Pakistan became interested in opening a trade route to them through Afghanistan. It had a new Prime Minister in Benazir Bhutto, the daughter of Zulfikar Ali Bhutto. She had come to power after the army, shocked by the death of President Zia, had agreed to the return of democratic politics. Benazir was young – she was thirty-six – Western-educated, with no experience of government, and was very distrustful of the army and particularly the ISI. It was the army, after all, which had killed her father. In her government one could see some marked tensions in policy towards Afghanistan. The ISI and much of the military establishment remained strongly in support of Hekmatyar, Islamist militancy and the Pathan elements in Afghanistan. Benazir herself was more inclined to coordinate her actions with whatever remained of American policy.

In Saudi Arabia there were no changes at the top of the government and we had no reason to change our policies. Our mission had been partly accomplished, but we still wanted to bring down the Najibullah regime and to install a new, stable, government in Kabul based on a united front of Mujahideen parties. We were starting to become a bit worried by Afghan and Arab Islamist militancy, as I shall explain later, and we would probably have endorsed some sort of compromise between Najibullah and the pro-monarchist Afghan parties had this been possible. It was talked about and in some ways, it appealed to us – Saudi Arabia is after all a monarchy and a conservative, 'status quo' power – but it was never seriously on the cards.

The first step towards the installation of a new government in Kabul, which was the central element of Pakistani and Saudi policy, seemed to be the formation of a provisional government. This would give the Mujahideen parties, and all the Afghan opposition, some formal international status, as well as creating a body which could assume power when Najibullah fell. So, at the beginning of 1989 the Pakistanis organised a Loya Jirga, or Grand Assembly, of Afghan leaders and tribal representatives in Rawalpindi. All the seven official parties attended, along with two Shia parties. The actual event was held in February. More than 3,000 Afghans came from all parts of the country and from the refugee camps. The meeting was financed from the CIA/GID/ISI budget, which covered administration and logistics as well as arms purchases, and it was quite expensive. The Pakistani government had to spread some money around to get a minimal degree of co-operation; indeed, some of the Afghan delegates went to Pakistani officials and asked for money as the price of their presence.

For days the members of the Loya Jirga argued. I was there, and it was an exhausting experience. It seemed impossible to find a formula which would satisfy everyone. Eventually the assembly was pushed into agreement by the forceful intervention of Jalaluddin Haqqani, who was Maulvi Younis Khalis's well-respected commander and tribal leader from the Khost region. He said there should be a vote by everybody present for all the posts at the top of government and all the ministerial posts. Anyone who wanted to put himself forward as a candidate could do so. The person who got the most votes would be President, the second Prime Minister, the third Foreign Minister, the fourth Defence Minister – and so on down a list of some fifteen or twenty ministries. The idea was accepted and everybody agreed that the outcome of the vote would be binding. I spoke to all the leaders and repeated to each that this time they really should stick to what they had agreed.

Each of the nine parties (including the Shias) nominated seventy people for election, which meant that there were 630 candidates. The vote was held. The person who came out on top was Hazrat Sibghatullah Mojaddedi of the Afghan National Liberation Front. His party had been the least effective in a military sense during the war, but it had a large number of supporters and Mojaddedi himself was well respected as a philosopher and a man of courage and principle. He also proved himself effective as a politician at the Loya Jirga. Most important, he held out the possibility of some stability in government because he was neither Burhanuddin Rabbani nor Gulbuddin Hekmatyar, and the delegates could see that if either of these two leaders of the major parties was elected President the result would be a total split in their ranks, and chaos. Second in the vote was Abd Rabb Al-Rasul Sayyaf, who passed the job of Prime Minister to his deputy, Ahmad Shah Ahmadzai. Third, with the post of Foreign Minister, was Gulbuddin Hekmatyar.

The first thing Hekmatyar said when he heard the result was, 'I don't accept it'. He had expected to be President. It fell to me to persuade him that he had made a promise and should stick to it. Personally, I had doubts about whether he was a natural foreign minister, but I had to do my best. I sat and argued with him for two hours, and eventually I succeeded. At the end I asked him, 'Are you sure you accept this post, because I'm about to report to the Pakistani Prime Minister and then I shall be reporting to King Fahd'.

'Yes, I give you my word, you are my brother,' he replied, putting his hand on his heart.

So, I went straight to Benazir Bhutto and I was telling her about the deal – it was scarcely an hour after I had left Hekmatyar – when an aide came in and said that Hekmatyar was saying on the radio that he was boycotting the government. 'Are you sure you heard right?' said Benazir.

In any event it was decided by us all that the government should be formed, with or without Hekmatyar, and so on 14 February 1989, the day before the final Soviet withdrawal, a formal announcement was made establishing the Afghan Interim Government. Saudi Arabia promptly recognised it as did the United Arab Emirates. We assumed that Pakistan would do the same and we hoped that America would follow. But the Americans hesitated. They wanted to see whether the interim government would hold together and whether its forces could capture a substantial city in Afghanistan, which would give it a physical presence in its own country. Benazir Bhutto followed the American lead. Possibly her confidence in the new government had also been weakened by Hekmatyar's behaviour.

Quite independently of any American thinking, the interim government itself and the ISI under Major General Gul also felt it would be a good idea for the Mujahideen to take an Afghan city. The place they chose was Jalalabad, which was only fifty kilometres from the Pakistani border. It was an obvious target. It could be supplied easily by the Grand Trunk Road, which ran over the Khyber Pass from Peshawar, and it would give the Mujahideen a base closer to their other areas of operations, particularly Kabul. Quite apart from giving the provisional government a foothold in its own country, its fall would be a great moral blow to the Communists.

The Mujahideen assembled 5,000–7,000 men and launched a conventional attack in March 1989. It was badly planned. There was no overall commander for the effort – instead, there were eight commanders who carried out their attacks with minimal coordination. The Mujahideen failed to penetrate the city's defences; their assaults were broken up by the Afghan government forces' armour, artillery and aircraft. The attack degenerated into a siege, with individual commanders launching their own operations at random. The Afghan army fought hard to survive. At the beginning of the battle some of the prisoners taken by the Mujahideen had been killed, and when news of this got back to the garrison it confirmed in the soldiers' minds that surrender was not an option. The battle went on intermittently for four months until June. It cost the Mujahideen 3,000 men killed and wounded, by far their biggest loss in any battle they had fought, and it used up their accumulated stocks of arms and ammunition. The Afghan army gained greatly in confidence. The whole operation was a disaster, and at the end of it, Major General Gul was removed from his post.

Equally bad, just after the end of the siege one of the senior commanders in Hekmatyar's party ambushed some of Massoud's forces and killed thirty-six men, including several of his friends. The attack was part of a feud which went back to the previous year when forces of the two parties had attacked the town of Taloqan, in the north-east. The city was captured, but as soon as they had it the two forces separated into opposing camps and began fighting each other. The fighting continued intermittently into the following year, until in the early summer a truce was arranged and sealed by the commanders on each side reading passages from the Holy Quran aloud to each other. It was after this, on 9 July, that the ambush of Massoud's men took place. Massoud was furious. He spared no effort in seeking revenge and he offered a reward of one million afghanis, around $18,200, to anyone who could find the men responsible. The offer quite quickly produced results. One of Hekmatyar's commanders, Sayad Jamal, and his brother were brought to Massoud and he had them hanged. This provoked a return to open warfare across much of the north-east.

The fighting between Massoud's and Hekmatyar's forces was only one – though particularly serious – instance of the many feuds that took place during the war. Feuding was a major problem from the beginning. It led to the deaths of hundreds of Mujahideen at the hands of their comrades-in-arms and it was a distraction from the war effort against the Soviets and the Afghan Communists. On all my visits to Pakistan I tried to get the parties and commanders to reconcile their differences, and the Pakistani government and particularly the Afghan Bureau did the same. The best we achieved was periodic truces.

After the Soviet withdrawal the problem grew worse. It seemed that Hekmatyar was trying to eliminate his enemies. He was kidnapping and murdering Mujahideen royalists, intellectuals and rival commanders. The man who tried to stop the violence at this point was Abdullah Azzam, the founder of the Office of Services. Azzam and his followers organised a religious group to travel around northern Afghanistan to mediate between Hekmatyar's forces and Massoud's – using principles from the Quran and the Sharia to persuade the rivals that what they were doing was wrong. The attempt failed. Azzam himself travelled to Takhar province, the area around Taloqan, and met Massoud. He tried to broker a fresh truce, but his efforts were thwarted by Hekmatyar, who continually denounced Massoud before audiences in Peshawar – saying, truthfully, that he had received help from French intelligence and, falsely, that he frolicked with French nurses at luxury camps in the Panjshir Valley.[1]

Then, on 24 November 1989, as he arrived at the Saba-i-Leil mosque to lead the Friday prayers, Azzam was assassinated by a car bomb. There were any number of suspects with plausible motives, conspiracy theories multiplied and the crime was never solved. The most likely culprits were the KHAD and Hekmatyar – and my own belief is that the man behind it was Hekmatyar himself.

Abdullah Azzam's death was a sad loss to the cause of moderation in Afghanistan and in the highly politicised world of Peshawar and the camps along the frontier. During his years in this region, he had seen the evil consequences of violence, personal ambition and the lack of proper authority in men's lives, and he had become a more thoughtful, less passionate, wiser man. He had come to believe that reason and negotiation were better than war as a means of solving the problems of the Muslim world. He did not take the position that all Muslim governments were illegitimate – as Bin Laden and Ayman El-Zawahiri were to do. After his death it was these two men who took over the Office of Services, working with allies in Hekmatyar's party. They overcame competition from Azzam's son-in-law, who also wanted to control it. They renamed the office Al-Qaeda ('the Base'), which was intended to evoke images of Bin Laden's battle against the Soviets at Jaji and also convey the idea that it was from here that they would begin a campaign of jihad to right the complaints and sufferings of Muslims everywhere.

In the following year Hekmatyar's behaviour sank to a new low. In March 1990 he reached an agreement with the Defence Minister of the Communist government, Shahnawaz Tanai, and they attempted a joint coup d'état in Kabul. Tanai had units of the Afghan air force bomb the presidential palace – they failed to kill Najibullah – while some armoured forces drove south to open the way for Hekmatyar's fighters advancing from the area around Jalalabad. The attempt was a fiasco. Within hours of the bombing of the palace it became obvious to the Afghan commanders in the capital that the coup was failing, so the waverers rallied to the President and Tanai's allies in Kabul were routed. Tanai fled to Pakistan, where he had friends and backers in the ISI.

The utterly unholy alliance between a hard-line Communist and a nominally devout Muslim that lay behind the attempted coup discredited everybody involved – particularly Hekmatyar and elements of the ISI – in the eyes of most of the Afghan resistance and the population at large, not to mention Saudi Arabia and the United States. I began to despair of the Mujahideen. A year before, at the time the Soviets pulled out, we had thought the Najibullah regime would fall within months and that we had an agreement on a provisional government which united an overwhelming majority of the Mujahideen. Now everything was in ruins. Hekmatyar was clearly trying to seize power for himself. The Mujahideen were in a state of civil war. And the Afghan army, or at least elements of it, had proved itself quite competent. The Najibullah government was given a new lease of life, which enabled it to survive for another two years.

Chapter 10
Interlude – the Kuwait Crisis

In early 1990 Bin Laden left Afghanistan and returned to Saudi Arabia. He clearly felt at this stage that his presence was not needed in and around Peshawar because his affairs were well established there, and that he should devote his energies to the struggle against the 'enemy' elsewhere. By the 'enemy' he seemed to have in mind not just the Communist government of Dr Najibullah and the Soviet Union, but anyone who 'did harm to Muslims' – and specifically at this time he had his eye on the People's Democratic Republic of Yemen (PDRY), which was the official name of what was generally called South Yemen. Since its formation after the British left Aden in 1967 the PDRY had been the Arab world's only Communist state.

Bin Laden came to see me in my office in Jeddah one day soon after his return. It was my first and only formal meeting with him. He explained to me that the force he had assembled on the Pakistan-Afghanistan frontier and across the border consisted of not only Saudis but also many Yemenis, and now that the Soviets had been forced out and the Mujahideen had begun fighting among themselves, most of these young men had returned home – to North or South Yemen, or to Saudi Arabia, where many Yemenis lived and worked. He referred to them as 'my Mujahideen'. He then said he would like the support of the Saudi government in having his Mujahideen drive the Soviets out of South

Yemen. It was an idiotic scheme – hopelessly ill-informed, dangerous and against the Kingdom's interests.

The Communist government of the PDRY had torn itself apart a few years earlier in an internal power struggle which had led to near civil war in some of the areas around Aden. East Germany, which had been more important than the Soviet Union as the direct backer of the state, had itself collapsed in the autumn of 1989, and the Russians were not continuing their financial assistance. The government in Aden had been dependent on funding from these two states. Seizing the opportunity presented by the weakness of the PDRY, Saudi Arabia and the Yemen Arab Republic (North Yemen) had begun political initiatives to see if it would be possible to change or modify South Yemen's government by peaceful means and bring it into the political mainstream of the Arab world. Soon after my meeting with Bin Laden, in May 1990, after the total collapse of the PDRY finances, South Yemen was united with the Yemen Arab Republic – entirely on the YAR's terms.

I explained to Bin Laden what was going on – I was surprised he did not understand it already – and I added that, if he were to attack the south, he might actually unite the factions in the very government he was hoping to destroy. To my surprise he totally failed to accept these arguments. He left my office, and that was the last time I ever saw him. He had seemed a very different person from the calm, gentle young man I had met informally several times in Pakistan. He had become haughty and arrogant, and very much a man with a mission.

I learnt later that he took his scheme to other members of my family, and in particular to Prince Ahmad bin Abdulaziz, the Deputy Minister of the Interior. Prince Ahmad gave him much the same reply as I had done. I gathered that, ideally, Bin Laden would have liked to meet Prince Sultan bin Abdulaziz, the Minister of Defence, who had been in charge of Saudi Arabia's relations with Yemen since he took up his post in 1962, during the civil war between the republicans and royalists in Yemen. On all Yemeni matters other Saudi government bodies referred to Prince Sultan's office. It seems that Prince Sultan had been too busy to see Bin Laden.

A few months after my conversation with Bin Laden my attention was diverted wholly from Afghanistan to Kuwait. On the night of 1–2 August Saddam Hussein's forces invaded Kuwait and occupied it. Although Iraq had been threatening Kuwait for some time – bullying it on the spurious charge that it had been taking oil from an Iraqi field near the border – the invasion came as a shock. When he heard the news King Fahd immediately telephoned Saddam Hussein, but was told, 'Sorry, the President is not available'. Then he telephoned King Hussein of Jordan and was told, 'He'll call you back'. At this level, this sort of offhand reaction is most unusual and very insulting. When King Fahd did eventually speak to the two other leaders later in the day, Saddam said bluntly that Kuwait had always been part of Iraq, which brought the conversation to an abrupt end. King Hussein said that he was 'totally surprised' by the Iraqi action, but that everyone should 'work for an Arab solution to the crisis' – which was obviously not going to be effective. Throughout their conversation the two kings addressed each other very formally as 'Your Majesty', which was their normal practice.

Two days later there was an Arab foreign ministers' meeting in Cairo at which the Arab world divided into two camps. The majority condemned the invasion – some of them rather reluctantly – but six delegations, from Jordan, Yemen, Sudan, Tunisia, Algeria and the Palestine Liberation Organisation, appeared to support it. This was all a very disillusioning experience for Saudi Arabia. Together with Kuwait we had given Iraq an enormous amount of financial and moral support during its war with Iran from 1980 to 1988. Our aid began in 1982 when the Iranians, having regained their own territory, began to advance into Iraq. Likewise, over many more years we had given much financial help to most of the states that now supported Iraq, to Yemen, Jordan and the PLO in particular. Their position – supporting the unprovoked aggression of one state against another – seemed to us to be totally immoral.

It was clear to us that if diplomacy did not succeed Saddam would have to be removed from Kuwait by military force. Saudi Arabia never thought of abandoning Kuwait. We have similar political systems, we are bound together in the Gulf Cooperation Council and we are virtually the same people – the dynasty that founded Kuwait in the eighteenth century, and which still leads it, were originally from Najd in central Arabia. Our two ruling families are distantly related. Sheikh Mubarak Sabah Al-Sabah gave my grandfather, Abdulaziz, shelter when he was forced to leave Riyadh in 1891 and he then backed him in the early campaigns that led to the creation of the present Saudi Kingdom. The two rulers at the time of the invasion, King Fahd and Sheikh Jaber Ahmad Al-Sabah, had a good personal rapport. Sheikh Jaber and most of the rest of the Kuwaiti government were given refuge in Taif during the period of the Iraqi occupation.

The American and British governments supported our stand from the start. King Fahd and President George H.W. Bush spoke on the telephone within hours of the invasion and it was at this point that the President promised in broad terms that he would give whatever support was needed to restore Kuwait's sovereignty.

It happened that I was in Washington at the time. I had been given permission in late July to take a holiday – because the Iraq-Kuwait crisis seemed then to be subsiding – and after a few days in Europe on 1 August I had flown with my family to Washington. Our plan was to go the next day to Argentina for a skiing holiday. Of course, when I heard of the invasion, at 7 p.m. US Eastern Time on 1 August, I telephoned the King to tell him I was in Washington, and because at that moment Prince Bandar bin Sultan, our ambassador to the United States, was also on holiday, the King told me to stay where I was.

My task was to get a view of what the Americans were thinking. I had meetings at the White House with the President and his National Security Adviser, Brent Scowcroft, and with William Webster, Casey's successor at the CIA. It was clear that the Americans were solidly behind us, and the main subject of debate seemed to be the number of troops that would be needed to remove Saddam from Kuwait if diplomacy failed. Apparently with each discussion of the crisis the Secretary of Defence, Dick Cheney, and the Chairman of the Joint Chiefs of Staff, Colin Powell, increased their estimate. They quite quickly reached the figure of half a million troops, and although this was not announced immediately, that was the number eventually deployed.

On 5 August Cheney flew to Jeddah to show the King satellite pictures of Iraqi troop positions, which I had already seen in Washington. They showed armoured forces comprising perhaps 200,000 Iraqi troops on the Kuwaiti-Saudi and Iraqi-Saudi borders. These did not at this stage suggest either attack or defence, but they were a cause for great concern. An invasion of the Saudi Kingdom seemed unlikely, and militarily difficult, seeing that it is an enormous country, a quarter of the size of the United States, with much bigger armed forces than Kuwait. Quite probably Saddam had deployed his troops merely with the purpose of frightening Saudi Arabia – but we could not be sure.

Saddam was a man who had built his career on being extremely violent and finding that violence paid, and he was also a gambler and unpredictable. He might have been thinking of occupying some of the Kingdom's oilfields, which begin only 130 kilometres south of Kuwait, and holding them as a bargaining counter; he would give them up in return for being allowed to keep Kuwait. We decided with the Americans that US troops should be sent to defend Saudi Arabia, and so began the huge deployment of forces from many nations that would eventually liberate Kuwait in February 1991.

It was only a matter of days after these events that Bin Laden made a strange reappearance. He asked once again to meet Prince Sultan, and this time the Minister of Defence agreed, out of courtesy rather than from any feeling that what Bin Laden would have to say would be relevant to the matter in hand. When they met Bin Laden explained that in his view Saudi Arabia had no need to call upon the Americans or anyone else to liberate Kuwait. It was wrong, he said, to allow non-Muslim forces into the Kingdom – in spite of the fact that the senior *ulema* (religious scholars) had already issued a fatwa stating that when threatened by an enemy Muslims were justified in accepting the help of non-Muslim friends.

Instead of the foreign forces, Bin Laden suggested that he and his Mujahideen could do the job. 'We threw the Soviets out of Afghanistan', he said, 'and we can do the same with the Iraqis in Kuwait.' It was a staggering proposal. It showed ignorance on every level. Bin Laden seemed completely unaware that it was political and economic pressure at home as much as military failure that had caused Mikhail Gorbachev in early 1986 to decide that the Soviet Union would have to leave Afghanistan. He had apparently forgotten that his Mujahideen and the other Arabs who had fought in Afghanistan were few in number and, compared with the Afghan Mujahideen, had contributed very little in a military sense. And he was ignoring the fact that, whereas Afghanistan is a mountainous country ideally suited to guerrilla warfare, Kuwait is completely flat and is perfect terrain for conventional forces. Bin Laden seemed to be living in a dream world.

Prince Sultan was polite but firm. He thanked Bin Laden for his proposal and talked about the great contribution the Bin Laden family had made to the physical construction of the Kingdom – Bin Laden had been the first Saudi company to undertake major road-building projects. He said that he would call upon Bin Laden if needed, but meanwhile he expected him to give his full support to the government at a difficult time.

It was certainly not obvious to Prince Sultan at the end of this conversation, but apparently Bin Laden was immensely surprised and hurt by the rejection of his proposal. It seems that the meeting and the previous rejection of his proposal about South Yemen were a watershed in the development of his thinking. In later years his manifestos suggested that he had felt personally humiliated by the rejection. Then, in his view, the government insulted him further by inviting more foreign troops into the Kingdom in the build-up to the liberation of Kuwait and, some years later, depriving him of his citizenship in response to his continuing criticism. He suffered from the sense of grievance and the delusions of the semi-educated man who has limited experience of the world but strong political and religious convictions.

After his meeting with Prince Sultan we heard nothing more from Bin Laden until the last weeks of 1990 and early 1991, shortly before the start of the military campaign to liberate Kuwait. He began preaching at the Bin Laden mosque in Jeddah and speaking at schools without the permission of the Ministry of Education. His themes were the predictable ones: Muslims should unite, solve their own problems, and not allow infidels to become involved in their quarrels; Afghanistan had been neglected since the Soviet withdrawal; Palestine was still occupied. After a few such sermons and speeches Bin Laden was invited to the headquarters of the Jeddah police and was advised to stop his activities. He was told that he was not a preacher, and that before he made any more speeches he should ask for permission. He was arousing people's emotions at a time when Saudi Arabia needed solidarity. Two months later, after the end of the war, he began preaching again, and this time he was summoned to the police headquarters and told more forcefully to stop. He obeyed this order. He was also told to inform the Ministry of the Interior if he intended to leave Saudi Arabia.

At this time Bin Laden's preaching was only one element of a broad problem of which we were becoming aware. It concerned some of the young Saudis who had been returning from Afghanistan and the frontier camps in the two years since the Soviet withdrawal. Most of these people had integrated perfectly happily back into Saudi society. But some had changed.

To explain this, I must describe some of the character of our society as it has evolved since the large flow of oil revenues began in 1974. It has been the policy of the Saudi government to spread its revenues as much as possible among its people; the same policy has prevailed in all the Gulf states. This practice has provided not just free healthcare services and education in the Kingdom, but also a range of subsidies, often amounting to nearly a hundred per cent of the cost, on certain categories of housing, electricity and water, domestic flights, telephone calls and basic foodstuffs. Businesses have been helped by low interest rates (two per cent) or interest-free loans, and anyone investing in agriculture in the 1980s and early 1990s benefited from a huge array of subsidies and a very high price at which the government guaranteed to buy grain. There are no income taxes in Saudi Arabia – other than zakat, the 2.5 per cent religious tax – and, until recently, no sales or value-added taxes. For many years, from the 1970s to the mid-1990s, the government virtually guaranteed any university or high school graduate a job – and a job holder was not necessarily expected to work very hard.

At the same time, the legal and social structure of Saudi Arabia, and much government spending, have been geared to maintaining the strength of family life, which is at the core of Islam. It was this objective which lay behind the limits then placed on the public roles and social activities of women – which were more a matter of custom than of written government regulations – and the limited number of entertainments available to young people outside the home. In a public sense, also, there is little scope for Saudis to engage in politics. People can criticise ministries and policies in newspaper articles and they can meet members of the royal family to discuss their concerns, but until the introduction of municipal elections in 2005 there was no opportunity for people to put their energies into political campaigning, lobbying, local politics or similar activities that occupy the more politically minded members of the Western world.

The whole system had created a society that was generous but rather bland, in which life was easy and not at all challenging. One can understand, therefore, what an impact life on the Afghan-Pakistani frontier could have on the young Saudis who went there. For the first time in their lives they saw poverty, suffering and real need – and they were able to do something really valuable to help. They also encountered powerful political issues of right and wrong as they saw the results of war, an evil political system that was forcing change upon a society, and the bombings and murders by KHAD agents. Everybody who went to the frontier felt that he was involved in some way in fighting this evil, and those few who joined the Mujahideen inside Afghanistan fought or came close to fighting in a real physical sense.

When they came back to the Kingdom these young Saudis found that, apart from their families, everything in their lives seemed unimportant; it is rather the same for everyone returning home from a war, or from a disaster area where they have been working for relief agencies. Most, as I say, adjusted, but some decided that the society of their own country was too soft and easy, and not sufficiently religious.

Many of this latter group, like Bin Laden, had gained a heady sense of power. They felt they had helped defeat the Soviet Union (without understanding anything about the internal failures of Communism) and thought they could go on to change the rest of the world, starting in Saudi Arabia. Strangely, in retrospect, we – the Saudi government and Saudi society as a whole – had never thought when we encouraged young men to go to Pakistan in the 1980s that it might change their political ideas. At that time, we were all united in helping the Afghans and fighting the Communists. Our attention, and for that matter the attention of our Western allies, was directed just to winning the war. Some of the people who had been radicalised by their experiences went back to Pakistan and Afghanistan; others in due course found their way to Bosnia and Chechnya and some Arab countries. Others began campaigning for change in Saudi Arabia. They joined a domestic Islamist opposition which emerged openly in 1990 and 1991 for the first time.

It was a period of free and open discussion in Saudi Arabia. The government published figures for the enormous sums it had given to Iraq during the previous ten years – more than $25 billion in cash and an equal amount in medical supplies, food and armaments. And it openly expressed its disenchantment with some other Arab governments. It began to reassess its foreign policy and defence spending. There was, likewise, much public criticism of government policies. Some asked why, when we had spent billions of dollars for military purposes we were still unable to stand up to Iraq on our own. The answer, in part, was that though our air force could have defeated the Iraqi air force – we had better aircraft and good pilots – our army was far too small. Saudi Arabia is not a military society. The government has never wanted to build a large army, there is no conscription and the public, as a whole, has not been hugely attracted by careers in the military services.

The radical elements returning from Afghanistan and the domestic Islamist opposition went far beyond discussion of these types of issues. They attacked the system of government and the whole basis of Saudi society. They did this mainly through preaching in the mosques and giving lectures, and through circulating cassette tapes. Many of these were rabid in their tone. Some made ludicrous allegations. One, called 'America as I

Saw It', denounced the United States as 'a nation of beasts who fornicate and eat rotten food'.

It was a common theme that American forces had come to occupy Saudi Arabia and to seize its oil. Anyone who had liberal, pro-Western views, including many of the well-educated technocrats who run our government, was liable to suffer the most personal and vicious attacks, backed by totally fabricated allegations. In any Western society these would have led to a libel action by the victim and the award of heavy damages. One of my sisters, who was involved in charity work, had been quietly pushing for a more public role for women. The charity she ran was denounced as a 'whorehouse' in a Friday sermon delivered by a preacher at a mosque in Riyadh. The next Friday I went to the mosque myself, and asking to speak, which any member of the congregation is entitled to do, I gave a quiet, reasoned and strong reply. I said that if the preacher had any evidence for his accusation, I would expect him to give it to me in a week's time. If he had none I would take action against him. No evidence was forthcoming and by the end of the week he had been dismissed from his post. Afterwards other preachers toned down their vitriol.

The attitudes of the domestic Islamist opposition – and of that in other Arab countries – were the product of the rather isolated and introverted world their members had created for themselves. Most of the preachers and the authors of the tapes had received rather little education. Their sense of self-worth, of their role in society, came only from their limited religious studies, and they saw the modern, more secular world outside as a threat to themselves and to what they knew and understood. It was this fear that particularly conditioned their attitude towards women. In the world they knew, women were confined to the home. As one of the leaders of the Front Islamique du Salut in Algeria put it at this time, 'A woman should be out of the house only three times in her life – when she is born, when she is married and when she is taken to the cemetery'. For this man and others like him the emergence of women playing a broader role in society was a challenge with which they had no idea how to deal.

At the same time, in a more aggressive, assertive way, the Islamist opposition wanted more power for itself. Saudi Arabia has always been a religious society, and one would think at first sight that there should be little need from anyone's point of view for it to become more so. By saying that the country needed an even larger Islamic content in the school curriculum, more mosques, more religious programming on television, a more Islamic tone in new government regulations and a wider application of Sharia law, the opposition was seeking to expand its role and, most importantly, to provide jobs for the growing number of graduates coming out of the religious universities. When it argued, 'Surely it should be the most Islamically educated members of society who should govern the country' and 'Society should be ordered in a truly Islamic fashion', it was saying, in effect, 'Back us, give us a greater role in government, support the creation of a fundamentalist Islamic state, and bit by bit we shall be able to take over the country and run it ourselves'.

The royal family and the government tolerated this opposition activity for several years. Obviously, we reprimanded individual preachers from time to time, and the police confiscated subversive cassette tapes when they found them, but it was not until 1994, when some religious figures in Buraidah, in Najd, launched what was virtually an insurrection, intending to create an independent extremist community under an Islamic cloak, that we put a number of the leaders in prison. Even then the Islamist political opposition continued, though in a less public way.

The upsurge in opposition at home made us much more conscious of all that was going wrong on the Afghan-Pakistani frontier. As the numbers of Arab volunteers – mainly Gulf Arabs, Palestinians, Egyptians, Algerians and Yemenis – there grew in the late 1980s they seemed to become more militant. It was in the summer of 1989, soon after the Soviet withdrawal, that we became particularly aware that they were involving themselves in activities that had nothing to do with what should have been the continuing war against the Najibullah regime. We got more reports of the desecration of graves and there were nasty confrontations between Arabs and Western aid workers. The militants, as noted earlier, seemed to feel that it was none of the Westerners' business to be working in an Islamic country. Among some of the militants a *takfir* mentality was developing. *Takfir* is the process of a Muslim withdrawing from the community of other Muslims whom he considers to be less pure than himself and considering those around him as *kuffar*, unbelievers.

Our concerns prompted us to start studying which Arab political groups were operating on the frontier and who were their members. We began to make lists of the people who had gone to the frontier – Saudis and others – and when we talked to our Pakistani colleagues we found they were doing the same. Our obvious starting point was to check the records of the people who had been given discounted airfares, but these covered only the later years of the campaign against the Russians. There were no other easily available documented sources, and the work was complicated by the fact that many of the Arabs had adopted pseudonyms. But we did what we could, using our own GID agents and the various other people on the frontier who we had come to trust. Our list was certainly not comprehensive. We shared what we compiled with the Ministry of the Interior, which was interested in following the activities of the militants who had returned home.

We were also unhappy about the direction of Saudi private-sector aid. We had begun to worry about this in the later 1980s when it seemed that too much of the charitable money that should have been used for relief work was going to the Afghan parties, and especially to the most militant fundamentalist groups. This led us to establish the National Public Committee for the Support of the Afghan People, under Prince Salman bin Abdulaziz, then the Governor of Riyadh, to coordinate and direct the flow of money from the charities. But this body did not control any of the money that was contributed directly by rich private donors – and much of this continued to go to the most radical groups. We tried to tell these donors that their money was creating something which was dangerous and beyond our control, but our words did not have much effect.

Our official payments were being reduced in line with US payments from the time of the Russian withdrawal in 1988–89. There was no single meeting to discuss this; we liaised with the Americans on an ad hoc basis, keeping each other informed of what we were doing. We were very much aware of the Americans' declining interest in Afghanistan, which was running a bit ahead of our own views. I remember in November 1990 I met the Deputy Director of the CIA, who explained to me that a recent cut in US funding meant that for the following three or four months no more support for the Mujahideen would be forthcoming from the United States. The inference was that for the time being it would be up to us to continue the support. The same day, 25 November, I sent a cable to King Fahd. I reproduce the relevant parts below because they provide an example of our thinking at the time:

Peace and blessings be upon you,

I inform Your Majesty that I was visited today by Mr. Himes, the Deputy Director of the American Central Intelligence Agency (CIA), the CIA's Pakistan representative, Mr. Himes' assistant, and officials from the Afghan State Intelligence Agency who notified me of the following:

The American government has committed to continue supporting the Afghan issue this year. Congress initially agreed to give the CIA a budget of 250 million dollars to fund the effort, of which 120 million has been spent up until now. The remainder will not be spent until next March (Ramadan) if Congress agrees.

The budget for the jihad has been depleted and, until the United States releases its budget, the Mujahideen will rely on the Kingdom for funding this year to maintain the flow of weapons and continue the fight until the Russians are forced to abandon the Najibullah government. The amount needed is 375 million dollars, the first part of which will be spent before next January to purchase weaponry and deliver it to the Mujahideen by February. This will allow the Mujahideen to continue their operations without interruption.

Your Majesty, the coming phase of the Afghan conflict will be decisive. We must not abandon our support for the jihad despite the current circumstances, as this would have negative consequences on our relations with Pakistan and give Iran the opportunity to undo everything we have achieved in Afghanistan.

I would like to ask for your permission to travel to Pakistan to meet with Pakistani and Afghan officials. The last time I met with them was months ago, before the formation of the current government headed by Prime Minister Nawaz Sharif. Please order the Ministry of Finance to release this year's Afghanistan support budget and have the first payment of the regular 135 million dollars released this month.

Also, please approve my trip to Pakistan and provide me with any further instructions.

May God protect you,
Turki AlFaisal

At the end of 1991, our official support under the original US-Pakistani-Saudi arrangements stopped altogether. Again, there was no formal meeting to announce this – the United States and Saudi Arabia simply informed each other that they were stopping. The end of US support for the Mujahideen had been agreed by the Secretary of State, James Baker, and the Soviet Foreign Minister, Boris Pankin, when they met in September 1991. They pledged a mutual cut-off of arms supplies – to the Mujahideen and Najibullah's government – effective from 1 January 1992.

After this, what further official Saudi aid that was given to Afghanistan was for purely humanitarian purposes. On 10 January 1992 Prince Salman sent a cable to King Fahd to say that the Ministry of Finance had agreed to extend the Saudi Red Crescent's operations on the Pakistan-Afghanistan border for another year and fund it with an additional $4 million. He said this would be the last year that the Kingdom would continue funding these operations and that the remaining projects would have to adhere to this final budget. Given the sensitivity and importance of Saudi Arabia's relief efforts in Afghanistan, Prince Salman advised ending operations gradually in order not to undo the Kingdom's gains over the past years and compromise its good reputation among the Afghans. He argued that there was a feeling that Saudi

Arabia had provided far more services to the conflict than any other party and was expected to maintain a presence longer than its peers. The King agreed.

In all we calculated that up to this time we had spent $2.71 billion on Afghanistan. But it was not just because of a wish to save money, at a time of low oil prices when we were still paying for the allied liberation of Kuwait in early 1991, that we had no regrets about the system of matched payments (entirely separate from the Red Crescent funding) coming to an end. The Mujahideen were now fighting mainly among themselves, and several of their leaders, notably Hekmatyar and Sayyaf, had been vocal in their support of Saddam Hussein during the Kuwait crisis. We regarded this as a betrayal. It was, quite simply, no longer in the Kingdom's interests to continue supporting these people.

Chapter 11
The Fall of Dr Najibullah

In the north of Afghanistan there was a character I have not yet mentioned in this story. He was Abdul Rashid Dostum, an Uzbek born in 1954, who had joined the KHAD after the Soviet invasion and been sent to Soviet Uzbekistan for intelligence training. When he returned the government posted him to his hometown of Sheberghan in the north-west of Afghanistan, where he established his own militia of 300 Uzbeks dressed in KHAD uniforms and loyal to the government, but immediately answerable to him. He gradually expanded his force.

After the Soviet withdrawal he became indispensable to the government of Dr Mohammad Najibullah as the guardian of the most northerly part of the road from Kabul to Termez on the border. At the same time, he established good relations with the governments of the Soviet Central Asian republics, Turkmenistan and Uzbekistan, and maintained these connections after they became independent when the Soviet Union collapsed at the end of 1991.

These governments saw him as a force against the spread of Islamic fundamentalism from Afghanistan into their own territories. The Russians, likewise, saw him as useful in this way, and they gave him a considerable amount of assistance. By 1992 he had built a force of 40,000 men, with tanks and artillery. He had established a fearsome reputation as a hard leader. On one occasion when members of his forces committed some violent crime he had them tied to the tracks of tanks and then had the tanks drive around the parade ground. The crowd that witnessed this punishment was suitably impressed, as were the journalists who saw the remains of the criminals scattered over the parade ground afterwards. The publicity he achieved only increased the fear and respect of his people.

In the first few weeks of 1992 Dostum fell out with Najibullah. The quarrel stemmed partly from disagreements about money, exacerbated at that time by Russia stopping military supplies to Najibullah's government. In addition, in the later months of 1991 Najibullah had appointed a Pathan governor to be his (nominal) representative in the north, which Dostum saw as an insult and a threat. He viewed the Najibullah government in general as being too pro-Pathan. Further to the east, in the Tajik provinces, Ahmad Shah Massoud noticed the tension between the two and opened 'diplomatic' contacts with Dostum. Najibullah heard about the contacts and Dostum, sensing this, began to fear that he might be arrested, or even that his life might be in danger. In late January, Dostum suddenly changed sides and joined Massoud – the first of several changes of allegiance he was to make in the years to come. The move shook the whole country. Some of his soldiers were so surprised by the new orders they received that they did not believe them and stayed at their government posts.

Now the combined armies of Dostum and Massoud's Supreme Council of the North were the most powerful force in Afghanistan – stronger than the Afghan army and much stronger than Hekmatyar's fighters. Najibullah could see the writing on the wall. He spoke to a group of reporters in his office in Kabul in March and appealed for support from the United States and 'the rest of the civilised world'. 'We have a common task – Afghanistan, the USA, and the civilised world – to launch a joint struggle against fundamentalism', he said, according to a report in the *International Herald Tribune*. 'If fundamentalism comes to Afghanistan, war will continue for many years. Afghanistan will turn into a centre of world smuggling for narcotic drugs. It will be turned into a centre for terrorism.'[1]

As it turned out, Najibullah was quite right – and indeed at the time much of the rest of the world could see he was right – but for obvious reasons nobody was going to help him. The United Nations mediator in Kabul, Benon Sevan, urged him to resign and give his support to a transitional government, and Najibullah agreed. He read a speech, written for him by Sevan, on national television, saying he would leave the presidency as soon as a successor government had been formed under United Nations auspices. But it was too late.

On 14 April 1992 the northern forces moved down on Kabul and camped about an hour's drive from the city. At the same time Hekmatyar advanced from the south. Massoud made it clear from the beginning that he wanted the two forces to co-operate in taking Kabul, to avoid bloodshed and destruction and for the sake of establishing a stable government. But Hekmatyar was set against agreement in any form. For the last few years he had been fighting a war against Massoud's forces, and he seemed to regard him as much his enemy as Najibullah. Maybe he also wanted to ensure that Pathans dominated the new government in Kabul; certainly, he must have realised that, if he took the city in co-operation with the northern allies, he would be the weaker party afterwards.

According to the private account of a member of his staff, he sat with them one evening and announced that he was going to take Kabul himself, kill the members of the Communist government and defeat any attempt by Massoud to challenge him. The men with him were Maulvi Halim Wardak, who was one of his most able commanders, Ansarullah Maulvizada, Fazil Mawla Latoon and Inayatullah Toufan; the last ran his communications and his radio station. Wardak very frankly disagreed with him. He said Hekmatyar risked causing enormous bloodshed, urged him to compromise with Massoud and reminded him of his failure to seize power two years earlier in his conspiracy with the Communist Defence Minister, Shahnawaz Tanai. Hekmatyar replied that he was not a man to compromise and swore he would fight. Again, Wardak told him that if he caused bloodshed he would only give himself greater problems in the future. Hekmatyar got 'upset and angry' and the meeting came to an end.

Later the same evening Toufan received a radio call from one of Hekmatyar's commanders who was already in Kabul. This man,

Commander Malang, said he had with him two ministers of Najibullah's government – the Defence Minister, General Mohammad Rafi, and the commander of the Kabul garrison, General Nabih Azimi. Hekmatyar did not trust Azimi, but he agreed to talk to Rafi, who told him, 'The weather at the airport is not good – we cannot fly to meet you to negotiate'. By this he meant that Massoud's forces, or sympathisers, had taken control of the airport. So Hekmatyar told him to try to come to him by car, which he did.

He arrived at Hekmatyar's headquarters the next evening, explained that Massoud's troops were already in the capital's northern outskirts and asked him to send his own troops to take control of the city. Hekmatyar agreed with pleasure – the defection of the Minister of Defence seemed like a guarantee of success. Almost everybody in his force volunteered and a large supply of light weapons was issued. He announced to his troops that they were going to seek out all elements of the opposition and execute them. The only man who was not enthusiastic about this prospect was Toufan, who had many relations in Kabul. By his own account he went away and cried.

Toufan and Wardak were not the only ones urging compromise on Hekmatyar. A large number of people from other Islamic countries, including me, had come to Peshawar to try to ensure a reasonably orderly takeover of Kabul. We organised a radio call between Massoud and Hekmatyar. Massoud could not have been more diplomatic and tactful. He flattered Hekmatyar and explained that the Communist government in the city had already collapsed and that they – the Mujahideen – had now achieved everything for which they had been fighting for the last twelve years. He suggested that the two of them should go to Peshawar, join with other Islamic leaders and then all enter the city together. Hekmatyar was utterly unyielding; he simply accused Massoud of allying himself with the Communists. And apparently, as he broke off the negotiations, he believed he could take Kabul the next day. His confidence was bolstered by the many recruits from Pakistani madrasas who he had recently absorbed into his forces.

On the evening of 24 April Hekmatyar had his troops wash the tanks, armoured personnel carriers and trucks in his forces. Green flags were put on them. He led the evening prayers and recited the verses of the Quran that the Prophet Mohammad recited after he took Makkah. My former press adviser, the late Jamal Khashoggi, then working as a journalist, was with his forces that night. He recalled later that as the Mujahideen went to sleep they felt they would be victorious: 'Everybody in the camp was happy – Hekmatyar was happy – it was great. I was thinking that next morning I would be marching with the victorious force into Kabul. But Afghans have the strange habit of turning off their radios when they go to sleep – as if war will stop. So, they switched off their radios and we all went to sleep – and we woke up early in the morning. Spirits were high. We prayed the dawn prayer. Hekmatyar made a very long prayer. The sun came up and the operator turned on the radio – and the bad news started pouring in.'

Massoud, too, had been negotiating with a faction in Kabul – and, as General Rafi had reported, this faction had taken control of the airport. During the night of 24–25 April transport planes flew in carrying Dostum's forces, and as the airport is not far from the most important government buildings, these buildings were quickly seized by the northern allies. In the morning Hekmatyar's forces grabbed what few buildings they could, but by the end of the day Massoud's positions were much stronger. Hekmatyar's forces were surrounded on three sides and slowly they were pushed out of the city. After a week they withdrew altogether and installed themselves in the mountains that overlook Kabul. Enraged and bitter, Hekmatyar began to bombard the city.

Najibullah took sanctuary in what remained of the United Nations compound, where he remained for the next four years. The body of the chief of the KHAD, Ghulam Faruq Yaqubi, had already been found on 16 April, lying in a pool of blood beside his glass-topped desk – on which still stood his Soviet hotline telephone and a model of a watchtower.

* * *

While these events were unfolding the people gathered in Peshawar had been concerned with more than trying to mediate between Hekmatyar and Massoud. When it seemed that Kabul was going to fall, Nawaz Sharif, who was Prime Minister of Pakistan from 1990 to 93, had assembled a large number of people who he thought might help negotiate the creation of a new Afghan government. They included the leaders of all the Mujahideen parties, apart from Hekmatyar and Massoud: Abdullah Naseef, the then-Secretary General of the Muslim World League; Hassan Turabi, the leader of the National Islamic Front, which had recently come to power in Sudan; Bin Laden, who had been given permission to leave Saudi Arabia when he had asked to come to Peshawar a few weeks earlier; Benon Sevan of the United Nations; Peter Tomsen, the US State Department's representative; and many other interested individuals from Muslim countries' governments and Muslim organisations, charitable and political. I was one of the assembled. I had been invited to stay in the house of the military governor of the North-West Frontier Province.

The negotiations that took place in Peshawar were more or less a free-for-all. There were all sorts of bilateral talks. The Americans were promoting, as they had been for some time, the idea of an independent commanders' shura as a means of moving power in Afghanistan away from Islamist parties. I doubt whether their idea, had it come to fruition, would have had the results they wanted. The Saudi position was that we had, with immense difficulty, worked out a formula for an Afghan government in Rawalpindi in 1988–89. We felt that this created a structure which none of the Mujahideen parties would be able to dispute – seeing that hundreds of Afghan deputies had voted for it. Therefore, we would now be very unwise to tamper with it, unless we absolutely had to. And it was our position that won the day. It was agreed, as it had been at the beginning of 1989, that Hazrat Sibghatullah Mojaddedi would be president for a year, and that he would be succeeded for two years by Professor Burhanuddin Rabbani, who would prepare the way for elections. The ministries would be divided among the main Afghan parties, which had been roughly the outcome of the vote at the beginning of 1989. The big difference was that Hekmatyar would not be given the job of Foreign Minister.

The formula was agreed by Burhanuddin Rabbani and his military commander, Ahmad Shah Massoud, and so, as soon as conditions allowed,

President Mojaddedi got on an aircraft and went to Kabul. I had already told Nawaz Sharif that I was not going to go back to Saudi Arabia without first having a look at Kabul, having focussed my thoughts on this city for much of the previous twelve years. Also, I felt that the arrival of the representative of a friendly foreign government days after the installation of Mojaddedi would give the government a little bit of extra legitimacy, adding to public confidence in it. Sharif's immediate response was, 'I won't let you go alone – I'm coming with you'. Arrangements were made very quickly and the ISI communicated to Hekmatyar that it would like him to stop shelling the airport, at least while the Prime Minister of Pakistan and I were there.

The next day we boarded two C-130 Hercules aircraft and flew to Kabul. It was a magnificent sight in the spring as we approached. Kabul is surrounded by mountains, which were still glistening with snow at that time of year, the air was clear, the sky was blue, and green leaves had already appeared in the orchards and gardens around the city. We both landed safely. Sharif had with him many of the religious, tribal and military dignitaries who had been in Peshawar. On the tarmac to greet us was President Mojaddedi, in traditional costume, with his own entourage of Afghan dignitaries.

Nawaz Sharif and I started to walk away from our aircraft – when all of a sudden a rocket exploded about a hundred metres away. Almost the entire assembly flattened themselves on the ground, in their robes and turbans – a sight that was both amusing and frightening at the same time. The two exceptions were Sharif and me because both of us felt that as the senior representatives of two foreign governments much involved with Afghanistan we had to be more dignified. I think we also sensed that Hekmatyar was just making a point and that the first rocket would not be followed by a general bombardment. We were right. We all got into cars and went to the Grand Mosque, where we prayed at noon, and then on to the newly tenanted Presidential Palace, where we had lunch with Mojaddedi before flying back to Peshawar the same day.

This is my last comment on Hekmatyar: I have to say he was a complete disappointment. During the jihad he was highly rated by us all – the ISI, the CIA and the GID. He had one of the most effective forces, with good field commanders; he got things done. But as for scruples, he had none whatsoever. When the Taliban later defeated his forces he took refuge in Iran, which he had previously denounced as a heretical state. Ten years later he was offering himself to the Afghan government, the Americans and any other interested party as the only man able to negotiate with the Taliban.

* * *

Sadly, as soon as the new government had been installed Afghanistan slid back into chaos. Mojaddedi stayed in power for only two months and then in late June made way for Burhanuddin Rabbani. For the rest of 1992 and 1993 Hekmatyar continued to bombard Kabul, out of pure frustration and spite. He had ample supplies of rockets and he killed and wounded thousands. He tried to have Massoud assassinated, but his henchmen got the timing of their target's movements wrong and the attempt failed. Within the city minor Mujahideen leaders fought each other, periodically switching sides. Rabbani's party, allied with Sayyaf's, attacked the Shia parties. Dostum's troops raped and murdered. Electricity failed, food ran out and disease spread. There were several attempts at mediation during this sad decline. I flew to Islamabad at one point, and the former ISI chief, Lieutenant General Hamid Gul, undertook some initiatives of his own – but we achieved nothing.

Abdul Rashid Dostum fell out with the Mujahideen leaders in power in Kabul. He noticed that they took the best jobs for their own supporters, and he began to feel that, as a former Communist, he was in danger. In January 1994 he changed sides again and entered an alliance with Hekmatyar. At the same time, he and his troops retired to the flat country of the north-west. He felt more secure there. His backers in the governments of Uzbekistan and Turkmenistan viewed the new government in Kabul in much the same way as he did – as unstable, violent and a potentially dangerous fundamentalist influence. They continued to back Dostum with supplies. He resumed his previous role as a buffer between the Afghans and the ex-Soviet republics as the lord, for a time, of his own little Uzbek state.

Chapter 12
Bringing Home the Volunteers

In October 1992, seven months after the independent government in Afghanistan came to power, we sent our ambassador to Kabul. He was General Mohammad Eid Al-Otaibi, who had spent his career in the army and the GID and then retired from my department to join the Ministry of Foreign Affairs so he could take up his appointment in Kabul. He was a robust character – tough and intelligent – who had already been much involved with Afghanistan while in the GID.

Otaibi was given three tasks: to bring back the young Saudis from Afghanistan, to promote peace in the country and to help reconstruction. The last of these tasks turned out to be totally impracticable because by the time Otaibi arrived in Kabul the government was hardly functioning. There was a nominal government, headed by this stage by Burhanuddin Rabbani, but it had no authority. Power lay with the nine parties, their armies and various other forces – most of them having their own independent relations with Pakistan, and several of them linked to some other foreign backer as well. There was one Shia party that was entirely under the control of Iran's Islamic Revolutionary Guard Corps. Abdul Rashid Dostum seemed to be working very closely with the Russians. Hekmatyar's party, which was actively at war with the government, operated hand in hand with the ISI. In the centre, Rabbani and Massoud, supported by Abd Rabb Al-Rasul Sayyaf, were bravely trying to play the role of government, but around them ministers, representing different factions, would come and go, giving or withdrawing their support according to their parties' petty needs of the moment.

Otaibi concluded that for the Saudi government to give budgetary help or project aid for reconstruction was out of the question because there was no central government worth providing with such support. He reported back to the Foreign Ministry that before the Kingdom considered giving aid there had to be a legitimate government under the control of one person, one party or a stable combination of parties.

Meanwhile, he set himself the job of bringing as much as possible of the private and charitable Saudi money that was going to Afghanistan under the control of his embassy. The flow of these funds had been much reduced since the fall of the Najibullah government early in 1992 because by then most of the donors could clearly see that their money was going largely to finance a civil war – the word in Arabic is *fitna*. But there were still some donors dealing with the different parties, either backing them directly – this applied mainly to Hekmatyar – or giving them money which was supposed to be used in the refugee camps but was ending up financing their militias. The continuing flow of money was leading to accusations of Saudi favouritism.

Massoud, who Otaibi liked and respected as the most sincere and patriotic of the Afghans, complained about Saudi support for Hekmatyar. He also accused the Saudi government of not having given him sufficient backing in the past. Otaibi's answer to the second charge was that we and the Americans had left the allocation of funds between the parties to the ISI – a policy which we were both now coming to think had been a mistake.

At first Otaibi sent messages back to Riyadh requesting that the charities be asked to stop their donations, but later he decided he had to talk to the charities himself. He returned to Riyadh and one evening invited to his home forty or fifty of the people, mainly ulema, who were most active in collecting money. He told them bluntly that what they were now supporting was *fitna*, not jihad, and that they should stop encouraging donations of any sort. If they did still find themselves with money to give, he said, it should go through the Islamic International Relief Organisation and the Muslim World League, which would hand it to his embassy. This speech brought the flow of charitable funds virtually to a halt – at least Otaibi found that the charities' payments to the parties seemed to stop, and no money came to his embassy. What did continue was some clandestine support from private donors for Hekmatyar.

While working on the cut-off of funding for the parties in early 1993 Otaibi had his embassy staff and the GID calculate how much money each of the parties had available. They did this by making enquiries with various sources in and around the parties themselves and by comparing notes with the ISI. The results, from Otaibi's notes on six of the major parties: Hekmatyar had $200 million, Gailani $200 million, Sayyaf $185 million, Mojaddedi $130 million, Rabbani and Massoud $17 million and Mohammadi $14 million – the last's money being 'cash under the bed', whereas the funds of the others were mostly held in bank accounts in Dubai. It was surprising, at first sight, that Rabbani and Massoud had such a small balance, in spite of having leased the emerald mines in the far north-east of the Panjshir Valley to French and German prospectors. The reason was simply that they maintained what was virtually a standing army, in parallel with the army of the Afghan government, and this cost them a great deal of money.

Otaibi's primary task, which was to bring home the Saudi Mujahideen, went ahead in parallel with his efforts to cut the flow of funds. It was the fighters – the Mujahideen – who worried us much more than the radicalised aid workers. Our overall view of the aid workers was that they were doing a good job, particularly if they were working for an international organisation or a major Saudi charity such as the Islamic International Relief Organisation or the Saudi Red Crescent. Anyway, most of these people were in the refugee camps on the Pakistani side of the frontier, which was officially outside Otaibi's territory. As for those who were in Afghanistan or were working for political parties in the frontier camps, our hope was that our efforts to cut political donations from Saudi Arabia would have the effect of making them redundant. They would be told by their backers in Saudi Arabia that there was no more work for them – or they would return home of their own accord.

In extracting the fighters, the first job was to calculate the numbers involved, and at the same time compile a list of names. All sorts of figures have been put forward for the numbers of Saudi Mujahideen – and it is difficult to know whether to include those people who went out for very short periods to 'get their feet dusty'. Likewise, it is difficult to draw a distinction between fighters and supporters – the latter being people who were closely involved with the parties and were certainly not aid workers, but may not have been in the front lines. Otaibi eventually decided that a maximum figure for the numbers of Saudi Mujahideen in Afghanistan at the time he took up his post was about 500. The calculation was done partly through the process of compiling a list of names, based on the list the GID had begun to compile in 1989. Otaibi's staff tried to work out which of those people who had gone to the frontier had joined Mujahideen groups and which had later returned to Saudi Arabia. Once he had a rough list of those who had not returned, he tried to find out who was alive and who was dead.

In the process of making these lists it became clear (predictably) that most of the Saudi fighters were with the militias of Sayyaf and Hekmatyar. When Otaibi approached him, Sayyaf was quite co-operative. He said he appreciated the Saudi government's concern and that therefore the Saudis in his forces should either return to Saudi Arabia or stay and take Afghan nationality. Hekmatyar was not helpful at all. He had with him about 200 Saudis – many of whom he had given military rank. He had taken their passports, and when he heard about Otaibi's initiative he told them that if they returned to Saudi Arabia they would be put in prison. The Saudis were useful to him. Some were good agents for collecting money secretly from private donors. Others he had allowed to become drug addicts, knowing that under the influence of narcotics they would be ready to carry out suicidal missions on his behalf.

Otaibi had been given a diplomatic staff of fifty-six – two from the Ministry of Foreign Affairs and the rest from the GID. The GID people were drawn intentionally from all over Saudi Arabia – from all the major towns and regions – and each of them was assigned to trace and contact those Saudis on the 'still-alive list' who were from his own town or region or tribe. Along with the names of his targets, or prospects, each man was given his own budget, a car and an Afghan assistant. They drove all over Afghanistan – and into the camps on the border. It was obviously dangerous work, but nobody was kidnapped or killed. Once a member of the GID team had got in touch with one of his prospects and established that he was willing to return to Saudi Arabia, the young man had to prove his identity. We gave him a fairly long questionnaire which he had to fill in, and we would then check it for plausible answers and compare it with what solid information we already had on him.

In all, during Otaibi's period in the embassy in Kabul (from October 1992 to September 1996) some 200 young Saudi Mujahideen returned to Saudi Arabia – 150 of their own accord and 50 through the efforts of the embassy. Twenty of these were from Hekmatyar's militia, which was by far the most difficult 'target' given that its boss did everything he could to prevent any contact between the embassy and his Saudis. Of these twenty, sixteen were drug addicts and had to be detoxified when they came back to the Kingdom. Most were frightened of returning, either because of their addiction or because they held radical political views. In fact, when the fighters returned to Saudi Arabia they were not imprisoned or charged with any crime. Some, though, were put under observation to make sure – or to try to make sure – that they did not get into trouble or get others into trouble. Those civilian camp workers who were known to be radicalised were brought into the Ministry of the Interior for questioning and then advised to go back to their families.

Otaibi describes the young men with whom he dealt as 'half educated – failures – lost souls'. They had gone to Afghanistan to look for a cause, a purpose in life. He remembers an encounter in a hospital in Kabul with a wounded young Saudi who had been given the rank of brigadier by Hekmatyar. The youth was very afraid of coming back to the Kingdom. He looked at Mohammad with wild eyes and said simply, 'I know why you are here. You're an agent.'

At the beginning of Otaibi's posting the embassy 'worked on' Khaled Al-Subei, another young Mujahid. He was persuaded through one of his relatives in the GID to return to Saudi Arabia, but a few months later Otaibi learnt that he had gone back to Afghanistan and had then moved north to fight in the later stages of the vicious civil war in the independent republic of Tajikistan. In 1993 he moved to Chechnya, where he married a local girl. Later he and his wife returned to Saudi Arabia – and he was accepted back by the authorities, with the usual warnings. But he could find no useful or fulfilling work and he joined an Al-Qaeda cell in the Kingdom. In 2005 he was killed in a shootout with the police in Riyadh.

* * *

The first major initiative for peace in Afghanistan during Otaibi's tenure in Kabul came from the Pakistani government of Prime Minister Nawaz Sharif in early 1993, in the month of Ramadan, which that year fell in February and March. My involvement began with Sharif telephoning King Fahd, telling him that he was attempting a new reconciliation among the Mujahideen, and asking him if he would agree that I should help in the negotiations. The King then promptly called me and told me to go to Islamabad.

The Pakistani Prime Minister had done an excellent job in assembling the Mujahideen leaders. The heads of six of the seven parties who had fought the Soviets were there, along with personalities from the government in Kabul. The only major figures not present were Maulvi Yunus Khalis and Ahmad Shah Massoud – but Massoud's interests were well represented by Burhanuddin Rabbani, who was both head of his political party and head of the government. There were also representatives of two Shia parties, one based in Pakistan and the other, the Hizb-i-Wahdat, closely linked to Iran. This second group, led by Ayatollah Fazl, had existed in Iran throughout the period of the jihad but it had not joined in the fight against the Soviets in any way. As soon as Kabul fell the Iranians threw the group into the Afghan cockpit – and to their credit both Mojaddedi and his successor, Rabbani, accepted the group as having a legitimate interest in the country and gave its members posts in their governments.

The peace negotiations among all these factions were just as slow, fruitless and exasperating as I knew in my heart – and against all my hopes – they would be. We talked for nearly ten hours a day, but the Mujahideen refused to agree on anything. After a few days of this Sharif started to despair. He came to the conclusion that there was no more he could do and turned to the assembly and said: 'Gentlemen, I've done everything I can to bring you together – and I have no more to say, nothing more to give. Let's finish this, and you can go home and do whatever you want.'

The stalemate was predictable but very depressing. I could not help feeling that it would be such a pity if after so much effort the conference was going to end in nothing. This thought made me remember a verse in the Holy Quran in which God says he is merciful to Muslims because he resolves fights between them and turns them from enemies into friends. I could not remember the exact words, but I turned to Ahmad Badeeb, my secretary, who was sitting next to me, and asked him to look it up. I knew he always carried a small pocket edition of the Quran with him. After a minute or so, while the delegates were talking and accusing each other, he whispered enough in my ear to remind me of the wording. It was verse 103 from the Surah Al-Imran. I interrupted the argument and said: 'Brothers, think of what God says to us in the Holy Quran':

And hold fast,
All together, by the Rope
Which God (stretches out
For you), and be not divided
Among yourselves;
And remember with gratitude
God's favour on you;
For ye were enemies
And He joined your hearts
In love, so that by His Grace,
Ye became brethren;
And ye were on the brink of the Pit of Fire,

And He saved you from it.
Thus doth God make
His Signs clear to you:
That ye may be guided.

Then I said: 'You should be ashamed of yourselves. You call yourselves
Muslims and you have fought jihad in the name of Islam, but you cannot
bring yourselves to stop fighting each other. And you should be ashamed
of yourselves in front of Nawaz Sharif who has spent so much time to bring
you together – but to no avail. Nothing has been achieved. God will not
forgive you for that.'

It worked like magic. The Mujahideen leaders turned to each other
and said, quite simply, 'We agree'. So, Nawaz had his staff bring out the
draft agreement he had prepared to reflect what seemed to be a possible
compromise, and had it read to them. 'Yes, we agree,' said all the delegates
one after the other.

The agreement contained five main provisions:

- There was to be a permanent ceasefire, to be monitored by the Organisation
of the Islamic Conference.
- Burhanuddin Rabbani was to remain President until mid-1994.
- Gulbuddin Hekmatyar's party would have the right to appoint a Prime
Minister, who would choose his own cabinet.
- A sixteen-member Defence Committee, with two people from each of
eight parties, would raise a national army and supervise the removal of all
heavy weapons from Kabul.
- An Election Commission would be established to supervise elections to
a Constituent Assembly in November 1993, approve a new Constitution
and hold a general election by mid-1994.

It was decided straight away that there should be a signing ceremony
at the Prime Minister's official residence in Islamabad. The next day,
7 March 1993, all was prepared. A table was set out on the veranda in

front of the house. Everybody who was party to the agreement attended and everybody signed. Nawaz Sharif then said to me that it would be a good idea if we could arrange for the leaders go to Makkah and sign again in front of the Kaaba – and I too felt that this would be a good idea. It was not just that this seemed to be the culminating moment of some thirteen years of effort; I wanted Saudi Arabia to be seen getting some credit for all the work we had put in. So, I telephoned King Fahd and told him that Nawaz Sharif wanted to bring all the Mujahideen leaders to Makkah.

The King was sceptical. 'Look how many times we have brought these people together, and then seen them break their word,' he said. I persevered. 'Oh, Long of Life,' I said, this being the normal Saudi greeting to a prince or to a person senior to oneself, 'with due respect, what you say is true, but it is also your duty as Custodian of the Two Holy Mosques not only to support this agreement but to allow the participants to sign in front of the Kaaba.' The King agreed, which pleased me very much, and he also said he would send some aircraft to fly everybody to Makkah.

I left Islamabad the next day to organise everything that needed to be done in Makkah. Two or three days later all the delegations arrived. They were accommodated in the best hotels and they signed their treaty in the guest palace overlooking the Grand Mosque. They were in a room which has a huge window looking directly down onto the Kaaba. After everybody had signed we arranged for the delegates to fly to Tehran, because the Iranians had said they would like to have a signing ceremony in their capital too – so that they could also get some credit – and we thought it diplomatic to agree to this. So all the delegates flew to Tehran and held a signing there. The agreement was as solid as anything on paper could be.

Yet on the very next day – when the commanders on the ground knew perfectly well that a general peace had been agreed – the fighting started again. The initial outbreak was between the Hizb-i-Wahdat and government forces, but the battle soon spread. The political terms of the agreement likewise fell apart. Hekmatyar became Prime Minister and remained in that post, in a nominal sense, until January 1994. But he immediately and predictably fell out with the President over the role of Massoud, who had been Minister of Defence. Hekmatyar refused to reappoint him; Rabbani insisted Massoud should remain in his post. There was a stalemate. The Rabbani–Hekmatyar combination was as ineffective and chaotic as every other Afghan government of the early 1990s had been.

I thought then, as I often did on Afghanistan, about why it was so impossible to stop the fighting in that country. And I came to the same conclusion as I always did. The problem was a combination of the lack of a single dominating personality, as well as naked personal ambition, distrust and fear, and the tribal or ethnic group mentality. The last is the belief of simple, uneducated people that their own group, tribe or village is good, honourable, trustworthy and friendly, but that people from another region, even a nearby town or village, who they really do not know at all, are bad, or cruel, or thieves or murderers, or in some other way threatening. This is a form of thinking which my grandfather, King Abdulaziz, and his sons have tried to stamp out in Saudi Arabia, and I hope they have succeeded. Elsewhere, we have seen its consequences in recent years not only in Afghanistan, but in Tajikistan, the Caucasus, Central Africa, Indonesia, the former Yugoslavia, Libya, Iraq and Yemen. The tribal mentality is something which seems to re-emerge in a society whenever its people are frightened and maltreated, and when they have seen the destruction of institutions, conventions and habits of behaviour which they have traditionally respected and which have made them feel secure.

After the failure of the 1993 peace initiative, we despaired of trying to get the Afghan factions to work together. We had already done much to discourage Saudi private donors from giving money to the different parties – albeit with only partial success – and now the government decided to order the closure of all the parties' offices in the Kingdom. The following is the order that King Fahd issued in early December 1993:

In the name of God, the Compassionate, the Merciful
Kingdom of Saudi Arabia
Court of the Prime Minister

No. 9524

Date: 2/12/1993   Secret

His Royal Highness the Minister of Interior
Cc His Royal Highness the Governor of Riyadh Province,
    President of the Afghan Affairs Committee
Cc His Royal Highness the Minister of Foreign Affairs
Cc His Royal Highness the President of General Intelligence

We refer to decree no. 12589 dated 2/11/1993 approving the envoy of Afghan President Burhanuddin Rabbani's request to raise his country's flag on the Afghan Embassy in Riyadh and officially open it. We refer to cables from HRH the Minister of Interior concerning the Governor of Riyadh's recommendation to close the Afghan leadership offices in the Kingdom. We also refer to Your Highnesses' support for HRH's recommendation as well as Your Highnesses' reference to HRH's meeting with the Afghan Chargé d'Affaires (who requested the closure of these offices and the consolidation of all activities under the embassy's supervision) and the regional governorates' occasional comments on the issue. We refer to the Governor of Riyadh's cable to the President of the Afghan Affairs Committee confirming the receipt of written acknowledgment by the Afghan offices' personnel pledging not to gather donations but stating that some personnel have not obliged. HRH has requested approval to close the offices. We refer to two cables from HRH the Minister of Foreign Affairs concerning the request that the Afghan Embassy in Riyadh coordinate with the relevant authorities in the Kingdom to bar individuals from gathering donations under the pretext of funding schools or orphanages in Afghanistan because this harms the Afghan government's and people's reputations – and it is the Afghan state that is responsible for taking care of its people's affairs. ...

We inform you of our approval of the Afghan Chargé d'Affaires' request to close all Afghan leadership offices in the Kingdom. We have no opposition to HRH the Governor of Riyadh Province summoning the office personnel and informing them that: the Jihad has ended in victory; they are now represented by their embassy; their offices are no longer needed; those who wish to remain in the Kingdom must find work, a sponsor, and cease gathering donations; those who wish to leave are to be sent to their home countries; offices will be closed permanently and returned to their owners regardless of whether they are offices or apartments.

Carry out what needs to be done.

Fahd bin Abdulaziz, Prime Minister of the Council of Ministers

Following this decree the Afghan parties' representatives were summoned to the offices of the Governor of Riyadh and required to sign a declaration as follows:

In the Name of God, the Compassionate, the Merciful
Kingdom of Saudi Arabia
Ministry of Interior
Governorate of Riyadh Province

No –
Date: 15/12/1993
Attachments: -

Declaration

We, the representatives of the Afghan Mujahideen of all parties that have had an active role in gathering donations for the Jihad, immigrants and orphans, agree to end completely all activities, permanently close all offices so that nothing remains, cease gathering any donations and remain in the Kingdom only on an individual residence basis; and we all require formal residency in the country. We hereby sign and swear:

1. Sayyid Ahmad Ridkul, Representative of the Islamic Union [Sayyaf], currently a student at the Higher Judicial Institute at Al-Imam University. We closed the office previously on 27/9/1993.

2. Sayyid Abdullah Abdul-Ahad, Representative of Hizb-i-Islami [Hekmatyar], on behalf of him (signed) Sayyid Habib Allah Khoja, currently a student at the Higher Judicial Institute at Imam Mohammad Ibn Saud Islamic University.

3. Abdul-Ahad Mullah Rejab, Jamaat-i-Islami [Rabbani], currently a student at the Shari'a College at Al-Imam University. We closed the office previously on 19/4/1993.

4. Waliullah Abdul-Hakim Sadat, Representative of Jamaat al-Dawa ila al-Quran wa al-Sunna, currently a student at the Language Institute at Imam Mohammad Ibn Saud Islamic University.

5. Twaqi Mourjan, Representative of Sheikh Jalaluddin Haqqani, currently working for Mulahi Homoud al-Otaibi.

Chapter 13
The Rise of the Taliban

After the collapse of the peace accord sponsored by Nawaz Sharif, conditions in Afghanistan got worse and worse. The country was more violent, chaotic and lawless than it had been during the war against the Soviet occupation and Najibullah – and now it was much more impoverished. Fighting between the government and Hekmatyar in 1993 and early 1994 killed about 10,000 civilians – two-thirds the number of casualties in nine years of Soviet occupation. In January 1994 Hekmatyar and Dostum attacked Kabul and reduced parts of the city to rubble. The country was divided among warlords – one or two major figures, but mostly petty characters – minor Mujahideen commanders and bandits.

These people were most active in the south, around Kandahar. They plundered homes, businesses and government property at will. They looted people's houses; they cut down trees in the towns to sell as firewood and they stripped the wires from telegraph poles and then sold the poles as firewood; they stole cars, trucks and factory machinery, mostly to sell to scrap merchants in Pakistan. Owners were thrown out of their houses and farms, which were given to the warlords' supporters. Young girls and boys were kidnapped and raped.

It was in response to this that a new militant group emerged in the region around Kandahar in the early months of 1994. The outside world knew nothing about it at the time. Its founders were idealistic men, many of them clerics, who had fought in the war against the Communists and were now frustrated and angry with what they saw happening in the country they thought they had liberated. After the spring of 1992, when Najibullah's government had fallen, they had returned to their homes or the madrasas in the towns of Kandahar province or in Quetta, which was just across the border in Pakistan. Several small groups began to discuss what could be done. In due course they made contact with each other – which was not just a matter of chance, because many of the people involved had fought side by side and knew each other already. They came to the conclusion that the answer to their country's problems lay in the literal enforcement of Islamic law, coupled with disarming the population. As most of the members of these informal groups were living in madrasas – schools in which they were studying and teaching Islam – they decided to call themselves Taliban, the plural form of *talib*, or student. The name had a good, clean, idealistic ring.

They quickly gathered around themselves young followers from the directionless and impoverished society of the frontier – 'children of the jihad', as they were sometimes known, born in the refugee camps and educated in the madrasas. They knew hardly anything of their own country, its history, geography, society or traditions. What they had learnt about – or half-learnt – in the madrasas was the pure, ideal Muslim society that had existed in the time of the Prophet Mohammad, and very briefly after him, in the seventh century.[1] They all adhered to the Hanafi school of Sunni Islam, referred to in a previous chapter.

The men who were to become the best-known Taliban leaders – Mullah Mohammad Omar, Mohammad Ghaus, Mohammad Rabbani (no relation to Burhanuddin Rabbani), Mohammad Abbas and Mohammad Hassan – had all been associated during the war with Maulvi Yunus Khalis's party. Interestingly, however, most of the second-rank figures, a more numerous group, came from the moderate parties, particularly the Harakat-i Inqilab-i-Islami of Maulvi Nabi Mohammadi. They were all devout Muslims, but their political background was the tribal society of southern Afghanistan rather than any established Islamist movement.

They were very much Pathans; their movement never had significant support among Tajiks or Uzbeks.

There is a famous story of how the Taliban became a military organisation and began its rise to power. In the way of such stories, it has no doubt been embellished over the years, and none of the participants has ever given an account of the event, but it has come to be widely believed and it is worth recounting. It tells how one day in the spring of 1994 some people from a village near Kandahar came to tell Mullah Omar that a local commander had abducted two teenage girls. It was reported that their heads had been shaved and they had been repeatedly raped. Omar was moved to action by this appalling story. He enlisted thirty of the students with sixteen rifles among them (an unusually low number of weapons to the man by Afghan standards) who attacked the commander's base and freed the girls. Then he hanged the commander from the gun barrel of a tank. His people seized a large quantity of arms and ammunition.

A few months later in Kandahar there was a confrontation between two commanders who were arguing over a young boy they wanted to sodomise. The confrontation, unsavoury from the beginning, degenerated into a small battle between the commanders' militias, and civilians were killed. Again, the Taliban intervened and the boy was released. Soon appeals started coming in for the Taliban to help in similar disputes. They were always successful and Mullah Omar's prestige grew because he never demanded any material reward. He asked simply that those he had helped should set up a true Islamic government in their community.

As these events were taking place the Pakistani government was reconsidering its Afghanistan policy. Its fundamental aim was to have a friendly government in the country to give Pakistan 'strategic depth' (as its generals put it) in its long confrontation with India, and to act as a buffer between itself and whatever governments might eventually emerge in Central Asia. In effect it wanted a friendly Afghanistan so that Pakistan would never find itself surrounded by hostile powers. It also very much wanted to open up a trade route to the new Central Asian republics, all of which were landlocked and could most easily get access to the Indian Ocean through Afghanistan and Pakistan. It saw itself not so much exporting its own manufactured goods as acting as an entrepôt and carrier. It envisaged its truckers, a very vigorous part of its economy, taking consumer goods northwards and bringing back agricultural produce, particularly cotton. There were also plans for oil and gas pipelines.

To achieve these aims the Pakistani government's policy since the later stages of the Soviet occupation had been to back Gulbuddin Hekmatyar, the most powerful of the Pathan party leaders. A Pathan-led government would have a natural appeal to Pakistan because it was itself a partly Pathan country, and Pathans made up a disproportionately large part of its armed forces. Hekmatyar, however, had lost credibility. He had proved himself untrustworthy, his extremism had divided the Pathan people – most of whom hated him – and he seemed to be losing ground militarily. Some Pakistani generals were continuing to back him, but the civilians in government and much of the military were beginning to consider other possibilities. They were thinking that perhaps they should give more backing to the government that already existed in Kabul, which was supposed to combine all of Afghanistan's ethnic communities and all its major political parties.

Quite separately from this debate, approaches had been made to some of the Kandahar commanders and Ismail Khan, the leader of the city of Herat, about trucks being allowed to pass through the western part of Afghanistan to Turkmenistan. It was thought that this might be less dangerous than the Grand Trunk Road and the Salang Pass route going from Peshawar through Jalalabad and Kabul. Initial contacts had seemed encouraging and Naseerullah Babar, the Pakistani Minister of the Interior, was organising a visit to Kandahar and Herat when suddenly the Taliban entered the picture.

They had been approached by what is generally known in Pakistan as the 'trucking mafia', the members of the big truck-owning syndicates. These people were already sending goods from Quetta into southern and western Afghanistan and they were tired of the extortion by Hekmatyar's men who controlled the frontier area. The practice of the frontier militia, apart from asking for bribes and stealing goods, was to insist that once the Pakistani trucks had crossed the border their goods should be unloaded and packed onto Afghan trucks. Then they demanded payment from the Pakistani shippers, part of which would end up in their pockets. The Pakistani truck syndicates therefore donated some money to the Taliban and promised them a monthly stipend if it would undertake to clear the roads. The Taliban responded on 12 October 1994: some 200 from Kandahar and the Pakistani madrasas took the small Afghan border post of Spin Buldak on the Quetta–Kandahar road. In the battle the Taliban lost one, killed seven and acquired another large supply of weapons.

It was within days of this event that Babar made his visit to Kandahar and Herat, but his negotiations made little progress. The Kandahar militia commanders were suspicious of his offer to repair the roads because they thought it might be a prelude to Pakistani military intervention. The Pakistani authorities nevertheless decided to try to push through a convoy from Quetta to Ashgabat, the capital of Turkmenistan, to see what happened. It consisted of thirty trucks, all with ex-military drivers.

The Kandahar commanders suspected the trucks were carrying arms and duly blocked the convoy, directing it to park in a village near the main road and demanding money and a share of the goods on board. The Pakistani government imposed a news blackout on what had happened and thought about various ways of rescuing the convoy, but eventually decided that the best answer might be to ask the Taliban for help. And this is what it did.

Once again Mullah Omar assembled a force and on 3 November 1994 attacked the people who had seized the convoy. The militia, possibly believing the attack was by the Pakistani army, fled. One of its commanders, Mansur Achakzai, was chased into the desert and shot, along with ten of his guards. His body was then hung from the gun barrel of a tank for all to see. That same evening the Taliban force moved on to Kandahar, where after two days of sporadic fighting they routed the militia forces that had previously controlled the city. They took tanks, other military vehicles and some MiG-21s and transport helicopters – Soviet equipment which had been given to Najibullah's forces. The Taliban now controlled an important Afghan town, and from then on it became a powerful force.

During the last weeks of 1994 the Taliban easily took control of the rest of southern Afghanistan, and in January 1995 their forces advanced north towards Herat, and north-east against Kabul. Here they were up against more experienced and better-organised troops than the militias they had defeated so easily around Kandahar, but at first they continued to do well. On 11 February they took the town of Mohammad Agha, forty kilometres south of Kabul, and trapped part of Hekmatyar's army. Three days later they occupied his headquarters, and the remains of his forces in the region fled east towards Jalalabad. The Taliban also pushed back the government forces under Ahmad Shah Massoud, who withdrew into Kabul.

There then occurred an extraordinary incident which was to influence Afghan politics for the rest of the Taliban period. Massoud turned his troops against the Hazara militia – Shias of Mongol origin – which had been in an unholy alliance with Hekmatyar and had been occupying Kabul's southern suburbs. He drove them out and in desperation they turned to the Taliban – even more unlikely allies than Hekmatyar, because the Taliban were Sunnis of the most austere, purist Deobandi persuasion. The Hazaras gave what positions they still held and their heavy weapons to the Taliban, but in the confusion of the handover their leader, Abdel-Ali Mazari, was killed. The Hazaras later claimed that he was being taken to Kandahar as a prisoner, and that when he tried to seize a rifle in an attempt to escape he was overpowered and then taken up in a helicopter and pushed out. His death damned the Taliban from then on in the eyes of the Afghan Shias and the Iranians – until the Americans invaded Afghanistan in 2001 and Iran and the Taliban found a common enemy.

It was against this background that I felt Saudi Arabia had to launch yet another attempt to make peace. There was nothing that made me think a new initiative might have a better chance than previous attempts; it was just that the situation in Afghanistan was so awful that I thought we had to do something. I spoke to King Fahd and we agreed that I should draw up a set of proposals and then try to muster the support of all interested foreign parties – Pakistan, Iran, Russia and the United States.

I worked on the peace plan with the help of Mohammad Eid Al-Otaibi. It had three main elements. First: all outside powers should impose a total arms embargo on all Afghan parties, and each country, together with the United Nations and the Organisation of the Islamic Conference, should station monitors on the borders. Second: all military forces in Afghanistan should be disbanded and their members invited to join a new army of national unity – and the outside powers should buy from the parties all weapons not needed by the army. The powers would also provide training for the new army. Third: an interim government should be established, including all the parties, but excluding all the party leaders. Then there would be elections for an Assembly which would produce a Constitution.

The crucial element was the second one – disarmament. We realised that it would be impossible to separate most of the individual Mujahideen from their personal small arms, but the idea of paying the party leaders for all of their more sophisticated weapons seemed a good one. It would involve Saudi Arabia and the United States paying for some of the arms for the second time, but for us this was a low price for peace, and I was sure the money would appeal to the Afghans.

I took the plan first to Islamabad, where I got the solid support of the government of Benazir Bhutto, in power for the second time, and met most of the Mujahideen leaders, including a representative of Gulbuddin Hekmatyar. It was here, too, that I met for the first time a member of the Taliban. He was Mohammad Rabbani, who was introduced to me by General Naseerullah Babar, the Pakistani Minister of the Interior. I knew that the ISI was not sure about the potential of the Taliban and, surprisingly, still had some faith in Hekmatyar, but the government, and Babar in particular, had clearly been won over. Babar suggested I should present my peace plan to the Taliban because he said they had recently gained much political weight and it would be a good idea for me to 'get them on board'. I remember his words of reassurance. 'These are my boys,' he said. 'They are good, they are sincere and they are the solution.'

From Islamabad I went to Kabul, where I met Burhanuddin Rabbani, Ahmad Shah Massoud and Abd Rabb Al-Rasul Sayyaf. Like everybody else I had spoken to so far, they agreed to my plan. I then returned to Riyadh and explained my plan to the CIA and the State Department – both of which gave their support – and received an Iranian delegation headed by Mr Tabatabai, the person responsible for the Afghan file in the Foreign Ministry in Tehran. It was now that I encountered a problem. My own strong view was that the arms embargo had to be the first step in the process; an effective halt to the flow of weapons would put pressure on the parties and make them more likely to be receptive to the rest of the plan. The Iranians, however, maintained that the first step should be the formation of a national government. It was difficult to see the logic of this. Presumably, they felt that at that moment in the internal wars of Afghanistan an arms embargo would be to the disadvantage of the Shia parties. We argued for a time and in the end agreed to disagree.

As a last step I travelled to Moscow to meet Yevgeny Primakov, who was then chief of the intelligence organisation that had taken over from the KGB. The Russians by this time had established quite good relations with the Burhanuddin Rabbani government. The main reason for the turnaround was the completely different type of government in power in Moscow. The Russians were able to argue that they had had a long and quite friendly relationship with Afghanistan going back to the nineteenth century, and that the invasion under the previous government had been an aberration and a mistake.

They also had an immediate and practical concern with the possible export of Islamic radicalism to the independent republics of Central Asia and to their own remaining Muslim territories, notably Chechnya. One way or another they were back in the Afghan political game – far more quickly than the Americans had re-engaged with Vietnam – and I hoped this would make them receptive to my plan. I thought they should have an interest in a stable, peaceful Afghanistan. They probably did, but perhaps they thought it was not likely to come about in the near future and that for the time being they would do better to stick to their existing policy.

Primakov said he thought the Saudi plan was a good idea but doubted that the flow of weapons could be stopped. In other words, he did not want to stop supporting the private buffer state of the solidly secular Rashid Dostum on the southern borders of Turkmenistan and Uzbekistan. Maybe he also felt that while the Afghans were fighting among themselves they would not have the time to turn their attention to backing Islamist movements among their brethren to the north. In any event the scepticism of the Russians, combined with the lack of support from the Iranians, doomed my peace plan. It meant that to the north and west there was no hope of sealing the Afghan border against the traffic of arms – and if those two borders could not be sealed nobody would be willing to close the others. And without an arms embargo, I had always maintained, there would be no point in pursuing the other elements of my plan.

* * *

For the next eighteen months the fighting in Afghanistan was as bad as, or worse than, ever. On 11 March 1995 Ahmad Shah Massoud, having regrouped his forces, launched a counterattack on the Taliban and pushed them out of Kabul, leaving hundreds of them dead. It was the Taliban's first major battle and their first defeat. Massoud was also concerned about the progress they had been making in the west, in the region south of Herat, so he sent 2,000 of his troops to the air base at Shindand, south of Herat, and had the air force bomb Taliban positions. The Taliban took further heavy casualties. Their image of invincibility was badly damaged. For several months their attacks came to a halt.

Then in August the Herati leader, Ismail Khan, believing the Taliban to be still disorganised, launched an ill-prepared offensive against them. His forces were ambushed and they retreated, inexplicably abandoning Shindand on 3 September. The Taliban troops were not heavily armed, but they were extremely mobile – their means of transport was the Japanese pick-up truck – and as the Herati forces retreated they were attacked from three sides. They panicked and fled. Khan abandoned Herat and drove to Iran, with his commanders and several hundred men. The Taliban took their second Afghan city – an ancient, beautiful and cultured place – which they proceeded to treat as occupied territory. They imposed a government and garrison of Pathans and closed all the schools. The government in Kabul blamed Pakistan for the disaster, claiming it had re-equipped the Taliban forces after their defeats in March and reorganised their command structure. A Kabuli mob attacked and sacked the Pakistani Embassy.

In the summer of the next year, 1996, the Taliban moved once more against Kabul. They managed to pay off several of the commanders in the east, including the head of the Jalalabad Shura. This enabled them to conduct a lightning campaign. They took Jalalabad on 10 September, seized control of the eastern provinces during the next few days and on 24 September captured Sarobi, forty-eight kilometres east of the capital. Then, without waiting to regroup, they swept into Kabul from the east and south two days later. They employed the same sorts of tactics – speed and an attack from more than one side – which had brought them the victory at Herat. The government troops in front of them ran back to the city and Massoud, not wanting to fight in the urban area, pulled his armour and artillery back to the north. Part of his forces, under his direct command, moved into the Panjshir Valley; another column under Burhanuddin Rabbani went to Taloqan.

As soon as their forces entered Kabul a small Taliban unit went to the United Nations compound, which had been left unguarded, murdered and mutilated Dr Mohammad Najibullah and his brother, dragged their bodies behind a pick-up truck round the walls of the Presidential Palace and then hanged them from a traffic signal.

In the next few days, the Taliban established a six-man shura to govern the city. Its members were Pathans – none of them had ever lived in the city and most had never visited it. They imposed an exceptionally severe and obscurantist regime. Women were banned from working, even though a quarter of the civil service, the entire elementary educational system and much of the health service were run by women. Girls' schools and colleges were closed. TV, videos, satellite dishes, music and all games, including chess, football and kite-flying, were banned.

For seven more months the fighting between the Taliban and their enemies continued. Massoud concluded an alliance with Abdul Rashid Dostum and the leader of the Hazaras, forming the Supreme Council for the Defence of the Motherland. His forces advanced back to Kabul, recapturing the Bagram air base. The Taliban were forced to enlist students en masse from the madrasas on the Afghan-Pakistani frontier. They pushed Massoud's forces back to the Panjshir and the north-east and advanced from Herat into the provinces of the north-west. Here they defeated a force sent from Iran by Ismail Khan.

In May 1997 the Taliban began what seemed to be a final campaign, directed against Mazar-i-Sharif in the north. This is the capital of a region of flat plains, part of the Central Asian steppe, which has most of Afghanistan's agriculture and almost all its industry, minerals and gas. Previously Dostum's forces had defended this area, but in May Dostum was deserted by Malik Pahlawan, his second-in-command, and by three other generals who believed that Dostum had murdered the brother of one of them. It may also have been that some Taliban bribes helped the desertions. Pahlawan understood that he would be entering a power-sharing agreement with the Taliban. Dostum promptly fled to Uzbekistan. Mazar-i-Sharif fell without a fight.

At this point the government of Pakistan decided to recognise the Taliban, rather than Burhanuddin Rabbani's administration, as the government of Afghanistan. Its reasoning was based on the conventional criteria employed by states giving recognition to new governments: the Taliban had become de facto the government of the country; they controlled the capital and almost all the rest of Afghanistan, except for the Panjshir Valley; and they were providing peace and security in the regions under their control. Given the awful suffering imposed on the Afghan people during the previous eighteen years, the imposition of peace and stability, under almost any conditions, seemed like a blessing.

The Saudi government was consulting regularly with Islamabad on Afghanistan, and the Pakistani government, now headed again by Nawaz Sharif, urged us to follow its lead. We quickly decided to do this, because our thinking was much the same as the Pakistanis'. It seemed to us that since the Taliban were in control of their country we would have to engage with them and this would be easier if we had diplomatic relations. We might even be able to influence them. The United Arab Emirates government felt the same way and likewise recognised the Taliban. In practical terms recognition meant only that we kept our embassy open when other countries were closing theirs. Mohammad Eid Al-Otaibi had left Kabul, after four years in the post, in September 1996, to take up a new post in Algiers – and we did not replace him. At the time it seemed best to keep our relations at the Chargé d'Affaires level – and this is how they remained.

In fact, recognition of the Taliban government was premature, because within days the new regime suffered a sharp and unexpected reverse. It handled Mazar-i-Sharif with extraordinary insensitivity and incompetence. It gave no posts to Malik Pahlawan and his colleagues, either in the city administration or in the central government, such as it was, in Kabul; and as usual it was utterly inflexible in the policies it imposed on the city. Women were driven off the streets, schools and the university were closed, mosques were taken over by Taliban imams and the Taliban troops began arrogantly to disarm the Uzbek and Hazara militias.

On 25 May a fight broke out when some Hazaras resisted being disarmed. The violence spread to the rest of the Hazara community and then the whole city rose against the occupiers. The Taliban troops, who did not know their way around the streets and alleyways, were cornered and crushed. Hundreds were killed and thousands captured. Many of the prisoners – Taliban and Pakistani students from the madrasas – were shot and then buried in mass graves. Some were locked in containers and left in the desert – to die of heat and suffocation. Pahlawan's troops retook the area around Mazar-i-Sharif, Ahmad Shah Massoud advanced out of the Panjshir Valley and the Hazaras rose up in the centre of the country around Bamiyan. For the first time Mullah Omar left his base in Kandahar to visit Kabul. He called for more troops from the madrasas. The situation looked so unstable that on the northern borders Russian troops, who had remained in the Central Asian republics after their independence, were put on alert.

For more than twelve months the Taliban remained under pressure. By September 1997 Massoud was only thirty kilometres from Kabul. Abdul Rashid Dostum reappeared and reasserted his control over the Uzbeks – and Malik Pahlawan fled to Turkmenistan. The Taliban government, meanwhile, totally failed to co-operate with the efforts by the United Nations to promote a ceasefire. It believed that the UN and all the Western powers were conspiring against it. It also greatly resented the fact that the UN would not give it the Afghan seat in the General Assembly, which continued to be held by Burhanuddin Rabbani's representative. United Nations staff in Kabul were harassed and arrested. The UN High Commissioner for Refugees office suspended operations in the country. In July 1998 the government closed the offices of all foreign non-governmental organisations in Kabul.

In the same month the Taliban attacked again in the north, once again helping its cause by paying bribes to some of Dostum's commanders, who switched sides. Dostum's remaining forces were routed and their leader fled again to Uzbekistan and then to Turkey. The Hazara force outside Mazar-i-Sharif was exposed by the collapse of the Uzbeks; it was surrounded and destroyed. On 8 August 1998 the Taliban troops re-entered the city. For two days they killed. They dealt particularly severely with the Shias. The new governor, Mullah Niazi, the same man who had ordered Najibullah murdered and mutilated in Kabul, announced that the Shias in Mazar-i-Sharif had three choices – convert, go to Iran, or die. The Taliban now controlled all of Afghanistan except the Panjshir Valley – and this is how things were to remain for the next three years.

* * *

The Taliban were always very much Pathan and very much from Kandahar Province, which – along with the two other southern provinces, Helmand and Nimruz – was the poorest, least developed and most desolate part of the country. It was not in any sense an educated movement. Its members had little understanding of Islam, no knowledge of Afghan history and no philosophy to guide their actions. Unlike the major revolutionary movements of the last 250 years the Taliban had no scholarly analysis of their society, history and religion; even if they had such an intellectual foundation it is likely – as in most revolutions – that most adherents would not have understood it. The Taliban were simply obscurantist. Most members of the movement – even among the leadership – knew only the rudiments of Islam, a few simple principles which seemed to justify the suspicion, fear and disdain they felt for the rest of Afghan society.

The Taliban troops – effective though they were – were the traditional tribal militia, the *lashkar*. The regular force never numbered more than 25,000–30,000, but its members could be increased rapidly before an offensive, drawing on the madrasas as much as on the Pathan tribes. There was always a coming and going of family members, who would sometimes change places at the front. This was not so different from the system that prevailed in the Mujahideen forces. The small number of people with technical skills, such as pilots and tank drivers, were recruited from the former Afghan army and were paid salaries.

The commanders of the Taliban armies – and most other senior government officials – were frequently changed. Dedicated and reliable characters were sent 'en mission' to different provinces and armies – just as trusted Jacobins were used during the Terror phase of the French Revolution. Mullah Mohammad Abbas, who was nominally Minister of Health, was second-in-command of the Taliban force in the north at the time of the first capture of Mazar-i-Sharif. He was then sent to the front north of Herat, and finally returned to his job six months later. Mullah Ehsanullah Ehsan, the Governor of the State Bank, also commanded a special Kandahari force. He was one of the people killed in Mazar-i-Sharif in 1997.

The ministries and institutions such as the State Bank remained in Kabul, which was always the country's capital. But the base of the Taliban and the centre of power in the country was Kandahar. The Taliban leaders never moved their families from the town and Mullah Omar left it only once.

1992. Mujahideen rebels take Kabul, Afghanistan.

1992. Rashid Dostum controlled the private buffer state on the southern borders of Turkmenistan and Uzbekistan.
Born in 1954 and solidly secular, Rashid Dostum was an Uzbek who joined the KHAD after the Soviet invasion. He joined Ahmad Shah Massoud, taking Kabul in 1992.

1 May 1992. Hazrat Sibghatullah Mojaddedi acknowledging a crowd of supporters.

29 May 1992. The author and Pakistani Prime Minister Nawaz Sharif arrive in Kabul and walk with Interim President Sibghatullah Mojaddedi.

29 May 1992, Kabul. After the fall of Kabul, Sibghatullah Mojaddedi, arrives at the airport with, on his right, Sharif Nawaz, Pakistan Prime Minister, and, to his left, the author Prince Turki AlFaisal Al-Saud.

7 March 1993, Islamabad, Pakistan. The author with General Muhammad Eid Al-Otaibi and his secretary, Ahmad Badeeb, Saudi Ambassador to Pakistan Yosuf Mutabaqqani, and Abdullah Mastour, the author's personal assistant, talking with Afghan leaders.

7 March 1993, Islamabad, Pakistan: Afghan leaders (sitting), along with representatives of several Islamic countries, pray after the signing ceremony for an Afghan peace agreement. Front row, from left: Gulbuddin Hekmatyar, Afghan warlord and leader of fundamentalist Hizb-i-Islami (Islamic Party), Burhanuddin Rabbani, Afghan President and leader of the Jamiat-i-Islami party, and Sibghatullah Mojaddedi, head of the National Islamic Front. Back row, from left: Siddique Kanjo, Pakistan Foreign Minister, Ala'eddin Borujerdi, Iranian deputy foreign minister, Nawaz Sharif, Pakistani Prime Minister, Prince Turki Al-Faisal, Saudi Arabia intelligence chief, Najibullah Lafrai, Afghan Minister of State for Foreign Affairs and General Muhammad Eid Al-Otaibi.

11 March 1993, Islamabad. Left to right, the author, Afghan President, Burhanuddin Rabbani, Pakistani Prime Minister, Nawaz Sharif and Gulbuddin Hekmatyar at a news conference.

1993. King Fahd of Saudi Arabia and Sheikh Abdulaziz bin Baz, Grand Mufti of Saudi Arabia in Makkah, meeting Pakistani Prime Minister Nawaz Sharif and the Mujahideen leaders after the signing ceremony for an Afghan peace agreement.

19 February 1994, Kabul. Two Shiite teenagers of the minority Hizb-i-Wahdat faction armed with Kalashnikovs, peer around their bunker during an exchange of small-arms fire with troops belonging to the Afghan President.

15 March 1994, Kabul. A man is captured by members of an enemy faction. Kabul's civilian population endured heavy weapon attacks killing thousands, and a food blockade imposed on the capital by forces allied to Gulbuddin Hekmatyar, the Prime Minister and General Dostum, the northern military leader, who were fighting the forces of President Burhanuddin Rabbani.

20 October 1996. Ahmed Shah Massoud's Mujahideen capture Bagram from the Taliban. Located about 60 km north-west of Kabul, Bagram is a key junction between the Panjshir Valley and the capital.

1998, Khost, Afghanistan. Ayman El-Zawahri, poses for a photograph with Osama bin Laden.

16 December 2001. Anti-Taliban Afghan fighters watch explosions from U.S. bombings in the Tora Bora mountains in Afghanistan.

Plaque given to the author by CIA head William Casey. The words in Arabic state 'Never Trust the Russians', a maxim of one of the Afghan kings.

7 October 2019, Riyadh. The author receiving the Afghan award of 'Ghazi Mirbajah Khan' decoration. From left to right, Dr Mohammad Humayon Qayoumi, Afghanistan Minister of Finance, the author, and Sayed Jalal Karim, Afghanistan Ambassador to Saudi Arabia.

At the top of the Taliban government was Mullah Omar and the Supreme Shura. The Shura, in principle, had ten members, but military commanders, mullahs and tribal leaders were often invited to its meetings, or invited themselves. Sometimes as many as fifty people took part. At the level below the Shura – and below the ministries – the Afghan government was simplified. All the senior civil servants of Tajik, Uzbek and Hazara origin were replaced by Pathans. Ministries worked just four hours a day, from 8 a.m. to noon. Government, in the sense that the modern world understands it, was not regarded as very important. In the provinces individual governors and commanders imposed their own taxes. Many of them became dealers in opium.

Altogether, the Taliban made an extraordinary movement. It began well but ended as totally uncivilised and impossible to deal with. Naseem Rana, who was Director General of the ISI from July 1995 to October 1998, tells a story of an occasion on which Taliban fighter aircraft forced down a Russian transport plane carrying arms and ammunition for Abdul Rashid Dostum's forces. The Russian government asked for the diplomatic assistance of Pakistan, and the Pakistanis told the Taliban that they could keep the arms and the aircraft but ought to hand back the crew. The Taliban totally failed to understand that this was the convention in such cases. The message they sent back to the Pakistanis said, in summary: 'First the Russians should give us a list of everyone killed and missing during the occupation – and then we shall release the crew – if the kinsmen of the dead Afghans agree'.

I have often seen reports claiming that I met Taliban officials to help them plan their military campaigns and to give them money. I must say that these reports are utter rubbish. I met Taliban officials on only three occasions: once when I was introduced by Naseerullah Babar to Mohammad Rabbani in 1995, and twice when I went to see Mullah Omar in Kandahar in 1998, as I shall describe later. Saudi Arabia never paid money to the Taliban. It is perfectly possible that the movement received some private Saudi money, as at the time our government did not monitor financial transfers, but it certainly got nothing from the state. During the early stages of the Taliban's rise to power our policy was that we would not finance Afghan groups to fight other Afghans. As far as we were concerned the need for fighting had ended with the fall of Dr Najibullah's government in 1992. Once the Taliban were in control of the Afghan government and had been recognised by Saudi Arabia, they might have been eligible for project and budget aid – but at this point we found ourselves in direct dispute over the shelter the Taliban were giving to Bin Laden.

Chapter 14
The Taliban and Bin Laden

Over the 1990s and especially during the early years of the Taliban government, I found my time increasingly occupied by the problem of Osama Bin Laden.

Bin Laden had been one of the many individuals who had assembled in Peshawar at the time of the fall of the Najibullah government in April 1992. I did not see him there and he played no role in the diplomacy that led to the creation of the Mojaddedi government, but while he was there he met Hassan Turabi, the ideologue of the government that had come to power in Sudan in 1989. This meeting led immediately to a new, more active phase in Bin Laden's career.

For practical purposes the new Sudanese government was a military regime headed by General Omar Bashir, but it had a veneer of fundamentalist Islam, and Turabi and his party, the National Islamic Front, provided this. The Front was an offshoot of the Muslim Brotherhood. Turabi wanted to spread Islamic revolution, and in particular to bring together all the different movements and parties that espoused this idea into some sort of union. He saw Bin Laden as a person who he would like to associate with his cause, not least because he was rich. He invited him to come to Khartoum and Bin Laden accepted. When the assembly in Peshawar dispersed Bin Laden flew directly to the Sudanese capital, in an aircraft lent by a rich Saudi businessman. He took a large entourage, mainly of Arabs who had been living on the Afghan frontier.

Bin Laden was fêted by the regime in Sudan. He was praised as a 'true Mujahid' and allowed to employ a body of retainers. He bought a large house in Khartoum and a farm north of the city. He gave money for a road-building project. The government announced that the sum was $10 million, but it was probably less. The original intention was that the road should be financed by Saudi government aid, but when the Sudanese government supported Saddam Hussein's invasion of Kuwait in 1990 the aid was suspended. The project was renamed 'The Road of Defiance' – and there was no doubt that the name was chosen as a small gesture of defiance towards Saudi Arabia. At the same time Turabi managed to sell Bin Laden a state leather-tanning factory. It seemed to us in Riyadh when we heard about these transactions that the Sudanese government was exploiting Bin Laden. I very much doubt he would ever have earned any income from the factory. He did, however, establish a contracting business and a trading company dealing in Sudanese agricultural commodities, and I expect these were profitable, if on a fairly modest scale.

At the end of 1993 Bin Laden issued his first public statement attacking Saudi Arabia, which he referred to as Declaration Number One. In this he set out his opposition to the Kingdom's invitation to American troops to help its defence in 1990, and he asked the King to terminate their presence and reform the government. He transmitted this declaration and the statements which followed it by fax to people and institutions in Saudi Arabia. International communications from Sudan were very poor and what he was sending would quickly have come under the control of the Sudanese authorities, so Bin Laden distributed his statements through London. He had a small office there, run by his representative, Khaled Al-Fawwaz. He would fax Fawwaz a statement, and Fawwaz would then organise its onward transmission to multiple recipients in Saudi Arabia.

The initiative coincided with the establishment in London of the Committee for the Defence of Legitimate Rights (CDLR), an Islamist propaganda organisation with an innocuous-sounding name, representing the views of two Saudi dissidents, Mohammad Al-Massari and Saad Al-Faqih. It was in part Fawwaz who helped these two establish their operation and taught them how to make multiple fax transmissions. The two operations exchanged names and fax numbers of potential recipients of their propaganda. To return the favour Al-Faqih bought a satellite telephone for Bin Laden.

The material that the CDLR transmitted was a mixture of (mostly old) stories of corruption and scandal and the political views of the organisation's founders. Its messages soon became repetitive and most of the recipients in Saudi Arabia found them rather boring, but it certainly upset the Saudi government. Bin Laden's own statements, similar in tone, were transmitted in the name of the Advisory and Reformation Committee. Among other ideas they proposed the break-up of the Saudi state and the creation of two new countries, or Islamic communities, Greater Yemen and Greater Hijaz, which would divide the Arabian Peninsula between them.

In response to the faxes the Saudi government instructed its ambassador in Khartoum to establish contact with Bin Laden and ask him to stop what he was doing. The message was that if he did not stop, legal measures would be taken against him, but if he ceased his activities and came back to Saudi Arabia all would be forgiven. The Bin Laden family likewise sent a stream of members to talk to Osama Bin Laden, including several of his half-brothers, an uncle, two sisters and his mother, but he was utterly unyielding. It was then that I realised how hurt he must have been by the rejection of his proposals in 1990 in the meetings he had with me, Prince Ahmad and Prince Sultan – though at no point did he say anything about these meetings. The family's efforts were organised very much in consultation with the government. At the beginning of the fax transmissions the head of the family had come to see us to say how ashamed they all were of what their errant member was doing.

Eventually, in March 1994, the Bin Laden family decided to disown Osama Bin Laden publicly, which it did by publishing advertisements in newspapers stating that 'this man is no longer a member of our family'. At the same time the government stripped him of his Saudi citizenship, which involved a decree issued by the King. His bank accounts in the Kingdom were frozen and his property sequestered and sold. The family had already isolated Bin Laden's share in its contracting business and put it in a trust. Many different estimates have been published of the amount of money that Bin Laden might have been able to transfer out of the Kingdom before his assets were frozen or seized. Most seem to be greatly exaggerated. My own estimate is that he is unlikely to have transferred more than $50 million.

At about this time there was a curious incident in which a small group of Sudanese 'Afghans' – Sudanese Mujahideen who had fought, or been close to the fighting, in Afghanistan – organised an attack on Bin Laden's house. The attack failed. Some of the assailants were killed by Bin Laden's guards; the others were arrested by the Sudanese police. Later they were put on trial and executed.

The episode was strange because it was never established what the assailants' motives were. Perhaps they had views that were more extreme than Bin Laden's and felt that he was not sufficiently revolutionary, or maybe they were involved in some feud that want back to their Afghanistan days. The Sudanese authorities accused them of being agents of the Saudi government, and at their trial they identified themselves as being members of the Ansar al-Islam, an established Sudanese group opposed to Turabi's National Islamic Front.

There is no suggestion that the Sudanese government organised the attack, but it certainly took advantage of it. It used it as a pretext for curbing the activities of the Ansar al-Islam and arresting a large number of its members – and it was also able to suggest to Bin Laden that the Saudi government was trying to kill him, which made him still more hostile to Saudi Arabia and more dependent on his hosts. We heard from our sources that he was becoming increasingly paranoid. He built a wall 2.5 metres tall around his compound, but Turabi, who was very much the controlling influence on Sudanese government policy at the time, would not let him put his own armed guards outside. He insisted on posting a Sudanese guard. This gave Turabi complete control over who had physical access to Bin Laden.

As might be expected, after the assassination attempt Bin Laden became more radical and more active in promoting revolutionary ideas. From the beginning of his time in Sudan he had been making donations to Islamist groups in other Arab countries, particularly Egypt. From 1994 he seemed to become more closely involved with these groups, and with Sudanese intelligence. He helped finance training camps for Islamist revolutionaries/terrorists in northern Sudan. At the end of 1994 the CIA discovered that his men were trying to organise the killing of its station chief in Khartoum. In November 1995 there was a car-bomb attack on a building belonging to the Saudi National Guard in Riyadh; the building was being used by an American team that was organising training and assistance for the Guard. The bomb killed five Americans and wounded thirty-four Saudis and other expatriates. It was the first attack of its kind on Saudi territory. The four young men who carried out the attack later confessed on Saudi television that they had been inspired by Bin Laden's ideas.

In February 1996 the United States withdrew its embassy from Khartoum because of threats made to American personnel and the lack of an adequate Sudanese government response to American protests and requests for protection. At meetings in Khartoum and Washington the Sudanese were told bluntly that if they wanted the American government to reconsider its decision and wanted to avoid sanctions being imposed on their country, they would have to change their policies. The core elements of the US demands were that Sudan should stop supporting Islamist revolutionary movements and expel Bin Laden. The Sudanese government was taken aback by the intensity of the Americans' anger.

In March the Sudanese President, Omar Bashir, came to Saudi Arabia on pilgrimage. He asked for a meeting with Crown Prince Abdullah, to follow up on diplomatic contacts that had been under way for some months. He explained that he would be willing to hand over Bin Laden, but when Prince Abdullah asked, 'When?', referring to the fact that the diplomatic exchanges had already gone on for quite a long time, Bashir said that he first wanted an assurance that Bin Laden would not be prosecuted. Such a guarantee was completely out of the question, given that Bin Laden had been encouraging and financing terrorist activities and trying openly to subvert the Saudi government, and Prince Abdullah explained this. His concluding words to the Sudanese President were, 'Nobody can be above the law'. This brought their meeting to an end. Bashir returned to Sudan and quite soon afterwards it seems that Bin Laden was told to leave.

Interestingly, the Sudanese also offered to hand over Bin Laden to the Americans, but the offer was turned down because, the Americans claimed, at that point they did not yet have sufficient evidence to prosecute him.

Bin Laden had only one place to go. He had been in touch with Maulvi Yunus Khalis in Jalalabad for some months, just in case he had to leave Sudan, and he had been told that if he needed to take refuge in Afghanistan, he would be welcome. So, in May 1996 a jet was leased from Ariana Afghan Airlines and in two flights it moved Bin Laden, his three wives, his children and a large force of followers and guards to his new home. He lived there under the protection of the Jalalabad Shura.

Once installed, Bin Laden lost no time in resuming his propaganda activities. In August he issued a long statement which he called a 'Declaration of Jihad on the Americans Occupying the Two Holy Places'. Among other matters this statement discussed how an alliance of his enemies had 'delivered him to his exile' and how the Saudi government had become 'the agent' of imperialist Jews and Christians. The statement was faxed by his representative to London newspapers. It was noticed but, being made up of the most bizarre and conspiratorial fantasies, little of it was published.

Very soon afterwards, in September, Jalalabad fell to the Taliban, which took over Bin Laden and his entourage along with the possessions and militia of Yunus Khalis. The new regime promptly sent a message to the Saudi government saying that it had 'inherited' Bin Laden and that it had 'given him refuge'. It did not offer to hand him back to us. We replied, in effect, that the Taliban could keep Bin Laden, but we would expect them to stop him from issuing anti-Saudi statements. This the Taliban undertook to do – but their promises were promptly shown to be worthless. Soon after the Taliban took Kabul that autumn Bin Laden gave first a press conference and then a long interview to an American television network. On both occasions we protested to the Taliban authorities and on both occasions we were told it would not happen again. We had the impression that Bin Laden was establishing rather good relations with the Taliban – an impression confirmed the following year when the entire Bin Laden entourage moved to Kandahar.

Both the Saudi and American governments were now seriously concerned about Bin Laden, not just because of his statements, though these were a continuous irritant, but because he seemed still to be encouraging anti-Saudi and anti-Western terrorism. When Prince Sultan, the Minister of Defence, visited Washington in March 1997 he proposed to President Bill Clinton that our two countries should establish a joint intelligence committee to collect information on terrorist activities in general and Bin Laden in particular. This committee would put on a formal and regular basis the exchanges we had had with the Americans for many years. The President liked the idea, and the next day he sent George Tenet, the Director of the CIA, to see Prince Sultan in the government guest house where he was staying. The result of their meeting was the creation of a committee on which all the intelligence organisations of both countries were represented, at the operational level. It met every quarter. Sadly, it did not achieve very much.

In February 1998 Bin Laden produced the longest and most elaborate of his many statements, which he issued under the aegis of the newly formed International Islamic Front for Jihad against Jews and Crusaders, a body apparently made up of Al-Qaeda and various associated groups in other Muslim countries. The new manifesto contained what had by now become standard material. It stated that '... for more than seven years the United States has been occupying the lands of Islam in the holiest of places, the Arabian Peninsula, plundering its riches, dictating to its rulers, humiliating its people, terrorising its neighbours and turning its bases in the Peninsula into a spearhead through which to fight the neighbouring Muslim peoples'. It ended with what purported to be a fatwa, a legal judgment, addressed to all Muslims: 'To fight and kill Americans and their allies, whether civilians or military, is an obligation for every Muslim who is able to do it in any country'. The statement and the 'fatwa' were sent to the editor of one of the Arab newspapers in London and they were broadcast by the Al Jazeera television network.

The Americans' response, in part, was to send Bill Richardson, their new ambassador to the United Nations, on a short visit to Kabul in March. He was accompanied by Tom Simons, the US ambassador in Islamabad. The two met Mohammad Rabbani, the Taliban's spokesman for foreign affairs, and over lunch they discussed the 'fatwa'. The Americans said that this constituted blatant incitement to murder and asked that Bin Laden be arrested and handed over to the United States. Rabbani and the other Taliban officials with him listened but avoided making any commitment. They merely assured the American party that Bin Laden was not a qualified Islamic scholar.[1]

For its part, Saudi Arabia continued to send protests to the Taliban about Bin Laden's activities, and they continued to ignore them. At one point the Taliban government was bold enough to ask for financial help; it was turned down flatly because it had not kept any of its promises about Bin Laden and was still fighting other Afghans. We were angry not only because of the stream of statements and interviews – there were several in late 1997 and early 1998 – but because in January 1998 our border forces had arrested a group of Bin Laden's followers who were trying to smuggle some Russian-made Saggar anti-tank missiles into Saudi Arabia from Yemen. Apparently, they were planning to use these in attacks on police stations.

The one small piece of good news we received around this time, in March or April 1998, was that the Taliban had taken Bin Laden's satellite telephone, which he used for some of his interviews, and replaced his guards with their own on his compound in Kandahar. These moves seemed likely to complicate, but not stop, his propaganda efforts. It was decided in conversations between me and Crown Prince Abdullah that it might help if I were to go to Kandahar and try to meet the Taliban leader, Mullah Omar.

We arranged a visit in June. I was accompanied by Sheikh Abdullah Al-Turki, who had recently retired as Minister of Islamic Affairs and was now Secretary General of the Muslim World League. We stopped in

Islamabad to pick up General Naseem Rana, the head of the ISI, who had agreed to accompany us to show Omar that we had Pakistan's support. It was the first time Sheikh Abdullah and I had been to Kandahar. We were struck by how dry, dusty and desert-like this region was, very different from Kabul and the North-West Frontier, which are quite green and colourful in early summer. In Kandahar there were broken buildings and the remains of war everywhere, as well as a very large number of trucks. Some of them were from Pakistan, covered in the extraordinary decorations that Pakistani truckers love; others were from Iran and from other parts of Afghanistan. We were escorted from the airport by the Taliban militia in a Land Cruiser with a few men with machine guns in front and one behind. After lunch we were taken to see Mullah Omar.

The meeting took place in a single-storey building – like most of the buildings in Kandahar – which we entered by a long corridor leading to a big, semicircular reception room. Here was the mullah. He was thin and tall, with a long beard, one eye and what seemed like an arm injury and possibly an injury to his leg – though I never saw him walk. He and his entourage were barefoot and wore mud-coloured clothes. They were sitting on rugs and cushions on the floor – there was no other furniture in the room. In all there were about fifteen or twenty people present and several went in and out during the meeting that followed. It was all quite friendly. We exchanged greetings and then I spoke at some length about what Bin Laden had been doing while he had been living in Afghanistan and about the undertakings the mullah's government had given that it would stop his activities. I ended by saying that I wanted Bin Laden handed over to Saudi Arabia.

Mullah Omar replied that he considered the security and safety of the Kingdom most important. He would never forget the help it had given to Afghanistan during the fight against the Soviet occupation, or the help it gave to Muslims everywhere. So, he said, in principle he was willing to give up Bin Laden, but at the same time he felt constrained by his obligations, having given refuge to the man. I replied that, though I understood his reservations, he should consider some of the passages in the Quran and the

Hadith which state that the security of the community as a whole should take precedence over the interests of an individual. I quoted to him a verse from the Quran. If I remember right, it was this:

> O you who have believed, if there comes to you a disobedient one with information, investigate, lest you harm a people out of ignorance and become, over what you have done, regretful. (49:6)

Sheikh Abdullah Al-Turki added some remarks in the same vein. Together we suggested that we should establish a joint committee of ulema from both our countries to draft a legal judgment which would allow Mullah Omar to surrender his guest. The committee would meet within two weeks. It was understood by everybody present that Bin Laden would be handed over, and that the purpose of the committee was simply to draw up a document which would give this move formal sanction. At the same time I made it plain to Mullah Omar that once we had Bin Laden relations between our countries would move beyond the stage of diplomacy, but no specific financial arrangement was offered, or asked for. And, I should add, we never thought at the time of the meeting, or earlier, of making any attempt to bribe any of the people around Mullah Omar. The idea would have been reasonable if it had had a chance of success, but from everything we had learnt the mullah's followers were utterly loyal and terrified of crossing him. It would also have been very difficult to identify who might have been the most influential and the most susceptible to financial inducements. The inner circles of the Taliban were mysterious and the people we met were nameless. The mullah himself, of course, was not interested in money at all.

In July 1998, a month after our visit, a personal adviser of Mullah Omar, Mullah Wakeel, came to Riyadh to reassure Crown Prince Abdullah and me that the Taliban leadership was in the process of selecting its members of the committee and that it was still on track to hand over Bin Laden. These are my minutes of this meeting:

Meeting of Prince Turki with a delegation sent by Mullah Omar to Riyadh 13 July 1998

The meeting held at 11:15 on Monday 13 July 1998 with the Afghan delegation included:

1. Mullah Wakil Ahmad Muttawakil, Adviser to Mullah Mohammad Omar, Amir of Afghanistan
2. Mullah Akhtar Mohammad Mansour, Minister of the Civil Aviation Authority of Afghanistan
3. Mullah Mutiyullah Akhund Zada, Official from the Afghan Ministry of the Hajj

From the Saudi side the meeting was attended by:

1. HRH Prince Turki AlFaisal, President of General Intelligence
2. HE Dr Abdullah bin Abdulmohsen Al-Turki
3. Salman bin Mohammad Al-Amri, Officer-in-Charge of the Saudi Arabian Embassy in Afghanistan

The Afghan delegation relayed its government's response on the topic of the rogue Osama Bin Laden who is using his position in Afghanistan to threaten the safety and stability of the Kingdom following the Taliban-controlled Afghan government allowing him to reside in the country. This was a response to what was requested of the Afghanis during the Saudi delegation's visit to Afghanistan.

At the start of the conversation, Mullah Muttawakil went over the current conditions in Afghanistan and the Kingdom's positions on the Afghan issue over the past twenty or so years. He expressed his Government's appreciation of Saudi Arabia's admirable support on the Afghan issue, which has turned it from just a single people's problem to a worldwide Islamic issue. The forces for good in the Islamic world have backed Afghanistan with direct support from the Kingdom. He expressed this by saying, 'Afghanistan is a country shared by both of us, and the Kingdom has spared no expense in supporting it. Indeed, Saudi Arabia is the capital for all Muslims and thus it is everyone's responsibility to protect it. Its standing alongside us confirms this. It was Saudi Arabia that recognised our government before anyone else. Veritably, those who do not thank others do not thank God.

'As you know, some Arabs came to Afghanistan at the onset of the jihad and have remained there until now. These include Bin Laden, who was located in Jalalabad before we took it over. He had a lot of potential and the previous groups supported him and considered him a brother. When we managed to take control of Jalalabad, the officer-in-charge of the embassy complained about Bin Laden's presence in the region and the fact that he was given the opportunity to be interviewed by journalists. We moved him to Kandahar where we had him vow not to take any action against the Kingdom or oppose it. What recently happened in Khost took place in coordination with the Kashmiri Ansar Group (which has a camp in Khost) and the help of others, the most prominent being the Pakistani journalist Yusuf Zay who works as a correspondent for several American and Western agencies and travelled to the United States immediately after the press conference. Zay has admitted his mistake in this regard.

'Mullah Omar summoned Bin Laden to Kandahar to discuss these developments with him, telling him, "You broke the vow you took and did something awful that affects us and others".

'Mullah Omar explained to Bin Laden that the journalists that interviewed him collaborate with the Americans, saying, "You claim to be against the Americans, so what kind of contradiction is this?" He went on to pressure Bin Laden to leave the country. Bin Laden responded, "God's land is vast, but I will depart and leave my children in Afghanistan." The meeting ended with this understanding.

'You all know now that the camps belonged to jihadist groups and are now used by Bin Laden and the Pakistani Ansar Group that fights in Kashmir. We made the decision to close these foreign camps whether they belonged to Ansar or not. We will not be able to expel these individuals; however, closing the camps will get them to leave Afghanistan, which suits everyone.

'One might say that Bin Laden helps us, but this is incorrect as his capabilities are modest at best. He has promised us on more than one occasion to provide support for projects, but he has proven incapable. When he requests a meeting with any official, we expect him only to ask for more assistance.

'We know that people come and go, but that states stay. No doubt you agree with us that our relationship with you is one of understanding and brotherhood and that we can overcome anything that tries to muddy it.

'As for Bin Laden's *fatwa* against the Americans, I met with him and told him that he is not a religious scholar and that he has not consulted with Afghan clerics on this issue. In response, he showed me written *fatwas* by Pakistani clerics, which we then told the Americans about. We believe that Israel and America are the reason behind the Islamic world's problems. Mullah Omar has said that it is imperative to stand up to the enemy of the ummah with action, not words, direct confrontation, not sabotage.

'We would also like to inform you that Bin Laden will be swiftly expelled from Afghanistan and will not be on our side. Others will accuse us of taking money to hand him over. He does have supporters inside Afghanistan as well as good contacts with a large number of individuals because of the financial support he has provided them. It would be better to examine this together and collaborate on coming up with a mutually beneficial solution. In Afghanistan, we agreed to apply pressure on Bin Laden to get him to leave the country. If you have another opinion on the matter, I am ready to continue our discussion until we reach a solution that satisfies everyone.'

At the end, it was agreed that discussions on the subject would continue, but we assured the delegation that it would be best to hand Bin Laden over to us and for them to get out of this bad situation, which would be in both of our interests. We will meet the delegation again in the coming days to continue the conversation.

S5/11/82-84

We then sent Salman Mohammad al-Amri, the Chargé d'Affaires at the Saudi Arabian Embassy in Afghanistan at that time, to Kandahar to follow up on this meeting, and three weeks later he sent me a cable, dated 10 August 1998:

To His Royal Highness Prince Turki AlFaisal
President of General Intelligence

Peace and blessings be upon you.

This is a follow-up on your instructions about meeting the Taliban leadership on the outcome of your visit to Kandahar and Wakil Ahmad Muttawakil and his delegation's visit to the Kingdom concerning the activities of Bin Laden and what the Taliban must do about this disobedient individual.

Accordingly, I would like to inform you that the meeting with Wakil Ahmad occurred last week. We discussed the measures that have been taken, and those that need to be taken. He explained that after returning from the Kingdom he met Mullah Omar and some of the Taliban leadership. They agreed to what he told them was discussed in the Kingdom. The meeting occurred at Kandahar airport. Subsequently, Wakil Ahmad headed to Islamabad and, based on what he claimed, on the agenda was a discussion about the camps located in Afghanistan that the Taliban claims belong to the Kashmiri Ansar Group and must be closed.

After discussing the topic with him, Wakil Ahmad promised me that their response would be ready within a week. He also promised me that he will contact me to let me know on what date I should travel to meet the leaders in Kandahar to get the response. I was actually ready to travel last Wednesday on the UN flight that goes to Kandahar twice a week. However, after reaching out to Wakil Ahmad, he informed me that the Taliban leadership had not come to a decision yet. Most recently, the trip has been postponed until tomorrow, Sunday. I will stay in Kandahar until I get the response that they promised me. From there, you will be contacted to review the latest findings.

Kindly review and pass along.
Respectfully yours,
Salman Mohammad al-Amri

Just three days before Salman Mohammad al-Amri sent this cable an event had taken place which I can see in retrospect may have been the key to our discussions with the Taliban coming to nothing – though dealing with that body was always so difficult and its leadership's thinking so opaque that it is difficult to be sure.

On 7 August there were two appalling bombings of American embassies in Nairobi, Kenya, and Dar es Salaam, Tanzania. Both involved truck bombs that exploded in parking lots next to the embassies. In all 224 people were killed, most of them Kenyan citizens who had nothing to do with the US embassy in their country. There was no doubting that Bin Laden was behind this attack. The CIA and the FBI had already been working to break up what they believed was an Al-Qaeda cell in Nairobi, and they had much material that now became very significant. More decisively, one of the perpetrators, who was travelling back to Afghanistan, was arrested as he passed through Pakistan; he confessed to carrying out the attacks at the behest of Bin Laden. The American government now sent a message to the Taliban leadership saying that it had absolute proof of Bin Laden's terrorist activities and that it wanted to arrest the man. The reply they got was that there was '… no proof' and that Bin Laden was 'being unfairly persecuted'.

So, President Clinton ordered retaliatory strikes. On the night of 20 August the US Navy launched seventy-five cruise missiles at establishments known to be associated with Bin Laden around Khost, Kandahar and

Jalalabad. They were camps used for training Bin Laden's own people for terrorist operations and for training Kashmiri/Pakistani militants for operations in the Indian part of the disputed region of Kashmir. The Americans had intelligence that Bin Laden was going to be in one of the camps at the time, a place he visited quite often and from which he had issued his long statement in February. As it happened, Bin Laden had been in a meeting in the camp that day – but several hours earlier than the attack. Possibly he changed the timing at the last minute as a routine security precaution. Instead of Bin Laden and his aides, the casualties from the missile strikes were other Arabs, Pakistanis and Afghans.

At the same time as the missiles were fired at the camps around Jalalabad the Al-Shifa chemicals factory near Khartoum was destroyed by a missile attack, causing one fatality and a number of casualties. It was believed, on the basis of soil samples taken by a CIA agent, that the plant was manufacturing precursor substances which might be used in the production of chemical weapons, which were a particular concern of President Clinton. In fact, it seems the intelligence was faulty. The plant made simple pharmaceuticals and the US government never admitted its mistake.

On 23 August 1998, three days after the missile attacks, I received the following cable from Salman Mohammad al-Amri regarding the Jalalabad attack.

Peace and blessings be upon you,

In reference to cable no. 3/w/3/30578 dated 23/08/1998 mentioned in cable no. 205/136 about the outcome of the American strike on the rogue group (Bin Laden). I would like to inform you that new information points to the following:

1. The death toll at Camp Zhawar (Badr 1), located approximately 6 kilometres from the border with Pakistan has reached 27 and there are 53 injured, a number of whom have been moved to Peshawar for treatment. Information indicates that approximately

15 of these are in serious condition. The dead can be divided into 3 groups:

    a.   13 Arabs: We do not know their nationalities or names. They were buried in their clothing and without being identified.

    b.   13 Pakistanis and Kashmiris from the Ansar Group.

    c.   1 Afghan.

2.   All of those killed and injured were from groups that received training at the above-mentioned camp. This includes the pro-Kashmiri Khalid bin Al-Walid Brigade, a number of whose trainees had their graduation ceremony at the camp. After eating dinner, Bin Laden left the camp for Jihad Wahl Camp at approximately 21:00 on Thursday evening. Missiles hit the site about 10 minutes after he departed.

3.   Most injuries occurred at the above-mentioned camp where the majority of the groups had come to attend the ceremony. One of the missiles hit a weapons depot near the camp mosque and led to the destruction of the depot and the weapons in it. Nobody was killed at any of the other camps even though they were directly struck, even the Khalden and Jihad Wahl camps. This owes to the fact that there were only small numbers of people in these camps at the time they were hit.

4.   The camps included:

    a.   Jihad Wahl which was set up by Hekmatyar during the jihad. It was vacant until last year when several training sessions were held there for Arabs and the Kashmiri Ansar Group, which receives support from Bin Laden and is called Camp Badr 2.

    b.   Zhawar receives new Arab and non-Arab trainees (Badr 1) and is loyal to Bin Laden.

     c.   Khalden was the camp of Sheikh Abdullah Azzam's service offices and was then taken over by the Palestinian Abu Zubaidah, who left it earlier this year. Currently, several Arabs and members of the Ansar Group live in the camp and some receive training there.

     d.   All of these camps are loyal to Bin Laden and we have produced a number of reports on them over the past years.

5.   These strikes have not had any impact on Bin Laden, but rather it is believed that they have been a turning point for the extremist groups loyal to him. Yesterday when Bin Laden reached Kandahar, he said that this strike had woken up all Muslims across the world and that they will support him both morally and materially to stand up to America. One of his advisers stated that this action will push them to carry out more operations against Americans wherever they may be found.

6.   The explosion heard in Jalalabad the same moment that the above-mentioned camps in Khost were struck was a blast from the same type of Tomahawk cruise missile that hit the Tora Bora camp, which Bin Laden left last year for Kandahar. The camp is now deserted and has no more than 7 Afghan guards. Intelligence indicates that none were harmed in the strike.

7.   An Italian died after being shot in Kabul yesterday, and a Frenchman was injured during protests and security disturbances that occurred yesterday in the majority of Afghan cities. The Frenchman was moved to Islamabad for treatment. Intelligence indicates that the two men were UN representatives: one was a soldier and the other a civilian. Kofi Annan released a statement to the Afghan Ministry of Foreign Affairs assigning it responsibility for the incident and requested that it protect foreigners working in Afghanistan. Four Arab individuals were

arrested and accused of committing the crime. They will stand trial in the coming days.

Please review and pass along.
Mohammad/35

During the second half of July and the whole month of August, while these events were unfolding, we heard nothing more from Mullah Omar, so in early September 1998 it was decided that I should go to Kandahar once more. I went again via Islamabad, where on 18 September I met Prime Minister Nawaz Sharif, along with General Naseem Rana. In accordance with what I had agreed with Crown Prince Abdullah, I now asked that General Rana should accompany me again to back up my message that what had been agreed in June had to be implemented. We flew on to Kandahar the next day in the Prime Minister's Airbus, which was able to land at this very provincial airport because the Russians had extended the runway. In all there were six or seven of us, including General Rana's deputy, an official from the Pakistani Foreign Ministry and an interpreter to translate between English and Pashto.

We were driven to the same building in which I had met Mullah Omar in June, and this time we went straight into a meeting with the mullah and much the same group of silent, nameless people who had been there the last time. General Rana began the proceedings by saying how important it was that agreements be honoured for the sake of good relations between all parties, and then he handed the discussion over to me. I ran through our previous meeting and ended by reminding Mullah Omar of his commitment. Much to my surprise he said simply, 'I never agreed to this'. I reminded him that in June I had summarised very clearly what had been agreed before I left, and he replied, 'No, it must have been a mistake in translation'. Next, he denied that his adviser, Mullah Muttawakil, had said in Riyadh in July that his government was in the process of selecting members of the joint Saudi-Afghan committee of ulema.

Then he launched into a tirade. He asked why Saudi Arabia was being so horrible to Bin Laden, who was 'a good Muslim' who had helped Afghanistan. Instead of asking for Bin Laden to be extradited, the Saudi government should put its hand in the hand of the Afghan people and fight the enemy which was occupying its own country. It was the United States that was pushing Saudi Arabia to put pressure on Afghanistan to hand over Bin Laden. The Saudi leaders were instruments in the hands of the Americans. They were helping the Americans inflict hunger on the Iraqi people. The Americans were in the Holy Places and it was very wrong of the Saudi ulema to allow their presence there. If Bin Laden could not carry out the task of expelling them, or was killed in the process, thousands of others would take over his work. Then the mullah went on to attack Iran for its aggression against Afghanistan. As he spoke his voice grew shrill. He sweated, almost as if he had a fever.

It was the most extraordinary rant, and there came a point when I was not prepared to listen to it any longer. I stood up and before I left the room I asked the translator to tell the mullah that I would not allow him to attack the Kingdom, its leadership, its ulema and its people in such a way, and that his broken promise and what he had said that day would eventually cause great harm to the Afghan people. I asked General Rana to be a witness to what I had said. The whole meeting did not last more than half an hour or forty-five minutes. The lunch that had been prepared for us was left uneaten.

On the flight back to Islamabad, during which the crew kindly shared their lunch with us, we discussed what had happened. Why had Mullah Omar changed his mind? We decided that either he had come much more under the influence of Bin Laden (and certainly what he had said sounded very much like 'Bin Laden-speak') or maybe he had been angered by the cruise missile attacks. Perhaps he had decided much earlier to go back on his commitment. After all, the American missile strikes had come well after we were supposed to have established the committee of ulema. It was interesting that at no point did Mullah Omar show any understanding that, now his movement controlled virtually all of Afghanistan, having finally gained control of Mazar-i-Sharif in the previous month, it would need to start building relations with the outside world and conforming to some international norms.

During the flight I drafted the report I would send to Crown Prince Abdullah. It read as follows:

To His Royal Highness Prince Abdullah bin Abdulaziz
Crown Prince, First Deputy Prime Minister of the Council of Ministers,
and Commander of the National Guard

Sir,

This letter is further to what I raised in no. 1/9/3/434 dated 13/07/1998 regarding the handing over of Bin Laden by the Taliban government.

I hereby submit to Your Royal Highness recommendations if the Taliban refuses to deport Bin Laden from Afghanistan or hand him over to the Kingdom.

1. Withdrawing our Chargé d'Affaires and telling officials there the reason why.
2. Ceasing all dealings with visitors from the Afghan government.
3. Having the Kingdom activate its contacts among all Afghan groups, particularly members of the Northern Alliance, who oppose the Taliban.
4. Having the Kingdom bring up the presence of Bin Laden and other terrorist groups in Afghanistan with the Organisation of the Islamic Conference so that the latter issues a resolution condemning the situation.
5. Urging relief organisations to cease work with the Taliban government.
6. Cut off relations with the group.

Sir, this must be brought to your attention. I wish you success.
Your servant,
Turki AlFaisal

I showed this draft to General Rana, and we discussed what Pakistan might do as well. It seemed it might be appropriate for Pakistan to reduce its diplomatic staff in Afghanistan and close some of its consulates, but not sever diplomatic relations because we needed to have at least one channel of communication remain open. I also suggested that Pakistan should stop whatever financial assistance it was giving to Afghanistan and mount a campaign to stop smuggling across the border. I wanted to make the Taliban suffer straight away because of its leader's broken promise. On our side, the Saudi government promptly implemented my recommendations. However, we continued humanitarian aid to refugees and continued to allow Afghans to come to Makkah and Madinah for pilgrimage.

We had no substantial contact with the Taliban from this time onwards. Naseem Rana, with whom I enjoyed working, retired from the ISI a month after our visit to Kandahar. Under his successor, General Khwaja Ziauddin, who had rather good relations with the Taliban, we received a message that Mullah Omar had been 'in a bad mood' the day he met me. That fact was obvious, and the message was not accompanied by any hint that he might be reconsidering his position on Bin Laden. There was no further message.

Whenever Taliban officials came to Saudi Arabia for Hajj or Umra we were willing to listen to what they had to say on an informal level, and we were always given the message that they wanted to restart relations. We always replied that we wanted Bin Laden first, and there our conversations ended. We also talked to the Pakistani government about what information it was getting from Kandahar, but we were always told that Mullah Omar was adamant that he would not change his mind. Certainly, this is what Bin Laden believed, because quite soon after my visit he gave a television interview to the BBC in which he gleefully described how I had failed to get Mullah Omar to give him up.

* * *

From the time it established control over the country the Taliban government became an international pariah. Most of the world was offended by its refusal to establish a broad-based government or observe diplomatic norms, by its brutality and by its appalling treatment of women. In December 1998 the United Nations passed a resolution in which it threatened sanctions on Afghanistan for its government's harbouring of terrorists, violations of human rights, promotion of drug trafficking and refusal to accept UN initiatives for a ceasefire between its forces and those of Ahmad Shah Massoud.

Speaking in a debate before the resolution, the US ambassador declared that Afghanistan-based terrorism had become an international plague. American policy at this time and for the next two years and nine months was to try to engage with the Taliban while squeezing them with economic sanctions. It rejected the idea of further missile strikes, given that the attacks of August 1998 had failed and further strikes would be bound to cause civilian deaths. Instead, it considered various plans for capturing Bin Laden, either by having someone in his entourage betray him so that he could be seized by an American snatch squad operating out of Pakistan, or by having American allies, notably Ahmad Shah Massoud's forces, ambush him and either capture or kill him. None of these plans came to anything. The ISI was nervous about getting involved and Massoud's forces were in the wrong part of the country.

Nothing improved in Afghanistan in 1999. Fighting continued between the Taliban and Massoud and the Hazaras. The country grew poorer and the government became increasingly unpopular. Most of the population resented having Pathan governors from Kandahar imposed on them. Everybody resented the government's conscription drive, the increase in taxes and the greed and corruption of some of the Taliban officials.

On 19 January 2000 the United Nations acted on its threat to impose sanctions. Security Council Resolution 1333 imposed a complete ban on the sale of arms to Afghanistan, the seizure of Taliban assets outside the country and a ban on international travel by Afghan officials. It also demanded the extradition of Bin Laden.

In October came an attack on the USS *Cole*, a very large, expensive and sophisticated guided-missile destroyer which was moored in Aden harbour. A small boat full of explosives blew up alongside it, knocking a twelve-metre hole in its hull and killing seventeen American sailors. The CIA could not find solid proof that Bin Laden had planned the attack, but it was quite certain he was responsible.

In February the following year, during a campaign against the Hazaras in the centre of the country, Mullah Omar ordered the destruction of giant statues of two Buddhas in the Bamiyan Valley. These were extremely important monuments of great cultural significance. There was an international outcry. A Muslim delegation, including Saudi ulema, travelled to Kabul to remonstrate with Taliban officials. It explained that under Sharia law a government should respect other religions in the country which it rules, as had been the practice since the time of the Muslim conquests in the seventh century. The reply of the Taliban was simple: 'You do not understand'. On 10 March Mullah Omar's orders were carried out and the statues were demolished by dynamite and tank fire.

In May the Taliban caused more international outrage. They closed the Italian hospital in Kabul, accusing the European doctors there of consorting with Afghan women. They also declared that all Hindus in the country should wear yellow badges. On this occasion they took some note of the outcry and after a few weeks modified the rule to state only that Hindus should always carry their identity papers.

Two months after this, in August, I resigned as Director of the General Intelligence Department. I was frustrated by my failure to extract Bin Laden from Afghanistan, and particularly by my failure in the past three years to make any progress at all in this direction. But the main reason I left the department was that I had been in the job for twenty-four years and I felt I was becoming stale. I had no idea at the time that the issue of Afghanistan which had dominated my time at the GID virtually from the beginning was moving towards its ghastly denouement.

Two important events followed. The first took place in Afghanistan and appeared to mark a decisive turn in the civil war. Since the spring Ahmad Shah Massoud had been putting increasing pressure on the Taliban army. In April he had made a visit to Europe. He had addressed the European

Parliament in Strasbourg, greatly impressed the European and American officials he had met and shown himself to be very popular among Afghans of all ethnic groups abroad. Hitherto the Americans had been reluctant to give him wholehearted backing because he was not a Pathan – i.e. not a member of the most numerous ethnic group in Afghanistan, which we all tended to assume would have to be at the centre of any stable government in that country. Now they started to see him as a very desirable and credible alternative to the Taliban. On his return to his country the United Front he had formed with Abdul Rashid Dostum, who had once again appeared in Afghanistan, and Ismail Khan, operating with Iranian support, launched a new campaign and made considerable progress. In June some of Massoud's units came close to Kabul.

In response the Taliban enlisted the support of Al-Qaeda. On 9 September two young north Africans with Belgian passports, posing as journalists, went to conduct an 'interview' at the United Front's headquarters in the Panjshir Valley. Using a bomb hidden in a video camera they blew themselves up and killed Massoud.

Two days later, as the whole world knows, four aircraft were hijacked by members of Al-Qaeda in the United States. One was heading towards Washington, D.C., where the hijackers were probably intending to fly it into either the Capitol or the White House, but its passengers tried to regain control of the aircraft and it crashed in a field in Pennsylvania. Another was flown into the Pentagon in Washington. And two were flown into the Twin Towers of the World Trade Center in New York. In all 2,996 people died and some 6,000 others were injured. The dead included 343 firefighters. For the United States the loss was not just human and material; the attacks were a colossal affront to the country's pride, prestige and security. They had to be avenged.

Chapter 15
Aftermath

Within hours of the attacks on 9/11 Mullah Omar issued a statement declaring that Bin Laden was not responsible – partly, it seems, to qualify the statement of his own Foreign Minister, Wakil Ahmad Muttawakil, who had denounced 'the terrorist attack' and whoever was behind it. Nobody, or very few people, in the outside world believed Mullah Omar. On the following day President George W. Bush called the attacks more than just 'acts of terror' – they were 'acts of war'. The State Department then demanded that the Taliban should surrender all known Al-Qaeda associates in Afghanistan and provide intelligence on Bin Laden and his associates. Mullah Omar and the senior Taliban leadership were approached on America's behalf by the Pakistani ISI. The Taliban refused to co-operate and repeated their refusal several times in different forms in the days that followed.

From late September, American and British intelligence officers and Special Forces began to be placed in Afghanistan, and with their support the Northern Alliance established control of one Afghan city after another. Kabul fell on 13 November. More countries joined the military effort and more American troops were flown in. The Taliban forces collapsed and Bin Laden and his Al-Qaeda supporters withdrew to Jalalabad, and then to the Tora Bora region near the Pakistan border where there were networks of caves. They were pursued by the allied forces and the places where they were thought to be were bombed relentlessly, but it seems the allies' intelligence was always a little out of date. Bin Laden and his associates were always a day or two ahead. Operations continued in a lower key through 2002. By this time there were eighteen countries involved in Afghanistan. In December 2001 the operation had been put under NATO and been given the name International Security Assistance Force (ISAF). It remained in Afghanistan for the next thirteen years.

It was not long after the establishment of ISAF, when it was already clear that Bin Laden was not likely to be found quickly, that the attention of President Bush and the American administration turned elsewhere – to Iraq. Saddam Hussein's regime had been under United Nations sanctions for ten years, and it had been very much the hope of the Americans, British and other allies who had joined the war to liberate Kuwait in 1991 that the sanctions would cause the regime to collapse. This had not happened, however, and the sanctions had been gradually relaxed.

By 2002 Iraq was being allowed to produce and sell as much oil as it liked. There were no controls on its imports of food and medical supplies – nor had there been from the start – and although other imports had to have UN approval, that approval was being given for almost everything except military materiel. However, to the great frustration and annoyance of President Bush and Tony Blair, the British Prime Minister, Saddam was smuggling out oil by road tanker to give himself revenue to spend as he liked, and conspicuously failing to spend his legitimate revenues for the benefit of his people. The Western press – gullible as always where human-interest stories of suffering are concerned – was reporting on the hardship of the Iraqi people and blaming it on sanctions. The sanctions regime had to be renewed every six months and the whole process had become an embarrassment for the Americans and British.

There were other factors in play. According to British and American intelligence, influenced a good deal by Israeli intelligence, which might well not have been wholly objective, Saddam was continuing his illegal programmes to build weapons of mass destruction. For President Bush there was also a personal matter, in that the day before his father visited Kuwait in 1993 the Kuwaiti authorities had discovered an assassination plot which appeared to have been arranged by the Iraqis. And lastly, on a most grandiose scale and influenced by the neo-conservatives in the administration, the Americans had conceived the idea that peace might be brought to the Middle East and altogether better government installed in the region by a programme of 'regime change', beginning in Iraq. So, on 20 March 2003, as the second stage of the 'War on Terror', American and British forces invaded Iraq, and with remarkable speed and ease overthrew Saddam Hussein.

Saudi Arabia, a staunch friend of the two countries, had been utterly opposed to the invasion. We had no love for Saddam – he was a brutal dictator, had killed thousands of his own people, had started two wars and, quite apart from his invasion of Kuwait, had been a standing threat to the countries of the Gulf. But at the same time we could see that overthrowing him would be bound to destabilise Iraq, however it was done. We also knew that if America then imposed democracy on the country that would involve a complete upending of the political order of the eighty years since the collapse of the Ottoman Empire at the end of the First World War. It would produce a Shia-led regime, which would lead to a great increase in Iran's influence in the region. Events have proved that we were quite right. The invasion quickly led to chaos, civil war, terrible bloodshed, a malign Iranian influence which then helped to consolidate a presence the Iranians already had in Syria and Lebanon, and – in response to the pro-Shia bias of the new Iraqi government – the emergence of the appalling ISIS.

I do not need to go in more detail through the miserable story of events in Afghanistan and Iraq in the two decades since the invasions. In neither country has the story yet come to anything which might seem a conclusion, in the sense of stable government and peace. I want, instead, to pick up some of the themes which I mentioned at the beginning of this book. There, I explained how the Afghanistan war produced Al-Qaeda, which became the first of a number of terrorist bodies that attracted young, naïve, ill-educated people of many nationalities, and espoused a sort of nihilistic thinking and purposeless violence which has become a curse of the world in the last twenty years. First I want to discuss how the events described in this book affected Saudi Arabia, and then I will look at the problems of the broader Middle East.

The attacks of 9/11 were as much of a shock to Saudi Arabia as they were to the rest of the world. Saudis were horrified to be told that fifteen out of the nineteen hijackers involved were from their own country; some people could not accept this fact. For a time our society as a whole refused to acknowledge that it was producing an underclass of semi-educated, disaffected religious fanatics – a body of potential and actual terrorists – and that it had to do something to correct this.

Nobody denied that Bin Laden and Al-Qaeda were terrorists, and that Bin Laden was a Saudi, but the man and his organisation were regarded as aberrations. Likewise, it was known that the four young men who bombed the National Guard building in Riyadh in 1995 were Saudis. But, again, the feeling was that any society may suffer the odd terrorist attack from time to time.

It was only when terrorist attacks began to occur regularly on Saudi soil in 2003 that it became apparent that the problem was more serious. The first major outrage was an attack by a group of terrorists armed with automatic weapons on a residential compound in Riyadh in May 2003. It was followed by another attack on a compound in November, and later there were further bombings of residential and government buildings, attempted bombings of oil installations, attacks on the police, and shootouts during police raids on terrorist cells – sometimes involving quite long sieges and several police casualties.

During the most intense period of attacks, between the first compound attack and the failed attack on an oil installation at Abqaiq in the Eastern Province in February 2006, the death toll reached 144 victims – foreigners and Saudis, including members of the security forces – and 120 terrorists. Since the beginning of 2006 our security forces have got on top of the problem, but we cannot guarantee that the war is over and there may be occasional attacks in the future.

The origins of our problems, I believe, go back to the 1950s and early 1960s. At that time Saudi Arabia and all the other Arab monarchies were under attack from Nasser's revolutionary socialist regime in Egypt. The Western powers too saw Nasser as a threat to their interests. Within its own country Nasser's regime turned against the conservative and religious opposition; its members were imprisoned and some of them were killed.

Saudi Arabia opened its doors to whoever was fleeing from persecution in Egypt – including many members of the Muslim Brotherhood. This seemed humane and politically sensible. From our point of view and that of our Western allies it was part of the fight against Communism and the related philosophy of hard-line Arab socialism. Once in Saudi Arabia a considerable number of the refugees, being rather well-educated, took careers as teachers or as civil servants in the Ministry of Education. Having a religious bias, they tended to increase the religious content of the school curriculum – and of course they tended in turn to give jobs to people who shared their religious and social views. As their students graduated with a religious bias in their qualifications, they went into the mosques or back into the educational system, and so Saudi education was infected by zealous interpretations of the Muslim scriptures. The way things were developing did not become evident until the 1980s.

Meanwhile, Islamism was developing as a political movement elsewhere. This can be traced back to the Arabs' defeat by the Israelis in 1967, which discredited the revolutionary republican regimes of Egypt and Syria, and Nasser's ideas in general. The defeat showed that socialism, the nation-state and pan-Arab nationalism produced neither strong modern societies with powerful armies nor economic prosperity.

The Arab world, and to some extent the wider Muslim world, began to think about the political causes of this failure. People had already seen that the European-influenced semi-democratic governments, dominated by the landowning classes, which had succeeded colonial rule in Egypt, Syria and Iraq, had been humiliated by Israel in the Arab-Israeli War of 1948. Then socialism and nationalism, both imported ideas, were discredited in the war nineteen years later. People began to look for a political idea which came from within their own society, and inevitably they found Islam. The prestige of Islamism as a political movement was increased by the success of the Iranian Revolution in 1979 when students, clerics and bazaari (the merchant classes) overthrew an absolute monarchy that was backed by a large army and had the moral support of the Western world. It was also enhanced by the success of the Mujahideen in Afghanistan in the 1980s. I must stress at this point that Islamism as seen in the world today is a political rather than a religious movement.

In retrospect it is not difficult to see how the expansion of religious influence in our educational system, which turned out increasing numbers of poorly qualified and sometimes unemployable young men, combined with the growing political prestige of Islamism, would produce a body of revolutionaries in Saudi society. The government's acceptance of religious influence in education and the media in the 1980s and the expansion in the numbers of minor religious functionaries at that time (topics I discussed in Chapter 6) no doubt encouraged the process.

Since 2003 we have been working to roll back these changes. This is a matter of changing society – altering the way some people think – and it can only be done slowly.

Most important for the long term is reform of the educational system. We have reduced the religious content of the school curriculum, and we have looked very carefully at what students are being taught in lessons on the various religious subjects. We have retired or retrained teachers we have found were inculcating extremist or intolerant attitudes. We discovered some cases, among teachers of secular as well as religious subjects, where they were telling their pupils the most extraordinary things. For example, they said that it was wrong to say 'Hello' to a non-Muslim. Since 2005–6 we have been sending more students to universities abroad as a matter of policy. As of 2020 there were more than 200,000 Saudi students studying on scholarships all over the world.

A similar critical appraisal has been directed at the Kingdom's mosques. In the 1980s we were very tolerant of what imams and *khatib*s (preachers) said in the mosques, but in recent years – from the early 1990s and increasingly since 2003 – we have taken note of extremist preaching. In the three years between 2003 and 2005 we dismissed a thousand mosque staff and sent three thousand for retraining with senior ulema.

We have taken steps to control charities and individuals transferring money abroad. In the months after 9/11 we instituted an outright ban on charitable transfers. We then established a new body, the Saudi Organisation for Charities Abroad, which had the job of monitoring transfers. Any person or institution wanting to make a foreign charitable donation had to explain to the organisation who would be receiving the money and what it would be used for. The organisation has since been merged into the King Salman Humanitarian Aid and Relief Center.

The emergence of women in more public roles since about 2000 has gained a momentum of its own. It has been the single most conspicuous recent change in Saudi society. Twenty years ago, in Saudi Arabia women worked in teaching and medicine, and – behind the scenes – as owners of businesses and leaders of charitable work. There was no rule preventing them from doing other jobs; it was simply the custom that they should not. And the custom reflected the views of a conservative society. Now women are appearing in managerial, clerical and secretarial positions, working as journalists, playing a leading role in domestic charities and campaigning for better legal rights for themselves. Women have been elected to the chambers of commerce and they can vote in municipal elections and stand as candidates. They are on the boards of public companies and state agencies, and in several cases chair these institutions. There are women in senior government posts, including ambassadorial jobs.

The innovations that have attracted the most publicity since 2015, under King Salman and Crown Prince Mohammad bin Salman, have been granting permission for women to drive, a series of decisions allowing women and men to mix in public places, including sports stadia and restaurants, and removing most Guardianship regulations. This means that women are now allowed to travel, accept scholarships abroad and marry without having to seek the permission of a male relative. The changes have been accompanied by the introduction of concerts, cinemas, theatres and other places of entertainment. The government has promoted entertainment 'events'. These changes have been very popular. The whole atmosphere of public places in Saudi cities – shopping malls, cafés, hotels – has changed. It has become softer, more human.

* * *

If I am rather encouraged by the ways in which Saudi Arabia is changing, I am much less happy about what has been happening in the world outside. In conclusion I feel I ought to say a few words about this and where possible suggest what might be done to improve the situation.

It is not only Al-Qaeda and other terrorist groups that have disrupted the Middle East since the beginning of this century. There has been also the 'Arab Spring' of 2011. This produced revolutions in Tunisia, Egypt, Libya and Syria and led to war in Yemen. In one country, Tunisia, the outcome has been a democratic government which is still somewhat fragile but which is a definite improvement on the regime that preceded it. In Egypt, after much violence and confusion, the country finds itself with much the same type of government as it had before. And in Libya and Syria the outcome has been chaos, war and disintegration.

While these events have been unfolding, we have seen a steady growth in Iran's malign influence in the Arab world. The Islamic Republic has done what it can to encourage opposition among the Shia populations of Bahrain and Saudi Arabia – though here it has not had much effect. It has intervened with worse effect in Yemen and Iraq, and with very serious effect in Syria and Lebanon. In Syria it has prevented the collapse of the brutal regime of Bashar Assad, whose refusal to concede in any way to the demands for reform of the initial demonstrations in 2011 was the cause of the civil war that followed. In Lebanon Iran has promoted Hezbollah, which has continually prevented the formation of a stable government embracing all the religious sects of that country, or indeed of a more modern non-sectarian government. In Yemen it is supplying the Houthi militias, which took control of the northern part of the country by force, with ballistic missiles and drones. The Houthis have been using these to attack Saudi Arabia since 2015. There have been literally hundreds of such attacks.

The Middle East has not been what might be called a 'happy' part of the world for two or three generations, since the end of the Second World War – but in recent years the events I have just mentioned seem to have been making matters worse and worse.

Clearly there are no simple solutions, but I can make a few comments.

First, regarding the campaign against terrorism: my belief is that we do not counter terrorism by war, except in a case such as that of ISIS where a terrorist body actually established a state of sorts. War as a policy in Afghanistan and Iraq produced only more violence. We work against terrorism through the police, intelligence, sometimes special forces, and diplomacy, shutting off sources of finance, and endless political initiatives. The aim has to be to restrict the terrorists' ability to operate. At the same time, where terrorists have a definable, rational cause, which has not always been the case recently, we have to undermine the support they receive by removing the grievances that produce that support. This process requires great patience. It took the British thirty years by these methods to resolve what one hopes will be the last phase of the conflict in Northern Ireland. There was much human suffering during these years, but the cost in destruction and lives was much smaller than we have seen in conflicts in the Middle East.

The citizens in any country, society and government at large have to be engaged in the struggle against the terrorists. There is a role for educational and religious instruction. I have already mentioned the Kingdom's reform of our educational system. There is the role of the media in all its forms, now especially through social media outlets. The government has established the International Center to Combat Extremism for this purpose. It canvasses social media outlets to counter any extremist narrative that may appear.

Then there is the rehabilitation of convicted terrorists by a process that in Saudi Arabia includes psychiatric therapy, religious challenges to the terrorists' convictions and reconnecting the terrorists with their families. The families are given a share in their well-being. The security forces are directed to deal only with suspected miscreants and those who are directly influencing them, and not with acquaintances simply because the terrorists know them. And, of course, there is intelligence sharing and political co-operation with other countries. The Kingdom took the initiative in 2014, holding a conference to combat the Islamic State in Iraq and Syria (ISIS); this resulted in the establishment of the International Coalition to fight ISIS led by the United States. Later the Kingdom initiated the Islamic Coalition to Fight Terrorism, composed of more than forty Muslim countries.

Second, the international community should work through diplomacy and sanctions to get Iran to cease its intervention in Arab countries. One can see clearly how this would improve the situation in Lebanon. The way ahead would also be a bit clearer without Iran in Yemen and Iraq, but in Syria the situation as of early 2021 is still so violent and confused that it is very difficult to define what an acceptable outcome might be. Russia's support for Assad is unacceptable because Assad is not just fighting terrorism but also, more often, brutally suppressing the legitimate demands of the Syrian people. The Kingdom initiated the Arab League's resolution on Syria, introduced to the UN Security Council back in 2012. This called for an interim government composed of the Syrian opposition and the government, represented by the Vice President, Farouk al-Sharaa. Alas, the Russians and the Chinese vetoed it.

Lastly there is the question of the Palestine-Israel conflict, which is at the root of the problems of the Arab and Muslim worlds. During my whole lifetime, not just the last thirty or forty years, this has been the great destabilising factor. It embitters and radicalises and it creates a popular feeling of Arabs and Muslims being separate from the West, rejected and disregarded by it. It legitimises extremism. Bin Laden's various proclamations mentioned Zionism, even though the target of his attacks was never Israel itself. The unit of Iran's Islamic Revolutionary Guard Corps that was led by Qasem Soleimani, who was assassinated by the Americans in January 2020, was named the Quds (Jerusalem) Brigade. It did nothing to restore Jerusalem to Palestinian control, but clearly its name helped legitimise it and win it support among some sections of the Arab population.

At the centre of the Palestine-Israel conflict is the utter injustice that has been inflicted on the Palestinians. More than a hundred years ago, when Jewish immigration into Palestine began, the Palestinians had their own country. It was not an independent state – it was part of the Ottoman Empire – but at least it was a place in which they made up virtually the whole population and which they could think of as their own territory – their home. Bit by bit they have lost it, and now most of those who have not fled are confined to the West Bank and a small strip of land around Gaza. Even in the West Bank their land is subject to rapidly expanding Israeli settlement, and planned annexation. Since the Israelis took over these territories in 1967 they have pursued policies designed to force as much of the population as possible to leave. Land has been seized, houses demolished and water supplies cut off. Acts of resistance, some involving the killing of Israeli civilians, have been followed by massive reprisals. Daily the population that remains is humiliated.

It is not just the Palestinians who suffer from this injustice. The whole Arab and Muslim world is angered by it and feels humiliated, alongside the Palestinians. It is angered by the almost entirely uncritical support that America gives to Israel, which seems to contradict normal American political values. America has traditionally been an anti-colonial power. It has supported self-determination for peoples and acted against countries that have seized others' territory.

The Palestinian-Israeli conflict has produced its own extremist groups. We have seen many of these emerge during the last fifty years – the most recent being Hamas. It has led to the destabilisation of Israel's and Palestine's neighbours, which play host to populations of Palestinian refugees. In the wider Arab and Muslim world the conflict has given legitimacy to the anti-American regime of Iran, which millions see as standing up to an America which supports injustice.

Saudi Arabia has consistently supported the various international initiatives to resolve the conflict. The late King Abdullah introduced an initiative of his own, which proposed ending the Israeli occupation of Palestine and the Syrian Golan Heights in exchange for recognition of

Israel not only by Saudi Arabia, but by the rest of the Arab world and by Muslim countries elsewhere. The plan was accepted by all the Arab and Muslim countries and by the rest of the world – with the exception of Israel.

I do not want to suggest that the Palestinian-Israeli conflict is the only problem of the Arab and Muslim world. I do not imagine that if this central issue were resolved the whole region would become stable overnight. But I am quite certain that until the this conflict is settled, in a way which the mass of the Palestinian people feel is just – whether that be a two-state solution, if that is still feasible, or a one-state solution – we shall not make much progress on the other issues.

Endnotes

Chapter 2

1. See Philip Mansel, *Sultans in Splendour: Last Years of the Ottoman World*, André Deutsch, 1988. I have drawn on this book in discussing the nineteenth- and early twentieth-century history of Afghanistan.

2. As a source on the uprising in Herat and the later military campaign against the Soviets I recommend Mohammad Yousaf and Mark Adkin, *Afghanistan the Bear Trap: The Defeat of a Superpower*, Leo Cooper, Pen & Sword, 1992. Yousaf was the head of the Afghan Bureau of the Pakistani Inter-Services Intelligence (ISI) in the mid-1980s, and he played in invaluable role in the ultimate victory of the Mujahideen.

3. The dialogue at the Politburo meeting is from 'Meeting of the Politburo of the Central Committee of the Communist Party of the Soviet Union', 17 March 1979, originally classified as Top Secret, translated by the National Security Archives in Washington, D.C. There is a longer summary of these conversations in Steve Coll, *Ghost Wars: The Secret History of the CIA, Afghanistan and Bin Laden, from the Soviet Invasion to September 10, 2001*, The Penguin Press, New York, 2004.

4. There is a graphic account of the murder of Amin in an excellent book by Monica Whitlock, *Beyond the Oxus: The Central Asians*, John Murray, 2003.

Chapter 3

1. Whitlock, *Beyond the Oxus*.

2. Ibid.

Chapter 4:

1. I have drawn the description of President Zia's intervention and the formation of the alliance, as well as other material in this chapter, from Yousaf and Adkin, op. cit., *passim*.

2.   Ibid., p. 106.

Chapter 5

1.   See Yousaf and Adkin, *Afghanistan the Bear Trap.*

2.   See Coll, *Ghost Wars.*

Chapter 6

1.   *Ifta* is the giving of *fatwas*, which are religious/legal judgments or opinions. *Dawa* is missionary activity or, more precisely, the spreading of a wider and better understanding of Islam among Muslims.

2.   The Sufis are Muslims who aspire to achieve a mystical personal relationship with God, through such exotic means as dancing themselves into a state of trance, repeatedly chanting the names of God and singing hymns and litanies. In their early days – the ninth century CE – they became associated with storytellers who wandered from village to village recounting tales of saints, miracles and mysteries. The storytellers wore robes of wool – *suf* – and the material gave its name to the wearers.

Chapter 8

1.   See Yousaf and Adkin, *Afghanistan the Bear Trap*, pp. 175–6.

2.   Ibid.

3.   See Whitlock, *Beyond the Oxus,* p. 135.

Chapter 9

1.   See Coll, *Ghost Wars.*

Chapter 11

1.   See Coll, *Ghost Wars.*

2.   See Whitlock, *Beyond the Oxus*.

Chapter 13

1.   There is an excellent description of the origins of the Taliban in Ahmed Rashid, *Taliban: The Story of the Afghan Warlords*, Pan Books, Macmillan, 2001. This has been the source of much of the history of the Taliban in this chapter. I have to say, though, that in the few places where it refers to Saudi Arabia its comments are not always accurate.

Chapter 14

1.   See Coll, *Ghost Wars*, pp. 385–6 and footnote 27 on p. 626.

Acknowledgements

Foremost, I thank Michael Field for co-authoring this book. He did all the legwork while I did much of the verbal work. In preparing the book he was much helped by meetings with the following people.

Turki AlFaisal, Riyadh, 2021

I am grateful to: Ahmad Badeeb, Prince Turki's Chief of Staff; Jamal Khashoggi, Prince Turki's former press adviser, who had worked as a journalist in Afghanistan; Mohammad Eid Al-Otaibi, from the General Intelligence Department, who was Saudi Ambassador in Kabul after 1992, and who was deeply involved in bringing home the Saudi volunteers in Afghanistan; Ahmad Hayat, a commander with Ahmad Shah Massoud's forces, who was a valuable source of information on the operations of the Mujahideen; Professor Burhanuddin Rabbani, President of Afghanistan, 1992–2001; Ahmed Rashid, author of *Taliban: The Story of the Afghan Warlords*; and Dr Zbigniew Brzezinski, President Jimmy Carter's National Security Adviser, 1977–81.

And lastly I would like to thank Eleo Carson, the editor of this book, who has brought great professional knowledge to the task and been immensely painstaking. It has been a pleasure to work with her.

Four books were particularly useful to me in providing background on Afghanistan and some of the events between 1979 and 2001. My conversations with Prince Turki and the other people mentioned here provided the material on Saudi involvement in these events, but left some gaps on the progress of the war against the Soviet occupation and the rise of the Taliban afterwards. These written sources helped fill the gaps. I would like to thank the authors and publishers of:

Mohammad Yousaf and Mark Adkin, *Afghanistan the Bear Trap: The Defeat of a Superpower*, Leo Cooper, Pen & Sword, 1992.

Steve Coll, *Ghost Wars: The Secret History of the CIA, Afghanistan and bin Laden, from the Soviet Invasion to September 10, 2001*, The Penguin Press, New York, 2004.

Monica Whitlock, *Beyond the Oxus: The Central Asians*, John Murray, 2003.

Ahmed Rashid, *Taliban: The Story of the Afghan Warlords*, Pan Books, Macmillan, 2001.

I strongly recommend these books to anyone who wants to read further on this subject.

Michael Field, 2021

Index

A

Abbas, Mullah Mohammad 144, 156
Adham, Kamal 14
Afghan army 20, 23, 29, 38, 42, 47, 51, 52, 54, 58, 96, 97, 103, 106, 123, 156
Afghan National Liberation Front 33, 101
Afghan War
air power 51, 96
ceasefire 53
changes in Soviet attitudes to 81–2
early years 49–59
economic impact of 50
operations in the southern Soviet Union 85–8
Paktia 58
Panjshir Valley 51–4, 97
sabotage operations 55–7, 95
Saudi involvement 68–9
Soviet army 50–1
Soviet casualties 96–7
Soviet military failure 96–8
Soviet strategy 49–50, 51–4
turning point and Soviet

withdrawal 81–98
Afghanistan
available funds of parties 132
border frictions with Saudis 70, 73–4
as a buffer state 8
characteristics of Afghans 36
civilian casualties 143
European dress 20
exiles 27–8
fighting around Kabul 124–8
history and society before the Soviet invasion 18–26
insensitive policy of the Soviet Union 36–8
instability xviii
Islamic militants 117–18
modernisation attempts 20–1
Najibullah, fall of 122–9
new government, formation of 100–3
peace initiatives 135–42, 148–51

Peshawar negotiations
127–8

plundering and destruction
143

political parties 30–3

races and linguistic groups
18–19

resistance to the Soviets 38

Soviet influences 21–5

Soviet invasion 1–13, 26

style of life 67

tribal mentality 139

uprisings 23, 28

Ahmadzai, Ahmad Shah 36,
102

al-Amri, Salman Mohammad
169, 172–4

Al-Faqih, Saad 161

Al-Fawwaz, Khaled 160–1

Al Jazeera television network
xx, 166

Al-Massari, Mohammad 161

Al-Otaibi, Mohammad Eid
130–2, 133, 134–5, 149, 154

Al-Qaeda xviii, xix, 66, 80,
105, 135, 165, 173, 183, 184,
186–7, 191

Al-Sabah, Sheikh Jaber Ahmad
110

Al-Sabah, Sheikh Mubarak
Sabah 110

Al Saud, Turki AlFaisal, Prince
41, 99, 127–8

and Bin Laden 78, 107–8,
161, 166–8

cable to King Fahd 119–20

early life and career 13–15

and Hekmatyar 91, 102,
104–5 128–9

and invasion of Kuwait
110–11

meetings with CIA and ISI
43–4

meetings with Taliban
leaders about Bin Laden
157, 166–73, 177–8

and peace initiatives 148–51

refugee camp visits 61

report to Crown Prince
Abdullah 179–80

resigns as GID director 182

role as government official
12–13

talks with Soviet Union
about withdrawal 90–3

Al-Subei, Khaled 134

Al-Suhaibani, Sheikh Saleh Ali
62, 65

assessing military
effectiveness of parties 62,
65

Al-Turki, Sheikh Abdullah 166,

168

AlFaisal, Saud 6–7, 11

Amanullah, King of Afghanistan 20–1

Amin, Hafzullah 24–6, 60

Andropov, Yuri 24

Ansar al-Islam 162

Arab Spring (2011) 191

Arafat, Yasser 34

Assad, Bashar 191, 193

Assad, Hafez 34

atrocities xix, 61, 152

Azimi, Nabih 61, 125

Azzam, Abdullah 75–8, 104–5, 176

B

Babar, Naseerullah 27, 146, 147, 149, 157

Bacha-i-Saqao, Habibullah Ghazi 20–1

Badeeb, Ahmad 5–6, 34, 48, 136

Balochistan 2, 3, 4, 39

Bashir, Omar 159, 163–4

BBC 1, 180

Bhutto, Benazir 27, 100, 102, 149

Bhutto, Zulfiqar Ali 3–4, 27, 100

bin Abdul-Wahhab, Sheikh Mohammad 70–1, 72

bin Abdulaziz, Abdullah, Crown Prince (later King) 14–15, 163–4, 194–5

bin Abdulaziz, Ahmad, Prince 108

bin Abdulaziz, Fahd, Crown Prince (later King) 1–2, 5, 11–12, 15, 35, 92, 99, 109, 110, 138, 164–5

   order for party office closures in the Kingdom 139–41

bin Abdulaziz, Khalid, King 1–2, 5, 11

bin Abdulaziz, Salman, Prince 118, 120

bin Abdulaziz, Sattam, Prince 62, 63, 64, 65

bin Abdulaziz, Sultan, Prince 14, 108, 111–12, 165

bin Baz, Sheikh Abdulaziz 62–6

Bin Laden, Osama xvii, xix, xx, 77–9, 80, 105, 107–8, 127, 158, 187, 193

   assassination attempt 162

   bombing of US embassies 173

   Declaration Number One 160

   'Declaration of Jihad on the

Americans Occupying the Two Holy Places' 164
disowned by his family 161
fatwa against United States 165–6, 171
in Jalalabad 164
promoting revolutionary ideas 162–3
in Saudi Arabia 111–13
Saudi assets frozen 161–2
Saudi requests for surrender of 166–73
in Sudan 159–60, 162–3, 164
and the Taliban 159–83
refuge with the Taliban 164–5
and Turabi 159–60, 162
US pursuit of 184–5
bin Saud Al-Thunayyan, Iffat bint Mohammad 13
Boko Haram xix
boron carbide 56–7, 84–5
Borovik, Artyom 98
Britain –2, 8, 19, 20, 21, 58, 88, 186
Brzezinski, Zbigniew 9–10, 11, 40
Bush, George H.W. 99–100, 110, 184, 185–6

C
Carter, Jimmy 8, 9, 10, 40, 57
Casey, William 44, 57, 68, 86, 90, 99, 110
cemeteries 73
charities and volunteers 60–74, 75
government agencies 62–3
military volunteers 68–9, 78
private funding and donations 61–4, 66–8, 118, 131–2
reception centre for 75, 77, 78
religious influences 70–4
returning volunteers 113, 114–16, 118, 130–42
Saudi ban on charitable transfers 190
volunteers, role of 65–7
Cheney, Dick 110–11
children 37, 55, 61, 66, 73, 77, 144, 164, 170
China 9, 11, 42–3
Christopher, Warren 11
CIA 8, 9–10, 24, 25, 42, 43, 44, 45, 46, 48, 57–8, 68, 82, 86, 87–8, 89, 93, 95, 99, 100, 101, 110, 119, 128, 150, 163, 165, 173, 174, 182
CIA/GID/ISI arms pipeline

12, 15, 39–48
funds 47–8, 57
scandals 43
sources 42–3
transport 44–5, 47
Clinton, Bill 165, 173, 174
Cole, USS 181–2
Committee for the Defence of
Legitimate Rights (CDLR)
160–1
Communism 3, 5, 22, 27, 28,
62, 71, 76, 99, 114, 188

D
Daoud, Sardar Mohammad 5,
21–2, 27, 28, 29, 31, 65
dawa 62, 66, 197n
Dostum, Abdul Rashid 122–3,
126, 129, 130, 143, 151, 153,
155, 157, 183
Durand, Sir Mortimer 4

E
education 66, 72
and religion 188, 189
Egypt 8, 34, 42, 44, 71, 75, 90,
91, 163, 188, 191
El-Zawahiri, Ayman 79–80,
105
executions 3, 22, 23, 122–3, 145

F
Faisal, King 1, 5, 13–14, 21, 28
fatwa 111, 165–6, 171, 197n
FBI 173
fitna (civil war) 131
Front Islamique du Salut 116

G
Gailani, Pir Ahmad 33, 47, 64,
91, 132
General Intelligence
Department (GID)) xvii, 2,
12, 13, 14, 15, 44, 48, 78, 101,
118, 128, 130, 132, 133–4,
135, 182
see also CIA/GID/ISI arms
pipeline
Ghaus, Mohammad 144
Gorbachev, Mikhail 81, 88, 98,
112
Great Game 1–2, 8
guerrillas 4, 5, 9, 15, 38, 40, 51,
55, 56, 89, 95
Gul, Hamid 94, 103, 129

H
Hadith 70, 72, 168
Hafizullah Amin 24, 25, 26, 60
Hamas 194
Haqqani, Jalaluddin 38, 58–9,
101, 142

Harakat-i-inqilab-i-Islami
(Islamic Revolutionary
Movement) 32–3, 144
Haramain Foundation 66
Hassan, Mohammad 144
Hayat, Ahmad 84–5
Hazaras 19, 148, 153, 154, 155,
181, 182
Hekmatyar, Gulbuddin 22, 28,
38, 42, 46, 47–8, 53, 63, 65,
91, 102, 121, 130, 143
character 29–30
charisma 68
and the fall of Najibullah
124–6, 128–9
and Pakistan 146
as prime minister 138–9
and Saudi militants 133, 134
subversive activities 104–6
Hezbollah 191
Hizb-i-Islami (Islamic Party)
28, 29, 32, 142
ideology 30
Hizb-i-Islami (Khalis's party)
31
Hizb-i-Wahdat 135, 138
hospitals 61, 65, 66
House of the Supporters 75–80
Household Nursery 37
Houthis 191–2
Hussein, King of Jordan 109

Hussein, Saddam xviii, 34, 121,
185–6
invasion of Kuwait 108–10,
160, 186

I

India 3, 4, 19, 20, 21, 72, 145
Inter-Services Intelligence (ISI)
2, 8, 12, 15, 41, 45, 54, 82, 87,
94, 100, 103, 106, 131
Afghan Bureau 41, 42, 43,
45, 46, 47, 50, 55, 59
Quetta incident 41
see also CIA/GID/ISI arms
pipeline
International Center to Combat
Extremism 192
International Coalition to Fight
Islamic State in Iraq and
Syria (ISIS) 193
International Islamic Front
for Jihad against Jews and
Crusaders 165
International Security
Assistance Force (ISAF)
185
Iran 8, 20, 24, 49, 25, 60, 85, 86,
93, 109, 119, 129, 135, 148,
151, 153, 155, 167, 178, 186,
191, 193, 194
Iranian Revolution xx,
188–9

Iraq xviii, xx, 7, 34, 109, 115,
139, 185–6, 188, 191, 192,
193
US/UK invasion 186
ISIS (Islamic State of Iraq and
Syria) xviii–xix, xix–xx, 80,
186, 192, 193
Islam xix, 3, 24, 32, 70–3, 76,
114, 137, 156, 159, 165
fundamentalism 123, 144,
150–1, 188
Islamism 188–9
Islambouli, Khalid 79–80
Islamic Coalition to Fight
Terrorism 193
Islamic International Relief
Organisation 66, 131, 132
Islamic Revolutionary Guards
Corps (Iran) 130, 193
Islamic Union for the
Liberation of Afghanistan
35
Israel 14, 171, 188, 193–5
Ittihad-i-Islami 35, 72

J
Jalalabad 31, 35, 40, 83–4, 89,
103, 105, 146, 148, 152, 164,
170, 173–4, 176, 184
Jamaat-i-Islami (Pakistan) 30,
63, 64, 75, 77

Jamiat-i-Islami (Islamic Group)
28, 31
jamming devices 56
jihad xix, 6, 23, 76, 105, 119,
128, 131, 135, 137, 141, 144,
164, 170, 175

K
Kaaba 35–6, 138
Kabul 1, 2, 3, 15, 19, 20, 22, 23,
24, 25, 26, 27, 28, 29, 30, 31,
33, 34, 35, 36, 38, 40, 46, 49,
52, 54, 55, 58, 60, 81, 84, 86,
91, 93, 96, 100, 103, 105, 122,
123, 124–6, 127, 128, 129,
130, 134, 135, 137, 143, 146,
148, 149, 154, 155, 156, 164,
166, 167, 176, 182, 183, 184
and the Taliban 151–3
Kandahar 3, 32, 33, 38, 45, 82,
85, 143–4, 145, 146, 147,
148, 154, 155–6, 157, 165,
166, 167, 170, 172, 173, 176,
177, 180, 181
Karmal, Babrak 22, 26, 82
KGB 22, 24, 29, 38, 45–6, 95,
150
KHAD 29, 38, 40, 45–6, 55, 56,
76, 82, 83, 95, 105, 114, 122,
126
Khalis, Maulvi Yunis 31–2, 38,

47–8, 58, 63, 83, 85, 91, 93, 101, 135, 144, 164

Khalq movement 22

Khan, Abdal-Rahman, Amir 19–20

Khan, General Akhtar Abdul Rahman 2–4, 5, 6–7, 39, 40–1, 94, 95, 99

Khan, Ismail 23, 146, 151–2, 153, 183

Khashoggi, Jamal 67, 126

Khomeini, Ayatollah xx, 25

Khrushchev, Nikita 33, 86, 93

King Salman Humanitarian Aid and Relief Center 190

Kosygin, Alexei 24

Kuwait xviii, xix, 107–21, 185–6
    Iraqi invasion of 108–10, 160
    and Saudi Arabia 109–10

L

languages 18, 19, 31, 66, 69

Latoon, Fazil Mawla 124

Lebanon xx, 186, 191, 193

Libya 139, 191

Loya Jirga (Grand Assembly) 20, 32, 99–106

M

Madinah 36, 68, 70, 71, 78, 180

madrasas 72, 125, 144, 147, 153, 154, 156

Makkah 34, 35, 36, 62, 63, 68, 71, 76, 78, 91, 126, 138, 180

Massoud, Ahmad Shah 22, 28, 38, 47–8, 51–3, 58, 104, 129, 130–1, 135, 139, 149–50
    and Dostum 123, 153
    and the fall of Najibullah 124–7
    and the Taliban 148, 151, 152–3, 182–3

Maududi, Abdul-Ala 30

Maulvizada, Ansrullah 124

Mazar-i-Sharif 38, 47, 49, 153, 154, 155, 156

Mazari, Abdel-Ali 148

Mohammadi, Maulvi Mohammad Nabi 32–3, 47, 64, 132, 144

Mojaddedi, Hazrat Sibghatullah 33, 47, 91–2, 101–2, 127–8, 129, 132, 135

Mujahideen xvii, 5, 6, 23, 38, 40, 49, 53, 189
    activities in the early years of the war 54–5, 57–8
    air attacks on 82–4
    attack on Jalalabad 103
    battlefield competence 46–7

disunity 35–6, 41–2
emergence of 27–38
feuding 103–4, 121
involvement of Saudi people
    68–9
loyalties 65
Military Committee 42
political parties 30–3
returning to Saudi Arabia
    113, 114–16, 118, 130–42
in the southern Soviet union
    87–8
Stinger missiles 82–6
summit meeting 1981 34–5
support from US 8–10,
    11–12
talks with Soviet Union
    91–4
Muslim Brotherhood xx, 75,
    79, 159, 188
    Islamic Medical Society 80
Muslim World League 64, 66,
    127, 131, 166

N
Nabi, Maulvi 46–7, 54–5
Najibullah, Mohammad 81–2,
    89, 91, 93, 96, 99, 100, 101,
    105, 106, 107, 117, 119, 120,
    131, 143, 144, 147, 158, 159
    and Dostum 122–3
    fall of 122–9
    murder of 152, 155
Naseef, Abdullah 127
Nasser, Gamal Abdel 75, 188
National Islamic Front 33, 127,
    159–60, 162, 165
National Public Committee for
    the Support of the Afghan
    People 65, 118
nationalism 188–9
NATO 29, 185
North-West Frontier Province
    3, 4–5, 27, 40, 60–1, 127

O
Office of Services 75–80, 104,
    105
Ojhri Camp 45, 83, 94–5
Olympic Games 7, 11
Omar, Mullah Mohammad 32,
    144, 145, 147, 154, 156, 157,
    166–8, 169, 170, 171, 172,
    177–8, 180, 182, 184
Organisation of the Islamic
    Conference 6–7, 34–5, 137,
    149, 179

P
Pahlawan, Malik 153, 154, 155
Pakistan xvii, xx, 2–4, 35, 39,
    100

Afghanistan policy 145–7,
180
military effectiveness of
parties 64–5
Soviet shell attacks on 40
support from Saudi Arabia
5–6, 11
Taliban, recognition of 153
treatment of refugees 60–1
Paktia 58–9
Palestine-Israel conflict 193–5
Panjshir Valley 19, 28, 31, 51–4,
58, 87, 97, 104, 132, 152, 153,
154, 155, 183
Parcham (Communist Party)
21–2
Pathans 4–5, 18, 19, 30, 31,
39–40, 45, 52, 61, 69, 124,
145, 146, 152, 157
People's Democratic Republic
of Yemen (PDRY) 107–8
Politburo 23, 25, 81
Primakov, Yevgeny 150–1
propaganda 9, 40, 46, 55, 86,
160–1, 164, 166
psychological warfare 45

Q
Quetta incident 41
Quran 30, 35, 66, 70, 72, 73, 79,
86, 104, 126, 136–7, 167–8

Qutb, Mohammad 75
Qutb, Seyyid 75, 79, 80

R
Rabbani, Burhanuddin 7, 22,
27–8, 31, 32, 33, 38, 47, 63,
64, 65, 85, 91–2, 102, 127,
132, 137, 140, 152, 153, 155
character 31
as head of government 129,
130–1, 135, 139, 149–50
Rabbani, Mohammad 144, 149,
157, 166
Rafi, Mohammad 125, 126
Rana, Naseem 157, 167, 177,
178, 180
Reagan, Ronald 29–30, 50, 57,
83, 84, 89, 93, 99
refugees 15, 16, 39–40, 48, 100
camps 60, 61
and Islam 73
numbers of 60
treatment of 60–1
Richardson, Bill 166
Russia 1, 8, 98, 123, 148, 150–1,
157, 193
see also Soviet Union
Russian Special Forces 26

S

Sadat, Anwar 14, 79
Saudi Arabia xviii, xx, 2, 68,
    100
  ban on charitable transfers
    190
  Bin Laden's criticism of
    160–1, 164–5
  border frictions with
    Afghans 70, 73–4
  character of society 113–14
  cooperation with United
    States 11–12
  declaration for
    representatives of Afghan
    parties 141–2
  donations to Afghan causes
    16, 61–4, 66–8, 118–21,
    131–2
  education system 188, 189
  false attributions 15–16
  as a financial free society 16
  free and open public
    discussion 115–16
  Islam 70–4
  Islamist opposition 115–17
  and Kuwait 109–10
  military involvement in
    Afghanistan 68–9
  mosques, appraisal of 189–
    90
  opposition to invasion of
    Iraq 186
  order for party office closures
    139–41
  and the Palestine-Israel
    conflict 193–5
  and refugees 61, 66–7
  rehabilitation of terrorists
    192–3
  requests for the surrender
    of Bin Laden 166–73,
    177–8, 180
  support for Pakistan 5–6, 11
  Taliban, recognition of
    153–4, 157–8
  and terrorist attacks 187,
    192
  weapons funding 5–6, 48, 57
  women in society 190
  young people returning from
    Afghanistan 113, 114–16,
    118, 130–42
Saudi Organisation for
  Charities Abroad 190
Saudi Red Crescent 65, 66,
  120, 132
Sayyaf, Abd Rabb Al-Rasul
  33–5, 36, 47–8, 68, 72, 102,
  121, 129, 130–1, 132, 133,
  149–50
Sevan, Benon 124, 127

Shams, Omar 14
Sharia law 70, 104, 117, 182
Sharif, Nawaz 127, 128, 135,
    136, 137–8, 143, 153, 177
Shevardnadze, Eduard 96
Simons, Tom 166
socialism 24, 188–9
South Yemen xix, 7, 11, 107,
    108, 112
Soviet Union xvii–xviii, xx, 1, 3,
    7, 8, 9, 39, 46, 57, 58, 71, 99,
    107, 108, 112, 114, 122
atrocities 61
attack on Bin Laden's
    compound 79
changes in attitude to the
    war 81–2
influence in Afghanistan
    21–5
insensitive policy in
    Afghanistan 36–8
invasion of Afghanistan and
    reactions to 1–13
occupying force in
    Afghanistan 50–1
operations in the southern
    Soviet Union 85–8
talks with Mujahideen 91–4
talks with Saudi Arabia
    90–3
talks with United States

about withdrawal 88–90,
    93–4
war casualties 96–7
war failure 96–8
war strategy 49–50, 51–4
withdrawal from
    Afghanistan 81–98
Special Forces (American
    and British) 55–7, 82,
    184
Spetznaz 51, 54, 58, 85
subversion 3, 38, 40, 45–6, 52
Sudan 109, 127, 159–60,
    162–3, 164
Sufis 64, 197n
Sunni Muslims xix, 19, 72, 86,
    144, 148
Supreme Council for the
    Defence of the Motherland
    153
Syria xvii, xix, xx, 7, 34, 186,
    188, 191, 193

T
Tajiks 18–19, 22, 25, 26, 30, 49,
    52, 86, 145
takfir 117–18
Taliban xvii, 15, 16, 32, 129
advances 147–8, 151–2
atrocities 152
and Bin Laden 159–83

collapse of military forces
184
commanders and senior
figures 156–7
cruise missile attacks on
Taliban camps 173–7
destruction of Buddha
statues 182
gives Bin Laden refuge
164–5
in Herat 151–2
and Kabul 151–3
Massoud's defeat of 151
meetings with Saudi officials
about Bin Laden 166–73,
177–8
name origin 144
nature of 156
Pakistan's recognition of 153
rise of 143–58
sanctions against 181
Saudi protests about Bin
Laden 166
Saudi recognition of 153–4,
157–8
Shura 157
and the 'trucking mafia'
146–7
world condemnation of
180–1
Tanai, Shahnawaz 105, 124

tape recorders 56
Taraki, Nur Mohammad 22, 23,
24, 25, 26, 28, 60
Tenet, George 165
Tomsen, Peter 127
Toufan, Inayatullah 124, 125
tribal mentality 139
Tunisia 109, 191
Turabi, Hassan 127, 159, 160,
162

U
ul-Haq, Mohammad Zia 2,
3–4, 5, 11, 39, 83, 99
character and looks 6–7
death 94
and the Mujahideen 40,
41–2
United Nations 29–30, 61, 88,
91, 124, 126, 127, 149, 152,
155, 166, 172, 176, 181, 185
United Nations High
Commission for Refugees
60, 66, 155
United Nations Security
Council 10, 193
Security Council Resolution
1333 181
United States xvii, xviii, xix, 8,
16, 99–100
9/11 attacks xviii, 16, 183,

184, 187

Bin Laden's embassy
bombings 173

Bin Laden's fatwa 165–6, 171

concern about Bin Laden
165

cooperation with Saudi
Arabia 11–12

cruise missile attacks on
Taliban camps 173–7

declining interest in
Afghanistan 118–19, 120

and invasion of Kuwait
110–11

plans to capture Bin Laden
181

reaction to Soviet invasion of
Afghanistan 10

security 10

Soviet fears of 24–5

and Sudan 163

support for Mujahideen
8–10, 11–12

talks with Soviet Union
about withdrawal 88–90,
93–4

weapons 57

weapons funding 48

Ustinov, Dmitri 23–4

volunteers *see* charities and
volunteers

Vorontsov, Yuli 91–3

W

War on Terror xviii, 186

Wardak, Maulvi Halim 124,
125

weapons 28–9

anti-aircraft guns 82

Blowpipe anti-aircraft
missile 43

chemical weapons 174

CIA/GID/ISI arms pipeline
12, 15, 39–48

cruise missiles 173–4

End User Certificates
(EUCs) 44

explosions 94–5

funds 47–8, 57

L-42 sniper rifle 43

mines 87

rockets 55, 87, 94–5, 128

scandals 43

Scud missiles 96

self-loading rifle 29

Stinger missiles 82–6

surface to-air missiles 82

transport of 44–5, 47, 95

Whitlock, Monica 37

Wilson, Charles 45–6, 57

V

women 18, 20, 22, 61, 73, 114,
116, 152, 154, 181, 182, 190
World Assembly of Muslim
Youth (WAMY) 66

Y

Yemen xx, 14, 107, 108, 109,
139, 161, 166, 191–2, 193
Yemen Arab Republic 108
young people xviii–xx, 66,
186–7
involvement in war 69
returning to Saudi Arabia
113, 114–15, 118, 130–42
Yousaf, Mohammad 30, 41, 42,
43, 47, 50, 83, 88, 94
*Afghanistan the Bear Trap: The
Defeat of a Superpower* 47

Z

Zabihullah 38

DEATH BY CONSEQUENCE

An Archie Freestone Mystery

GRAHAM HARDY

Death by Consequence is a work of fiction set in Pewsey,
Wiltshire early in 1949. All the characters mentioned are purely
fictional and have no connection to anyone having lived in the
village at that time or since.
Pewsey is a real village, some of the names, characters and
businesses in this book are either the product of the author's
imagination or used in a fictitious manner.
Any Military establishments named are purely fictional and
bear no resemblance to any actual establishment.

Illustrations by Graham Hardy

DEDICATION

To my wife who always believes in me.

DEATH BY
CONSEQUENCE

An Archie Freestone Mystery

GRAHAM HARDY

DEDICATION

To my wife who always believes in me.